PRAISE FOR *WEB3*

"*Web3* is a brilliant and timely book that should be read by anyone who wants to understand how the next generation of the Internet can help us build a better city and future."

—*Francis Suarez, mayor of Miami*

"Tapscott's new book describes with clarity and foresight how crypto networks will transform more than money and financial services—they will remake entire industries. Leaders must understand this new innovation or risk getting left behind."

—*Kristin Smith, CEO of Blockchain Association*

"With the rise of generative AI, the metaverse, and the next generation of blockchain, Web3 is now a breakthrough platform for innovators to rebuild the world of business and the global economy for a new era of prosperity. This extraordinary book shows how."

—*Klaus Schwab, chairperson of the World Economic Forum*

"Tapscott does a brilliant job of dissecting the impact of Web3. From one of the leading voices and thinkers in blockchain technology, this is a must-have in any library, digital or otherwise."

—*Angie Lau, editor in chief and co-CEO of Forkast Labs*

"Alex Tapscott has written the book we have been waiting for. *Web3* is the essential guide to the Internet's next era for business leaders, policymakers, citizens, and everyone who cares about economic freedom and the future of commerce."

—*Hon. J. Christopher Giancarlo, former chairman of the US Commodity Futures Trading Commission*

"Insightful, lively, and fun to read. Every person who is curious and cares about the future of commerce, culture, and society should read this book."

—*Yat Siu, cofounder of Animoca Brands*

"A must-read for anyone looking to stay ahead of the curve. With Tapscott's track record of seeing into the future, we should all pay attention."

—*Tyler Winklevoss, CEO of Gemini*

"This book is a must-read for all curious souls who care about the exciting ways Web3 will shape commerce, culture, and society."

—*Pplpleasr, multidisciplinary artist*

"*Web3* highlights how digital ownership, blockchain, and spatial computing will reinvent business and industries. Tapscott provides an important primer for leaders as they navigate this new future."

—*Paul Daugherty, group chief executive,*
technology, and CTO of Accenture

"Engaging with Tapscott's insights is like activating an over-the-horizon radar for your brain."

—*Matt Roszak, chairman and cofounder of Bloq*

"An accessible, well-researched, and thorough overview of Web3 technology and its many use cases."

—*Tim Beiko, Ethereum core developer*

"This book will be key to understanding what lies ahead, illuminating the path from fringe movement to mainstream disruption."

—*Roneil Rumburg, cofounder and CEO of Audius*

"Web3 has the potential to disrupt the experience economy by merging the digital and physical worlds, enabling fast-moving companies to WIN. Tapscott's vision for the future empowers leaders to put technology to work as Web3 matures in the years to come."

—*Bill McDermot, CEO of ServiceNow*

"An essential read for anyone looking to learn about why Internet with built-in ownership, or Web3, is so important."

—*Aleksander Leonard Larsen, cofounder and COO of Sky Mavis*

"Delightful! A wave of innovation is about to change our lives—a chance for a better tomorrow if we participate in shaping it today."

—*Beryl Li, cofounder of Yield Guild Games*

"Tapscott's new book, *Web3*, is a revelation. Innovators everywhere would be wise to read this book before charting their course."

—*John Ruffolo, founder and managing partner of Maverix*

"An indispensable tool for understanding Web3 at a time when the dream of a more decentralized, user-controlled Internet is on the cusp of becoming a mainstream reality."

—*Camila Russo, founder of The Defiant and author of*
The Infinite Machine

"Alex Tapscott provides a comprehensive and understandable look at Web3 and its promise of permissionless innovation, decentralized ownership, and creative and economic opportunity for all. For innovators and adopters, policymakers, entrepreneurs, and the tech-curious, this is an indispensable guide to our future."

—*Perianne Boring, founder and CEO of the Chamber of Digital Commerce*

"Tapscott masterfully illuminates the path to our digital future, which perfectly aligns with Dubai and the UAE's digital ambitions. A much-needed guide to the Web3 era."

—*Marwan Al Zarouni, CEO of Dubai Blockchain Center*

"Web3 envisions a decentralized Internet that empowers individuals and transforms industries. Alex Tapscott has made another timeless classic."

—*Jirayut "Topp" Srupsrisopa, founder and group CEO of Bitkub*

"As an investor and author, Alex Tapscott has tech in his DNA. His new book combines tech-savvy with highly practical insights and a sure sense of where the technology is taking us. *Web3* is truly required reading, a compelling, practical blueprint for the future."

—*Stuart Crainer, cofounder of Thinkers50*

"A delightful and engaging book that has the potential to reset the entire conversation about crypto, showing how a new Web and Internet is an unprecedented and powerful force for prosperity."

—*Tamara Haasen, president of Input Output*

WEB3

Charting the Internet's
Next Economic and
Cultural Frontier

ALEX TAPSCOTT

HARPER
BUSINESS
An Imprint of HarperCollins*Publishers*

HarperCollins books may be purchased for educational, business, or
sales promotional use. For information, please email the Special Markets
Department at SPsales@harpercollins.com.

FIRST EDITION

Designed by Bonni Leon-Berman

Library of Congress Cataloging-in-Publication Data has been applied for.

ISBN 978-0-06-329995-5

23 24 25 26 27 LBC 5 4 3 2 1

For Eleanor, Josephine, and Amy

CONTENTS

INTRODUCTION

Silicon Valley was once called a tech Galápagos for the unique blend of talent, money, technology, culture, and government research and development that led to the diverse species of tech entrepreneurs who went on to found today's mammoth Internet companies.[1] The World Wide Web was invented by English computer scientist Sir Tim Berners-Lee at CERN, or the European Organization for Nuclear Research, in Switzerland, but it was commercialized in America.

This time is different. Web3, the subject of this book, is emerging at a time when technology tools and human capital are more distributed than ever. In 1993, as the Web's pioneers were forging the first frontier online, half the world had never placed a phone call. Now more than two out of every three people on earth has a smartphone connected to the Internet.[2] To build on science fiction author William Gibson, the future is already here, and its talent and technology are almost equally distributed. If Web1 and Web2 democratized access to information and made it easier to meet and collaborate online, Web3 equips us with a more powerful toolset to earn money, own assets, and build wealth on a globally level playing field, decentralizing power and influence in the process. If the spread of technology truly makes the world "flatter," then Web3 will be a steamroller.

I first started writing about Bitcoin in 2014, before the word *Web3* entered the vernacular. An investment banker by trade and a CFA charterholder in traditional finance (what my Web3 friends would call a "TradFi" person), I thought I was investigating a new *financial* technology.

In 2015, I began a much larger research project with Don Tap-scott, my father. We published our findings in a book, *Blockchain*

Revolution. During that research, I had the epiphany that this new general-purpose technology was ushering in a new Internet of value that would change everything. That was not obvious to outsiders at the time, and we faced many doubters then as now. In 2016, when *Blockchain Revolution* came out, the entire market value of all digital assets, what we refer to as *tokens* in this book and the foundational asset class of Web3, was about $10 billion. If the whole industry had been a publicly traded company, it would have barely cracked the S&P 500 index. The Gap, seller of khaki pants, was worth more than the whole Web3 industry. Today, Web3 assets are more than 100 times that. The book struck a chord and benefited from impeccable timing (hey, better lucky than smart!), with twenty translations worldwide.

Since 2016, I have traveled to nearly forty countries, visited every continent except Antarctica, and met with local entrepreneurs, policymakers, business leaders, and everyday people. What has struck me most is how globally distributed Web3 innovation is. Airplanes have become time machines, shuttling me to various "futures": To Istanbul, where many citizens prefer to transact and store value in digital currencies. To Singapore, the beachhead of Asia's burgeoning Web3 industry. To Thailand, where Internet users are experimenting with Web3's toolset to bootstrap new jobs online. To Dubai, where the government has made Web3 the linchpin of a broader plan to attract global talent and capital. To London, where in June 2023 British Prime Minister Rishi Sunah shared his determination to "turn the UK into the world's Web3 centre."[3] Wheels down in Toronto, which was a leader in Web3 for a moment, I feel like Marty McFly landing in a 1950s cornfield.

In my travels, I've also seen how common misconceptions of the technology have spread, propagated by some media, business, and government leaders. They've raised the barriers to Web3 entrepreneurship. This, too, is a global phenomenon, with old-paradigm power brokers everywhere struggling to embrace the new. They point to the 2022 collapse of FTX, a prominent cryptocurrency exchange, and the bankruptcies of crypto lenders like Celsius and Voyager, to justify their concerns about Web3—that this new technology, while innovative and useful when controlled by central banks or big companies, is a net negative to society when left to the free market.[4] It gives speculators new ways to gamble and criminals new tools to evade law enforcement. In actuality, we can blame the collapse of these companies not on the technology but on the hubris of those wielding it.

The events of 2022 have smeared new mud on the windshield, increasing my sense of urgency for a comprehensive analysis of what's going on. As with any new industry, many startups are trying to build this future, and many will end up as footnotes to the transformation. That's normal. Though this book features the stories and insights of dozens of creators, builders, and dreamers, it's not about the fortunes of any one organization, person, or company. I won't be sharing industry gossip or predicting the price of any asset in this book. To be sure, tokens are key to Web3. Many of them will grow immensely valuable, especially those that represent ownership in the underlying protocols or some of the most disruptive organizations. But if you are looking for price targets or investing advice, look elsewhere. This is a book of enduring concepts, not of buy-in/cash-out strategies. I use data as points of comparison in time. This is such a vibrant and volatile space of innovation that readers will need to consult my sources for the latest data.

This book is also not an exhaustive study of every player in this new industry. To do so in the time allotted would be impossible. A decade ago, book authors could call up every founder in the space during manuscript development. No more. In this book, I attempt to bridge the islands in the archipelago of Web3 knowledge, to paraphrase historian Irene Vallejo's library metaphor.[5] In layperson's terms, I connect the dots.

That said, this book draws from half a decade of research, investment, practice, and collaboration in Web3. In 2017, Don and I launched the Blockchain Research Institute, which has conducted more than a hundred research projects on the impact of blockchain and Web3 on every industry, from healthcare and financial services to energy and entertainment. This research has informed many of the ideas in this book.

I also conducted more than fifty interviews for this book. Web3 is first and foremost an economic frontier, and so I wanted to speak to the business-minded pioneers like Yat Siu, cofounder of Animoca Brands. Siu got his first job as a teenager at Atari in the 1980s, and stumbled into Web3 in 2017, later staking his company's future on it and underwriting many of Web3 gaming's biggest innovators. A decade ago, Jeremy Allaire had the idea of creating the "HTTP for money," an Internet-native payment tool for dollars and other currencies. His company, Circle, created the stablecoin USDC, which through 2022 powered a cumulative *$8.6 trillion* in on-chain transactions.[6] Another pioneer, Sunny Aggarwal, dropped out of the University of California, Berkeley after a computer science teacher refused to let him skip a test to attend a Web3 meetup. He went on to found Osmosis, a decentralized exchange that powers frictionless peer-to-peer transactions in dozens of different assets. On my podcast, *DeFi Decoded*, yet another inventor, Anatoly Yakovenko, explained how he realized that Apple and Google's smartphone monopoly was choking off Web3 application development on his platform Solana. So Yakovenko launched a competing phone and operating system.

We spoke with technologists, and so-called "core developers" who are building the essential infrastructure of Web3. We caught up with Tim Beiko, a core developer at Ethereum, who worked with others to roll out a network upgrade known as "the merge," roughly like swapping out the engines of a supersonic jetliner carrying $200 billion in cargo midflight without upsetting the drink cart. Our discussion with Kevin Owocki and Scott Moore of Gitcoin, which has provided millions in grants to social entrepreneurs in Web3, was illuminating and inspiring. Jimmy Wales, the founder of Wikipedia, was open-minded about Web3 but skeptical about Wikipedia's benefitting from it. Several executives told us how they have evolved from thinking that closed-ended "enterprise blockchains" were the killer app of this technology, to realizing that public networks were the real innovation, as with the Web. Web3 skeptics shared their gripes (some legitimate) with me.

Venture capitalists Jesse Walden of Variant Fund and Arianna Simpson of Andreessen Horowitz described how their own personal journeys led them to Web3. Chris Giancarlo, the former chairman of the US Commodity Futures Trading Commission, weighed in on the direction of Web3 regulation and policy, as did Sheila Warren and Kristin Smith, who head up advocacy groups Crypto Council for Innovation and the Blockchain Association, respectively, in Washington, DC.

Web3 is also a cultural frontier, something apparent in conversations with Web3 artists like the pseudonymous pplpleasr, who is reimagining storytelling, and Jessie Nickson-Lopez, a screenwriter for hit shows like *Narcos: Mexico* and *Stranger Things*, who moonlights as a Web3 entrepreneur with her startup MV3. She wants to remake Hollywood. Several videogame executives in the Philippines and elsewhere told me how Web3 empowers cash-starved developers in the Global South with tools to fund new projects, elevating the creative power of typically marginalized groups. Culture needs a new business model. Web3 makes that possible. An eight-year-old Filipino artist named Sevi, who sells his paintings as NFTs to a global audience, raising enough money to pay for his autism treatment, put the societal impact of Web3 in stark relief. These interviews, my own wide reading, and the millions of dollars of Blockchain Research Institute research form the basis for this study of Web3.

This book is for everyone who cares about the future and wants to play a role in shaping it. Perhaps you're a student weighing your career options, or an executive trying to understand what Web3 means for your business. Maybe you're underemployed in Africa or India, and you see an opportunity to plug into Web3's global labor pool and work for one of its native digital organizations, known as DAOs. Maybe you're a social entrepreneur in the not-for-profit sector, and you're evaluating different ways to raise funds or engage with young constituents. You could be an artist or storyteller exploring how Web3 tools can reward your creativity. Perhaps you're a politician who wants to attract investment in your city, state, or country. Or maybe you're a citizen who feels that the Web and the world could be better and fairer.

Web3 is the Internet's next economic and cultural frontier. Some frontiers are for experts only and require vast amounts of capital or superhuman strength, like climbing Mount Everest or journeying to Mars. All frontiers present their share of risk and rewards. But the most bountiful of frontiers in history have often been pushed by everyday people, or at least the ones brave enough or driven by circumstances to pack up their belongings and hit the trail. Even the heartiest explorer needs a guide. With humility, I hope this one proves useful.

PART I
DISRUPTIONS

CHAPTER 1

The Web Is Entering a Third Era

Every so often, a new technology emerges, upending the social order and transforming the economy in profound and unexpected ways. Johannes Gutenberg's invention of the printing press in 1440 democratized books and knowledge (for the literate) and, nearly eighty years after its invention, helped Martin Luther spread his ninety-five theses challenging church dogma, ushering in the Reformation. It also created an era of broadsheets, pulp fiction, pornography, and print advertising. James Watt's steam engine in 1776 turbocharged the nascent industrial age, radically reshaped the natural world, and gave rise to new industries like railroads and telegraphy, giant corporations like Andrew Carnegie's US Steel and John D. Rockefeller's Standard Oil, and trade unions like the American Federation of Labor (later the AFL-CIO). The commercialization of Italian inventor Guglielmo Marconi's wireless communications by the Radio Corporation of America in the 1920s with live news and corporate-sponsored programming created a new mass media and consumer culture and changed politics profoundly as both autocrats and politicians in democracies harnessed the airwaves, reaching into the homes of the poor and the emerging middle class, to spread fear and hope in equal measure.

In the second half of the twentieth century, the Cold War and the space race accelerated the convergence of computing and communications, giving us another breakthrough: the Internet, initially conceived in the 1960s to keep the US command centers operational in the event of an attack, and later commercialized with Tim Berners-Lee's invention of the World Wide Web and Marc Andreessen's Mosaic web browser in the 1990s. The Internet, and the Web specifically, has already altered our world in profound ways. Now it is entering a new era that promises once again to transform all industries, society, and culture.

The first era of the Web, now known as Web1 (1992–2002), the so-called Read-Only Web, was a broadcast medium that recast information such as mail, magazines, catalogs, newspapers, and classifieds, digitally. *Wired*, a print magazine, launched the banner ad business, and corporations everywhere replaced their interoffice mail department with email and marketing material with websites. Users could read information online but not interact with it. Web1 democratized access to information for those with connected computers but was static and unidirectional. Users were passive receivers of someone else's content. Some of the best-known Web1 entities, such as Encyclopaedia Britannica Online, AOL, Lycos, and AltaVista, borrowed from pre-Internet counterparts.

The use of the words *page* and *mail*, as in a "web page" that one "published" and "electronic mail," says it all: the mental model was rooted in paper and publishing. Web1 creations were *skeuomorphic*, that is, digital versions of preexisting products, services, or their business models.[1] Sometimes the first version of a new product or service resembles the old version on one or more dimensions, because either the designer or the designer's targeted audience can't quite imagine a totally different future. More often, designers and entrepreneurs leverage aspects of the old to help their audience transition to the new, so that the new feels more familiar. For example, manufacturers of the first electric lightbulbs shaped them like candle flames. Computer icons of trash cans, file folders, and mailbox applications are another example. For years, the first Tesla cars had prominent front grilles, even though electric cars don't need them.[2]

"The superpower of Web1 was it harnessed the power of third-party developers and so it was a system governed by open protocols," said

Chris Dixon of venture capital firm Andreessen Horowitz. "Anyone could come and build stuff—websites, app layer, and infrastructure layer across the board. It had this community-driven development, which I think is a very powerful force."[3]

The crash of the dot-coms in 2000–2001 created a need for a new kind of Web. Thanks to some important technology innovations, the Web became a medium for collaboration and computation, called Web2, or the Read-Write Web (2002–2020), with tools for creating, sharing, and discussing content, unwittingly programming the Web in new ways.[4] To use computer programming jargon, we all could "write" to the Web, adding our own content. Internet-native communities and organizations formed. Consider Wikipedia. Its cofounders, Jimmy Wales and Larry Sanger, invited volunteers to contribute or translate entries, building an important global resource in the process. Wikipedia and other volunteer organizations stewarded but didn't control or own their sites' utility and development.[5] In contrast, social media giants like Facebook and Twitter enabled individuals to create and publish their own content, form groups, and collaborate online, but users couldn't attach clear ownership rights to their content, and they lacked any say in the governance of those platforms. As a result, "the economic interests of the biggest Internet platforms [were and] are poorly aligned with their most valuable contributors: their users."[6] Web2 and mobile combined to form natural monopolies in several areas, from search to social networking, e-commerce to mobile operating systems. Said Dixon, "We used to have CBS, NBC, ABC. Now we have Facebook, Google, Amazon, Apple."[7]

The Failures of the Old Web

Tim Berners-Lee's great invention is still a force for tremendous good in the world, but it has fallen short in key respects, as Berners-Lee himself acknowledged. Thirty years after the World Wide Web went live, he wrote in the *Guardian* about its legacy, including the "perverse incentives" that encourage "ad-based revenue models that commercially reward clickbait and the viral spread of misinformation" and "the outraged and polarized tone and quality of online discourse."[8]

Facebook's Mark Zuckerberg joined Jeff Bezos of Amazon and Sergey Brin and Larry Page of Google as the magnates of the new oil: user data generated from user attention, which was fracked, analyzed, and sold to advertisers. With the marriage of personal digital assistants, cellular telephony, and 3G connectivity came the smartphone, putting supercomputers online in the hands of billions. The smartphone camera made everyone a documentarian of their own lives, streaming a deluge of data. Mobile combined with the Global Positioning System unleashed so-called "sharing economy" platforms to package and peddle other people's excess capacity. Sharing economy is, of course, a misnomer: With Uber Technologies Inc., for example, drivers share their time and resources but do not participate in the upside of the platform and have no say in how Uber governs it. Likewise, riders make these networks valuable, but they have no economic or governance stake in Uber unless they're institutional investors or Uber insiders.[9]

Berners-Lee shares Web3 proponents' concerns about Web2. However, he is unenthusiastic about blockchain, one of the core technologies of Web3, as a solution to these problems. "Blockchain protocols may be good for some things, but they're not good for Solid," he said, speaking of his own project to decentralize the Web and improve privacy while putting data in the hands of Internet users. In his view, blockchains are "too slow, too expensive, and too public. Personal data stores have to be fast, cheap, and private."[10]

Berners-Lee has also shared his frustration with the public's conflating or confusing "Web3" with what he called "Web 3.0," meaning the "semantic web," where computers could read and process data from the Web to the benefit of all.[11] He said we should just ignore "Web3" because it's not really the Web at all. In a sense, he's right. Web3 as a concept is emerging; it is a radical departure from the original technology and architecture of the Web. Further, Berners-Lee's Solid could help solve the problems of data capture and ownership that he and others have identified with Web2. When the inventor of the World Wide Web speaks of its future, we should listen.

WEB2 ADVOCATES THOUGHT the new writable Web would remove gatekeepers. Instead, Web2 giants simply became new gatekeepers. When the government of Australia introduced a new law requiring Facebook, Google, and others to pay Australian news outlets to feature their links, Facebook responded by blocking all news content in a country where 39 percent of people get their news from the service. It did this in the middle of forest fires and the COVID-19 pandemic, effectively shutting off access to the national weather service and government health officials.[12] People were awaiting word on vaccination distribution. The government capitulated and offered Facebook various concessions.

With reams of data at their disposal, Web2 platforms devised ever more sophisticated tools to profile and target users in ways that Nielsen couldn't easily deliver for CBS, NBC, and ABC, even at its zenith. Social media specifically targeted those receptive to certain messages, regardless of their truth, amplifying extremism, harming public discourse, spreading misinformation, and, according to many scientists who've studied it, altering the chemistry of the mind.[13] An internal audit of Facebook concluded, "Our algorithms exploit human brain's attraction to divisiveness" and were "driving people toward self-reinforcing echo chambers of extremism."[14] So far such warnings have not spurred much soul-searching in the C-suites of Web2.

As more commerce moved online, Web2 businesses as well as banks and payment firms like Visa and Mastercard also became all-powerful financial intermediaries of the digital economy. Meanwhile, the value of all the collaboration and communication accrued to centralized platforms such as Apple, Google, Facebook, Amazon, and others as they harnessed user data, app developer data, and brand data to create immense value for themselves within their walled gardens.

This model worked well for a time, but it overwhelmed users with ever more targeted ads and page recommendations, and it exposed their data to hackers.[15] "Imagine if General Motors did not pay for its steel, rubber, or glass—its inputs," economist Robert J. Shapiro told the *New York Times*. "That's what it's like for the big Internet companies. It's a sweet deal."[16]

As natural monopolies, Web2 giants stifled competition as they consolidated network power. Founded in the 1990s and 2000s, these companies were flexing their muscles, killing off or acquiring up-start competitors. For example, Facebook snapped up FriendFeed in 2009, Friendster's patents in 2010, Friend.ly in 2011, Instagram and a wallet app in 2012, and WhatsApp and Oculus VR in 2014, to name a few. But it didn't stop there: it bought technologies for location discovery, facial recognition, speech translation, fitness and activity tracking, voice recognition, emotion detection, biometric identification, and a brain-machine interface that translates neural impulses into digital signals—setting the company up to collect the most personal data yet for profiling each user.[17] An attempt in 2013 to buy Snapchat for $3 billion failed. From Facebook's perspective, these deals were sound decisions; in other eras, corporate giants used their buying power to roll up competitors. But for Internet users today, the model looks more like a Faustian bargain and an increasingly unsustainable status quo in need of a major rethink.

Birth of the New Web

Following the financial crisis of 2008, just as the mobile Web was taking off and Web2 giants were consolidating their power online, an inventor named Satoshi Nakamoto surfaced to lay the foundation for another era of the Web. Satoshi released the Bitcoin white paper and then bootstrapped the first publicly available tool to send value over the Internet peer-to-peer with nothing more than a computer and an Internet connection.[18] Before Bitcoin, this was not possible without trusting a middleman. Bitcoin became public infrastructure for payments the way email and the Web became public infrastructure for information. What was remarkable about Bitcoin was that it worked, setting the stage for much bigger commercial, cultural, and political upheaval.

The Web is entering a third era, Web3, the Read-Write-Own Web (2020–), which can democratize tools for owning of the Web's key platforms, organizations, and assets and align incentives of users with the technologies they use. Web1 and Web2, though very different, were still *information media*. Together they make up the first era of the Internet. With Web3, the Internet is entering a second era—the Internet of value. In our book *Blockchain Revolution* Don Tapscott and I explained how the Internet is entering a second era. A revolutionary technology known as blockchain is ushering in an Internet of value where assets can be represented digitally, owned, transacted, and secured peer-to-peer. Blockchain is bringing a new Web and a new Internet.

Web2's missing piece was digital property rights. All of us who use the Web create value—virtual goods or digital assets that have value. We "write" to the Web and create value, but Web2 giants instantly expropriate that value. Users don't own the virtual goods they create, they can't monetize their data or manage their privacy, and they have no say as stakeholders in how the services they use are run. Every time you tweet, form a group on Facebook, upload a photo to Instagram, make a TikTok video, or publish to YouTube, you are creating value that you can't fully capture. Every time you do almost anything online, you leave a trail of intimate data about you—what you buy, eat, say, where you go, who you associate with, how you look, what interests you, which causes you support, how you access information, and how long you spend reading certain material. Get the picture?

Sometimes you even pay real money to create value for the platforms you use. Consider videogames like *Fortnite*, where you must buy that game's digital goods to fit in and compete effectively. But you can't take them with you. If the game developer gets acquired and shutters your favorite title or changes its code, you may lose your assets forever. We are not owners but renters online. Arianna Simpson of Andreessen Horowitz said, "Those aren't really assets in the traditional sense. You don't have ownership; there are no property rights.

They exist inside someone else's universe at their privilege."[19] This is bad for the user and limits the economic potential of the Web. Despite these limitations, Internet users still spend $100 billion a year on digital goods that they don't truly own. Matthew Ball wrote in his book *The Metaverse*, "The virtual hat, plot of land, or movie that a user buys cannot truly be theirs because they cannot ever control it."[20] Property rights laid the groundwork for prosperity in the industrial age. Digital property rights—ownership online—will underwrite prosperity in the information age.

Ownership of digital assets, or tokens, is the foundation to Web3. It gives people an economic stake in their digital existence. Ownership enables new models of finance, as individuals leverage their digital assets to earn, save, transact, or invest peer-to-peer, foreshadowing the biggest upheaval to finance and money in centuries. Kevin Owocki, Ethereum pioneer and founder of Gitcoin, said, "Property rights in the digital realm are not something that we've had before. If you think property rights were important for the evolution of finance in the real world, then you should think they're important for Web3."[21] With ownership also comes new forms of identity: Internet users can use Web3 tools to prove attributes about themselves, their Web3 identities complemented with biometrics and proof of government ID, what videogame entrepreneur Beryl Li calls "proof of humanness."[22] Finally, ownership gives users a say in how platforms and services operate. Governance rights promise a more representative and fairly run Internet where platforms are accountable to users. Simply put, Web3's leaders posit that Internet users should have privacy in transactions, sovereignty over their digital self, and property rights for their assets online.

Web3's leaders and advocates are also diverse, global, and young and empowered with technology tools that existed only in the domain of science fiction a generation ago. Dispersed technology will distribute power, influence, and value creation in Web3. Though there is no single "Web3 culture" any more than there is an "electricity culture," some common themes run through this community of users and developers. Early adopters are, by their nature, experimenters who aren't afraid of "reimagining the economy from first principles," even if they're playing with new and untested tools.[23] Like Web1, Web3 has a jaunty, even irreverent vibe. The stakes are high and consequences weighty, but the memes are lighthearted. When everyone calls you crazy, it helps to have a sense of humor. Web3 is also open. "It's not just that it's open source or permissionless," said Tim Beiko, a developer of the popular Ethereum platform. "When you build something on Ethereum, anyone can then interact with it." Not only can they see the code, "but they can plug into your thing directly. That creates a huge culture of openness and collaboration."[24]

Web3's builders are a capitalistic bunch competing aggressively in an open market. But, in general, Beiko's sentiment holds true. The one exception would be hard-core Bitcoiners who (to paraphrase a line from Tracy Kidder's 1981 Pulitzer Prize–winning book, *The Soul of a New Machine*) harbor very strong feelings about bitcoin, like Cossacks toward their horses.[25]

Life, Liberty, and the Pursuit of Digital Property

Property rights are foundational to a free society, democracy, and a functioning market economy, a concept first articulated during the Enlightenment but expanded greatly through the centuries. Today they are a cornerstone of a modern society and market economy. Property rights, documented in contracts enforced through the consistent and impartial rule of law, anchor all investment, capital formation, and innovation. Indeed, contracts are the foundation of every asset class, every corporation, and all economic activity. The countries that govern these best reap the rewards of greater investment and innovation. This makes intuitive sense: Why would anyone allocate capital to a new business or any other investment for that matter if they were not sure of their ownership?

While exiled in Paris during the English Civil War in the seventeenth century, English scholar Thomas Hobbes wrote his seminal work, *Leviathan*. In this work, Hobbes advocated for a strong central authority, but rooted in law and the state rather than a single person, arguing human beings' existence was "solitary, poore, nasty, brutish, and short."[26] A few decades later, during the Glorious Revolution, which affirmed the primacy of Parliament over the divine right of the monarchy, John Locke published his *Two Treatises of Government*. His view of man's natural state wasn't so pessimistic, and his concept of government was rooted more in the rights of the individual, not in the absolute authority of the state. Rights derived from private property, not government fiat.[27] Of course, that was not how things worked. What was Locke's remedy for the inconveniences of the state of nature? Property rights.

Web1 was not some barbarous state of nature—more Adam and Eve than Cain and Abel. Still, it was anarchic and disorganized, and it lacked a way for people to verify themselves without sharing personal information, as well as express digital property rights, represent community ownership, and develop other mechanisms to coordinate, organize, and fund the creation of value online. Web2 companies created a simple model where we get access to a gated and curated experience, and in exchange we contribute data to building these valuable platforms and agree to forgo any upside from our content or labor. We also agree to the terms of service without negotiation and often without reading them. We have no input into the platform's evolution, its other participants, and so forth. To paraphrase Locke, despite our labors, our "property" isn't properly ours. Instead, the platform markets our digital personhood to the highest bidder. In this respect, Web2 is more orthodox than enlightenment, more feudal than capitalistic. Surfing the Internet is more like *serfing* the Internet as we willingly forfeit privacy and data rights for the security of the digital estate.[28] However, under authoritarian regimes, Web2 applications can be instruments of social control and political repression.[29]

Web3 technologies, on the other hand, can be instruments of economic, social, and political freedom. Rather than relying on governments to enforce our rights, blockchains can do it for us. Privacy is "one of the most important things that Web3 can do over centralized systems," said Sunny Aggarwal, a serial crypto entrepreneur.[30] Digital bearer assets, known in the industry as *tokens*, enable us to hold and port valuable digital goods from platform to platform online. These goods can be currencies, securities, and other financial assets as well as collectibles, intellectual property (IP), our identities, our data, and the as-yet unimagined. Online there are no fixed hectares of property to claim. Only an infinite frontier. "Cyberspace is likely to be in due course the richest of economic realms," said James Dale Davidson and Lord William Rees-Mogg in their seminal book, *The Sovereign Individual*.[31]

The word *token* as a noun is an odd one for defining such a foundational concept. The *Oxford Advanced Learner's Dictionary* defines a token as a visible or tangible representation of a fact, quality, feeling, or voucher that holders can exchange for goods or services or use to operate machines.[32] For better or worse, the technology world has adopted the term and, as you will read, it turns out to be appropriate.

Chris Dixon explained how the token is the building block of Web3, just as the website was the building block of Web1 and Web2. Like a website, a token is a container, he said. "It can hold code. It can have images. It can have music. It can have text, whatever a creative person thinks of. The key property here is instead of being a hyperlink and delivering information, it can be owned. It can be owned by a user. It can be owned by a smart contract. It can be owned by a service."[33] The "smart contract" in question here is not the static and analog agreement that we can "sign" digitally using Web2 apps like DocuSign. For all their convenience, e-signatures are a Web2 invention: *read* the contract, *write* your signature. By contrast, smart contracts are self-executing and immutable peer-to-peer agreements written in code that do not require lawyers, banks, or other intermediaries to enforce the terms. In contrast, most of today's contracts are quite dumb. Smart ones can do a lot more, like hold money or other assets, like a digital trust account without the lawyer.

Brett Winton of Ark Investment Management put it simply: "We have a default mechanism by which we can digitally possess something, prove that we possess it, and transfer possession to another person, in a way that everybody can agree upon."[34] Finally, we have an instrument for possessing and proving possession of digital goods and identity, and as the saying goes: possession is nine-tenths of the law.[35]

The Triumph of Our Digital Commons

In a 1992 presentation, research scientist David D. Clark expressed the ethos of the Internet pioneers for those who hadn't been involved (as he had) since the 1970s: "We reject kings, presidents, and voting. We believe in rough consensus and running code."[36] Clark's declaration captured the quasi-anarchic spirit of Internet standards development in the 1970s and 1980s, which carried into the ethos of openness and freedom of Web1.

The creators of the Internet's early killer apps, like email and instant messaging, relied on open-source software funded by the US government and academia. No corporation owned the key platforms or oversaw the development of the early web.[37] As the Web matured and gained new functionality and hundreds of millions of new users, a new breed of companies emerged to exploit the commercial opportunities on top of these digital commons.

The ecologist Garrett Hardin coined the phrase "tragedy of the commons" about nineteenth-century farmers who grazed their animals on common land. All the farmers had incentives to maintain the land. But without rules regulating its use, and with all farmers driven by their own self-interests to feed their cows, they depleted the land. Hardin was also a nativist and racist whose land use thesis informed a zero-sum view of humanity that advocated for eugenics and against immigration.[38] Still, we cannot overstate his influence on everything from climate science to economic theory. Many others have extended cynical versions of his theory to other public goods, from roads and waterways to drinking water and food supplies, and used this "tragedy" as justification for private ownership or at least external governance of important resources.[39]

Our online public goods are not raw resources but open-source protocols, that is, software in the public domain, developed and maintained by volunteers who share the right to use, copy, adapt, and distribute the programs (called *source code*) to anyone who wants to use them. The Internet showed us that we could come together voluntarily to build open-source public goods of tremendous value. Open-source projects add hundreds of billions annually to the global gross domestic product (GDP), improve labor productivity, and help with startup formation.[40]

Kevin Owocki of Gitcoin told us, "As a software engineer, when I want to build a new website, I don't build my own web server, database server, or cloud host. I use open-source software. What's beautiful about that is, we're all standing on the shoulders of giants. We can all go faster because of these open-source Legos."[41] While building open source is clearly possible, maintaining it is a lot harder. Owocki also pointed out that, because the projects are not well monetized, the people who maintain them either burn out or work corporate jobs to fund their open-source passion projects.

This misalignment of incentives and economic rewards keeps open-source projects from competing effectively with corporate ones. As Michael J. Casey wrote, "For-profit companies steered their resources toward the commercialized proprietary applications that ran on top of open protocols."[42] Companies have the financial resources to poach top talent and donate to nonprofits that shape their direction.

Web3 tools not only empower individuals with property rights online through the ownership of digital goods, but also provide a workable model to launch and sustain open-source projects by giving developers an economic incentive to work on them full-time. Users and developers are different groups, but their interests align as economic stakeholders online.

If tokens are containers that can hold anything we value, then we can also program them with certain economic rights for contributors and rules for how to govern public goods. Nobel Prize–winning economist Elinor Ostrom researched communities that governed communal assets effectively. She identified eight principles, from setting clear usage boundaries to codifying simple governance, which led to sustainable resource management.[43] We can program rules and incentives into governance tokens along with economic rights so that open-source developers can turn their passion projects into full-time gigs. This essential infrastructure and these services for Web3 are open source: no corporation could capture them nor exclude others from building on them, thus bolstering individual ownership rights online.

This concept of community ownership extends to other realms of business and society. In Web3, people can pool their assets and manage them via new Internet-native organizations called DAOs, or decentralized autonomous organizations.

Six Transformations to Business and Our World

In this book, we look at Web3's nascent impact on our world. We explore some topics as if they were concentric circles, focusing narrowly at first on the concept of *assets*, and expanding outward to *people*, to *organizations* and *enterprises*, then to *industries*, the *human experience*, and *civilization* as a whole. I explain what all this means for young entrepreneurs or innovators pressing forward with their pathbreaking ideas, but also for those in the leadership suites of industry, government, education, and more.

At no point has our planet been more interconnected and interdependent. Web3 will affect all of us equally but in different ways. It presents challenges and opportunities for all. First, in **chapter two**, we lay out the blueprint and architecture for Web3. At the ground floor of the Web3 superstructure are blockchains. Not exactly a sonorous term, nevertheless blockchains are the foundation of Web3. They are virtual computers with unprecedented capabilities. In this chapter, we dive into what this means and how innovators are applying it in Web3 today.

In **chapter three**, we start our analysis of the core transformations with a deep dive of the core building block of Web3: digital assets, or *tokens*. Without assets, there can be no ownership. Digital assets give Internet users a direct way to participate in the growth of the digital economy, which will soon be the richest of economic realms. Our token taxonomy covers eleven kinds of digital assets that have gained traction in Web3 so far: cryptocurrencies, protocol tokens, governance tokens, oracle tokens, interoperability tokens, securities tokens, corporate tokens, natural asset tokens, stablecoins, non-fungible tokens (NFTs), and central bank digital currencies (CBDCs). Collectively these types make up nearly 100 percent of all digital asset value and have already found product/market fit. For example, stablecoin transaction volumes hit $7.2 trillion in 2022, a 19 percent year-on-year growth from 2021.[44] Nevertheless, cataloging the different "types" of tokens will soon be as useful as cataloging the ways we use websites—pointless. Further, if tokens are to Web3 what the website was to Web1, then many (though not all) of today's tokens will end up with the early dot-com websites—footnotes to this transformation.

In **chapter four**, we talk about people—the impact that Web3 will have on users newly empowered with ownership of their assets online. In Web2, platforms owned or co-owned and controlled the property of creators; and musicians, artists, writers, and others have suffered. In a Web3 world, all individuals who create value can own and benefit from their contributions. For example, musicians can publish content on platforms like Audius with its 7.5 million users and earn a share of the platform used, with an economic stake in its success and a say in its governance. NFTs are unique digital goods that express value of cultural assets and among other things enable visual artists to bypass galleries and sell directly to fans on platforms like Magic Eden, Rarible, or OpenSea.[45] When buyers resell their assets, the artists can earn royalties in perpetuity, all programmed on-chain. Hollywood is optioning rights to creating stories around early NFTs such as Bored Ape Yacht Club. As the saying goes, movies are the billboard for ancillary rights.[46] One insider quipped, "Hollywood adapts everything" today.[47] Some enterprising screenwriters who founded the NFT startup MV3 are rethinking the nature of storytelling, selling characters in their stories as NFTs to early fans and inviting them to write backstories for their NFTs, changing how fans participate creatively and economically in the process of storytelling and world-building. "Owning your own storm trooper" was not possible in Web2. "If bitcoin is a store of value, then NFTs are a store of culture" that will profoundly alter the creative industries, according to Yat Siu, executive chairman of Animoca Brands, a global leader in blockchain, gaming, and the open metaverse.[48]

But this is not just for creative types. All Internet users will have greater custody over their virtual selves. Each of us creates a mirror image of ourselves as we navigate and transact in the digital world. This trail of "digital crumbs" is the stuff of our digital identities.[49] In Web2, we create this data, but the digital landlords take it from us. With Web3, we can each recapture our digital selves in something called a *self-sovereign identity*, where we can each manage our identities responsibly for our own benefit. Today, accessing most of Web3 requires no formal verification: it is open and permissionless. We need no third party to prove who we are. By giving users tools to accumulate and control an asset base and reputation, Web3 innovators are creating tools for us to build out our own self-sovereign identities.[50]

If corporations were the foundation of the industrial age, then *decentralized autonomous organizations*, or DAOs, may prove to be the foundation of Web3 and the next digital age. In **chapter five**, we discuss the new Web3-native organizations and how they're transforming business and disrupting traditional enterprise. The limited liability company was a powerful machine for raising growth capital and spreading risks across a group of shareholders, which is why they worked great for an age of capital-intensive undertakings. Web3 is starting to change the deep structures and architectures of the firm itself, bringing new decentralized models of how we innovate and create wealth in society. DAOs are the default structure for most Web3 apps. Collectively Web3 DAO treasuries control billions of dollars of assets.[51] Web3 also forces us to rethink management science—how we organize capability, work together, and collaborate for shared success. How can business leaders respond? As Harvard professor Clayton Christensen observed, the market opportunity of new technologies is so ill-defined that business leaders often choose not to embrace them until it is too late.[52] Or they double down on existing technologies and tinker on the margin.

Some of Web3's supposed defects may turn out to be it biggest strengths, another challenge for incumbents. Christensen wrote, "The attributes that make disruptive products worthless in mainstream markets typically become their strongest selling points in emerging markets."[53] Consider one staple of Web3: self-custody of tokens in wallets. Owners can hold and control their assets personally. In a marketplace where customers have relied for so long on intermediaries like banks to custody and move assets, self-custody can feel like an inconvenience. But for others—especially those in the developing world, where sometimes corruption is rampant, where terrorists and paramilitary groups hold sway, and where local legal and financial infrastructures are woefully underdeveloped or underenforced— self-custodying assets securely, conveniently, and digitally can be a superpower. For young Web3-native users, self-custody is neither an inconvenience nor a superpower, but an expected function of their mobile user experience—control of everything, everywhere, all at once.

Web3 is transforming not just firms but all industries. In **chapters six and seven**, we look at two industries where Web3 is having the greatest impact today: financial services and interactive entertainment (gaming).

First, finance is going through the biggest upheaval since the invention of double-entry bookkeeping. For as long as human beings have been transacting with strangers, banks and other intermediaries have acted as trusted middlemen in the economy, moving, storing, and lending money and keeping records. That is changing thanks to decentralized finance, or DeFi. This is about far more than fintech, which is merely a new coat of paint on the old edifice of finance— digital wallpaper slapped on legacy infrastructure. DeFi extends Satoshi's concept of peer-to-peer electronic cash to lending, trading, investing, managing risk, and more, all of which operate on top of distributed networks, not corporations. These innovations are possible thanks to a breakthrough called a *smart contract*, an immutable, self-executing agreement written in code and settled on a blockchain such as Ethereum. Every industry will feel DeFi's impact, because finance is the cardiovascular system of the global economy, the lifeline of all other industries.

Second, Web3 is also helping reimagine the user experience for gamers and consumers of interactive entertainment, the second case study of this chapter. In the same way that free-to-play gaming transformed gaming by lowering the barriers for amateur gamers to play, integrating mobile gaming and revolutionizing the revenue model for the whole industry, Web3-based gaming will reimagine content, including the virtual goods bought in games, as an asset that users can truly own rather than a consumable experience they only pay for. This too will change the gaming experience, bring in new players, and reimagine the revenue model for studios.

In **chapter eight**, we go beyond individual industries to explore the much-hyped world of the metaverse, a shared, immersive, persistent virtual space that many expect will become a new and important plane for the human experience. Nearly everyone agrees that this is going to be big. Morgan Stanley predicts the metaverse will be worth $8 trillion by 2030.[54] Citibank believes that number will be closer to $13 trillion, which, for perspective, approaches China's 2020 GDP. Citi also believes the metaverse will have five billion users in less than a decade, and will be an engine for new business growth, entrepreneurship, and employment.[55]

But the metaverse is deeply misunderstood. "A lot of people are trying to put metaverse in this box where it's only about high fidelity and 3D assets," said Aleksander Larsen, cofounder and chief operating officer of Sky Mavis, maker of the game *Axie Infinity*, when really "it's a social construct where ownership is one of the foundations to real engagement. It's all about the people who are engaging and how deeply they are engaging with each other."[56]

If the desktop computer was our gateway to Web1 and the smartphone our portal to Web2, virtual reality (VR) and augmented reality (AR), along with the digital wallet, may be how many experience Web3. These technologies will usher in what technologist Dan Mapes calls a "spatial web" integrated into our natural environment.[57] Most of the major investments into VR and other immersive online experiences are happening inside big companies like Apple, with its Vision Pro headset; Facebook, with its Oculus Quest; and Microsoft. But to give the metaverse a "second life," we need Web3 tools of digital property rights and self-sovereign identities. Otherwise we run the risk of Web2 giants like Facebook, who see the metaverse as simply a new frontier to build a walled garden for existing users, harvesting their data and perpetuating the same ad-based model that made them successful in the smartphone age. Beware. "When big tech tries to co-opt the word *meta*, it's totally ridiculous to me. It reeks of desperation," said Larsen.[58]

The metaverse could become an Orwellian monster that reinforces existing inequalities, structures, practices, and forms of oppression. Innovators must hard-code property rights and self-sovereign identity into the metaverse, something Web2 giants would rather not see happen. Whereas the Web had its origins in government as well as volunteer and nongovernmental organizations (NGOs) such as the Institute of Electrical and Electronics Engineers (IEEE), private businesses are pioneering the metaverse "for the explicit purpose of commerce, data collection, advertising and the sale of virtual products," said Ball.[59] The winners will build the metaverse on shared infrastructure that functions as a public good and imbue it with digital rights. Only open-source Web3 tools like digital assets make this possible. In this chapter, we look at what builders are doing to pioneer the open metaverse for all.

Finally, we look at the physical infrastructure needed to power the Web3 metaverse. Call it DePIN, for decentralized physical infrastructure. It includes computation, Internet connectivity, graphics rendering, and more. The total addressable market for Web3-enabled decentralized physical infrastructure—from wireless networks to cloud computing—is estimated to be worth $3.8 trillion by 2028.[60] Executives in all industries should take notice.

In **chapter nine**, we look at how Web3 builds economic bridges online between distant markets, putting people and creators around the world on a more level playing field to fully realize their potential. By buttressing digital property rights, lowering barriers to financial access, and strengthening economic ties between people and organizations online, Web3 empowers those living in the Global South. We look at several examples of how Web3 is helping creators, business-people, and everyday citizens connect to the global economy. We also examine how Web3 threatens currency issuers in these parts of the world, where mass adoption of digital goods and specifically stablecoins could accelerate the collapse of their local currencies. In his book *The World Is Flat*, Thomas Friedman examined how globalization was creating opportunities for people in the Global South while also exploring the downsides. Web3 builds on that concept, "flattening" the world further by giving people a new digital toolset to earn money and connect more fully to the global economy. We explore what leaders in business and civil society can do to harness this technology for good.

The final part of the book takes a frank look at the problems and challenges of getting from here to there. Web3 is not without its critics—and loud ones at that. Some see little more than a buzzword conjured by billionaire venture capitalists or a clever rebrand of cryptocurrencies that—in their view—only money launderers and other criminals use.[61] Because of the Bitcoin blockchain's carbon footprint, they assume all Web3 applications waste energy or they dismiss Web3 native assets as toys.

In **chapter ten**, we discuss the soul of this new machine, a soul that seeks self-actualization. When we wrote *Blockchain Revolution*, the new machine was trying to survive, not self-actualize, per Maslow's framework. Now it can dream bigger as it rests up to clear the many hurdles ahead.

The failure of crypto exchange FTX in 2022 revealed the need for a comprehensive policy framework for Web3, digital assets, and companies that build services on top of these technologies. Government can help by creating the conditions for innovation to occur. But some fear that, in the absence of comprehensive Web3 legislation, US regulators are regulating by enforcement, choosing targets arbitrarily and interpreting their mandate too broadly. Lawmakers on both sides of the aisle condemned the U.S. Securities and Exchange Commission after the agency sued Coinbase in June 2023. The suit, if successful, would bring many, if not most, digital assets under the agency's jurisdiction.

FTX's collapse revealed another problem: that most new Web3

users began by buying into an asset class on a centralized exchange and then remaining there, favoring convenience over self-custody. We could say something similar about depositors of Silicon Valley Bank (SVB), including many startups and even large businesses that stood to lose almost everything, had the US Federal Deposit Insurance Corporation not stepped in.[62] For many, self-custody was not a realistic option, especially because their loan agreements with SVB bound them to hold their cash at the bank, too. The perception that SVB's collapse would cause widespread calamity and collateral damage in the economy spurred the government to act. In contrast, no one rescued the thousands of depositors, businesses, and investment funds that held assets on FTX; some of them lost everything.

Roneil Rumburg, founder of Web3 music platform Audius, told us that the collapse of FTX will "lead to more time/resources spent toward improving the usability of fully self-sovereign, decentralized tooling for managing digital assets."[63] But he was quick to point out that while "it's possible to be a self-sovereign crypto user today, the usability bar for doing so is still so high that it's out of reach for many mainstream users."[64]

Historian Niall Ferguson argued that Web3's steeper learning curve could create opportunities to centralize power, re-creating the Web2 dynamic but for money rather than information, where decentralized finance is "currently about as user-friendly as personal computer software in the pre-Windows era. So long as that remains true, crypto exchanges will have a role." He also underscored the possibility that, as in Web2, "a single exchange will become the dominant player, centralizing what was supposed to be a decentralized network, just as Amazon centralized e-commerce, Google centralized search, Facebook centralized social networking, and Twitter centralized outrage."[65]

There are other challenges: Does Web3 need its own hardware to dislodge the smartphone operating system duopoly of Apple and Google? What other technical upgrades do we need to usher in in a Web3 world? Many of these criticisms are valid. We are early and many Web3 applications are not yet ready for prime time, though that is changing rapidly. Criminals do use these assets, though with less enthusiasm than they spend stacks of cash.[66] The experience of interacting with Web3 can be clunky and confusing to new users. The explosion of innovation has led to numerous conflicting standards, with blockchains like countries with their own rail gauges. Every time we switch from one country to the next, we must switch gauges. That's risky, and we can derail. Can the technology coalesce around a single set of standards?

Every technological leap forward improves the reach of criminals. Exponential times lead to exponential crimes. Scammers have adopted Web3 tools, just as they embraced email, clickbait, text messages, and robocalls to rip off the vulnerable. Ponzi schemes specifically are what economists call a "negative externality" of Web3 that innovators and advocates must address.[67] Web3 holds a mirror up to society, reflecting its best and worst. Its unique properties make it particularly useful for do-gooders and dirtbags alike: it lowers barriers to spinning up new digital assets and promoting them passionately to a global audience.

That's why we need to assess "each crypto asset, blockchain, and project . . . on its own merit," said Hester Peirce, a commissioner of the US Securities and Exchange Commission (SEC). "Talking about crypto as if it [were] a monolith obscures important differences."[68] Obscurity is to scammers what water is to fish. How we act will heavily shape the development of this technology. As Ferguson argued, "The bursting of the Mississippi and South Sea Bubbles did not mark the end of equity financing and stock trading, any more than the many financial panics of the nineteenth century marked the end of joint-stock banking."[69]

That leads us to regulation of this new asset class, which challenges many existing legal and policy rubrics for the financial industry, as we will explore. Because of government's light touch in the West, Web2 entities have become some of the most powerful and profitable corporations in history, first undercutting the prices of brick-and-mortar incumbents and then acquiring potential rivals before they grew too menacing. Web3 innovations help to address the most glaring of Web2 shortcomings, such as the centralization of power and the manipulation and monetization of users' personal data. Even so, dis-lodging them will sometimes feel like a quixotic undertaking, "tilting at windmills," in the words of a prominent venture capitalist (VC).[70] Some critics call Web3 the "Wild West," but we have only just crossed the Appalachians. Ours is a journey through undiscovered country.

Such criticism has also exposed the cultural and generational fault lines between Web2 and Web3. The Internet was just for pornography, said early critics.[71] Upstart minicomputer companies, which sought to challenge IBM's mainframe monopoly, were cast as ravenous kill-ers. In *The Soul of a New Machine*, a computer executive told author Tracy Kidder, "I'm not sure IBM with its organization, can compete in the traditional minicomputer market. It's like putting a goldfish in a bowl with a piranha."[72] Later the PC caimans swallowed those same minicomputer piranhas whole. In 1977, the year Steve Jobs and Steve Wozniak launched the Apple II, the CEO of minicomputer juggernaut Digital Equipment Corporation, Ken Olsen, said, "There is no reason for any individual to have a computer in his home."[73] This cycle predates computers. Feudal lords would have doubtless scoffed at the notion that the "the small, dull, vulgar group of merchants and traders and money lenders" would somehow usurp them in power, and while it took centuries, capitalism became preeminent.[74] History doesn't repeat but it rhymes. In this chapter, we sort the myths and misconceptions from the real implementation challenges.

Finally, in the **conclusion**, we outline what readers can do. These formative years of Web3 are epochal times. We may look back on them as historians have looked back on previous upheavals. British historian Eric Hobsbawm said the "short twentieth century," which began in 1914 with the outbreak of World War I, ended in 1989 with the col-lapse of the Soviet Union.[75] The scales of geopolitics tilted dramatically that year, with a less dramatic impact on business, society, and daily life in the United States. Indeed, in retrospect, the present moment may itself mark the end of the *long* twentieth century and the dawn of a new era, and with it, a new economic and cultural frontier online.

CHAPTER 2

Blueprint for the Ownership Web

Web3 did not spring from the mind of a single genius tinkering away in a garage somewhere; rather, it emerged from centuries of innovation in computing.[1] One of its forebears was Alan Turing. In 1948, he wrote, "We do not need . . . an infinity of different machines doing different jobs. A single one will suffice." He imagined replacing "the engineering problem of producing various machines for various jobs" with "the office work of 'programming' the universal machine to do these jobs."[2] His work inspired inventions like the Ethereum protocol and its native programming language Solidity.

Nor did Web3 spill out of the institutional machinery of large corporations, with "teams of faceless organizational engineers contributing incremental advancements," as many advancements of the early digital age seemed to come from companies like Bell Labs and IBM.[3] Unlike the first era of the Internet, Web3 did not come predominantly from government-funded research programs. Instead, Web3 has emerged from thousands of contributors, sometimes collaborating, and sometimes competing, in a long and organic process of experimentation, with breakthroughs and dead ends, some great leaps forward and some steps back, that continue to move the technology and its applications onward. This story, which is as much about social engineering as it is about computer engineering, will continue to play out.

As Walter Isaacson wrote, "Innovation occurs when ripe seeds fall on fertile ground."[4] Like the earth beneath our feet, we stand on stratum upon stratum of technological innovation, each with unique markers of its age. This technology "stack" contains different building blocks from different times that form the basis for all digital innovation. Web3 may be the "new, new thing" but its terroir is complex and generative—and, in some cases, goes back decades. Jesse Walden, cofounder of Variant Fund, said, "This layer cake stacks up to a positive sum that is greater than its individual parts. It gives developers more tools to build applications that take advantage of all the specialized features of each layer in the stack."[5]

Sometimes the right idea, person, or group of people arrives at the right time to sow the seeds of something new.[6] Isaacson pointed out that the first lunar landing was possible only because powerful microchips for rocket guidance systems had become small enough to fit into the nose cone of a rocket, and the space program made the microchip industry viable.[7] In 1965, NASA was buying 72 percent of all chips manufactured in the United States, helping to underwrite the nascent industry and its imminent commercial applications.[8]

There is another lesson here—not only can governments cultivate the conditions for innovation and entrepreneurialism to occur, but they can also financially support and actively use this technology while enterprise develops commercial applications. History bulges with great examples. To incentivize investment in new and unproven technologies, the US Constitution gave inventors limited monopolies on their ideas through patents, and the federal government gave the earliest steamship entrepreneurs monopolies on commercial trade on America's waterways.[9] For a period, early inventors and entrepreneurs extracted monopoly rates as rewards for delivering working boats. Likewise, government set up public-private partnerships with railroad pioneers, putting up taxpayer capital, smoothing the railbed for construction, and by eminent domain, compelling property owners to sell their land for public works projects.[10] In the first era of the Internet, long before "the Web" as we know it was invented, government was a backer and user of the ARPANET and other early iterations of the technology. So far, we have not seen that with Web3, but that could change as the technology matures. To paraphrase Victor Hugo, nothing in business is more powerful than an idea whose time and technology have come.

Web3 Primitives

How should we think of these building blocks of Web3? Nature provides an analogy: Web3 is like an organism or ecosystem of organisms such as a coral reef, growing from a small beginning into a vast connected organism. Just as different species of coral make up a reef, different kinds of Web3 innovations make up this interdependent technology ecosystem. What to call them? How about *primitives,* so irreducible and elemental that developers use them to compose all-new things.[11]

Blockchains are a great example of this. They are the clever configurations of different building blocks, some of which we've had for over a decade, but we needed creative people to fit them together into novel and, in this case, revolutionary combinations. For example, two of the core primitives of blockchains—the *hash function* used in proof of work, which helps store transaction data on-chain, secure the network, and improve privacy and more, and the *digital signature,* which validates and authenticates the ownership and integrity of a digital asset—were pioneered in the mid-twentieth century and commercialized in other kinds of software in the 1980s and 1990s.[12] If we combine them with a peer-to-peer network, then we've got a new architecture for moving, storing, and securing value. The European Union is considering the hash function SHA-256 (used in Bitcoin) for its "digital euro" because experts believe it to be quantum resistant, meaning even the most theoretically powerful computers could not hack it.[13]

Equally important are so-called "virtual machines," which we can use to execute code in a distributed manner across many nodes in a blockchain network like Ethereum, and whose creators called it the Ethereum virtual machine (EVM). However, just like the hash function and the digital signature, virtual machines have a long history, dating back to the 1930s.[14] In the 1960s, IBM developed its virtual machine, on which users could run multiple programs, with each running in its own virtual environment.[15]

Perhaps the most "primitive" of Web3 primitives—cryptography—dates back to the fifth century BCE. The first applications of cryptography were not only for military or state secrets, but also for sensitive commercial information. Ancient Egyptian merchants swapped out letters for symbols ("substitution ciphers") to stymie unintended recipients, and the Mesopotamians used a system of numbers and symbols to encode their messages. Some historians believe that merchants invented writing to communicate long-distance.[16] As the name might suggest, cryptography is essential to cryptoassets, what we call *tokens*, and thus to Web3. Among other purposes, we use cryptography to encrypt and secure transactions, protect user data, and verify the integrity of the blockchain, so that only the sender and the recipient of the transaction can view its contents, but everyone can confirm its occurrence.

Web3 stands on the shoulders of giants, with today's innovators configuring some immortal primitives into new forms. Today Web3 is, along with artificial intelligence, one of the most exciting area of computer science, with new, completely native primitives emerging. Just as Steve Jobs combined cathode-ray tube monitors, graphical user interfaces, mouses, and keyboards with his proprietary operating system into the *personal* computer, so too are Web3 entrepreneurs combining the old and the new into new tools that decentralize power, improve privacy, and offer Web3 users better capabilities like proving ownership and controlling digital assets.

According to Ali Yahya of Andreessen Horowitz, blockchain protocols are powerful because they "let us create programs that, in a sense, have lives of their own. They are self-executing programs, free from interference from the people who originally wrote them, from the people who control the hardware running them, and from the people who interact with those programs while they're running."[17] What are the Web3 native primitives, the building blocks of this new Internet?

1. Tokens: How We Represent Value Digitally

A tabula rasa for programming nearly anything of value, the token is foundational to Web3. People are reimagining everything in tokens, from money to art, securities to carbon credits. Citing his colleague Albert Wenger's blog post on monetizing protocols, Brad Burnham of Union Square Ventures called them "the native business model of open-source software."[18] As Wenger noted, the only way to make money from open-source protocols was to "create software that implemented it and then try to sell this software (or, more recently, to host it). Since the creation of this software [was] a separate act, many of the researchers who have created some of the most successful protocols in use today have had little direct financial gain."[19] Tokens give developers a way to monetize their contribution to open source and an incentive to keep contributing because their stake grows more valuable as more businesses build on top.

Tokens fall into different categories, such as fungible tokens and non-fungible tokens (NFTs), where a fungible thing is an item that we can easily replace "with another item that is practically the same, such as wood or paper currency," in a legal contract.[20] Different blockchain platforms, such as Solana and Cosmos, support different tokens. For simplicity, let's focus on Ethereum. Two standards on Ethereum are ERC-20 for fungible tokens and ERC-721 for NFTs. These two represent most of the value of assets on Ethereum, and we can program them to represent whatever we want, from loyalty points to votes in an election. Not all tokens are created equal: where ERC-20 tokens are all identical in utility, value, and functionality and are therefore fungible, the units of an ERC-721 token are not.[21] For example, an entrepreneur launching a new Web3 project may want to incentivize a new user with a token: the user earns the token by using the platform, and the token gives the user a say in how the community runs the project. These "governance tokens" are indistinguishable from each other, and so they are fungible. By contrast, ERC-721 tokens representing art or other unique digital goods are provably unique, provably distinct, and therefore not fungible, not contractually interchangeable.

2. Consensus Algorithms: How We Agree on the State of a Decentralized Network

For tokens to have value, we must ensure they cannot exist in two places at the same time. If we can copy tokens as we copy information on the Internet, then they cease to be scarce. We need a way to maintain the "state" of the network to avoid this so-called "double-spend problem."[22]

Enter consensus algorithms, used to reach agreement on the state of a distributed system without the need for a central authority. The history of consensus algorithms dates to the 1980s and the development of the Byzantine generals problem, first posed by computer scientists Leslie Lamport, Robert Shostak, and Marshall Pease. In this analogy, a group of generals is trying to coordinate an attack on their enemy.[23] With their armies spread across different locations, the generals must communicate through human messengers. How do they agree on a plan of attack if their messengers can lie, or if one general can influence the outcome? The solution must tolerate these shortcomings of the system; that is, it must be "Byzantine fault tolerant" for most of the generals to remain loyal to the plan. But how?

First, the generals agree on a "consensus algorithm" that they will all use to determine the state of their decentralized armies, so that none of them must rely on a single general to make the call. Some examples of consensus algorithms include proof of stake (PoS) and proof of work (PoW). Let's say all our Byzantine generals have invested their money in this attack. If they fail as a whole, then they lose their individual investments. If one or more generals go rogue and act alone, then the collaborative generals can still win the war, but the rogues will pay a price. The consensus mechanism rewards the generals for doing what's best for the collective armies. Roughly speaking, this is how proof of stake works: market participants in Ethereum, Cosmos, Cardano, and other such PoS networks stake their assets to the network in exchange for a return on that investment (this return is known as a *staking reward*). They get paid if the network functions normally, and so their interests align with everyone else's. Sometimes they must tie their assets up, as in the case of Ethereum, while in others, like Cardano, they can swap in and out instantly.[24]

Alternatively, imagine the generals have marshaled huge resources—soldiers, weaponry, and so forth—for this important attack. They would have done that only if they wanted it to succeed. Their interests align with a positive outcome. They have put in the work, so to speak. In Bitcoin, certain participants commit computing power rather than assets. We call these participants "miners" because their mining unlocks new bitcoins from the network the way pickaxe mining unlocked gold from the ground. Their computers use energy, cost them money, and divert them from other productive usage, and so they receive new bitcoins as incentive to keep the system going.

Both systems have benefits and weaknesses. In Ethereum's PoS mechanism, a single actor can control (if not own) enough tokens to control the network through delegation whereby users unable or unwilling to do it themselves simply assign it to some bigger, more sophisticated actor. Bitcoin's proof of work makes such concentration much harder, but it uses a considerable amount of energy and does not scale well. These are implementation challenges we will address later. For now, both systems work to replace a central authority with a networked state.

3. Smart Contracts: How We Automate Commercial Agreements

Yahya added so-called "smart contracts" to the list of core primitives. The Bitcoin blockchain, which kick-started Web3, is good at moving, storing, and securing bitcoin, but limited in functionality. In the years after the Bitcoin blockchain's launch, many enterprising developers explored ways to program the network to do more, such as record land titles or secure transactions in other assets, what were known then as "colored coins." These efforts fell short because Bitcoin was not programmable. If blockchains are "new computers with new capabilities," as Chris Dixon said, then the Bitcoin blockchain was missing one feature: it was not a general-purpose machine as Turing described it, in that we could not program and reprogram it to do a wide (possibly infinite) variety of tasks.

Enter smart contracting platforms, such as Ethereum, which we can program to do more complex tasks. A *smart contract* is a special type of decentralized application, according to Nick Szabo, who coined the term in the 1990s. It can be "a machine with rules that we could have defined in a contract but instead wrote into a machine," like those vending cans of soft drinks.[25] Szabo wrote, "We can trust the code to run properly without having to trust the owners of any of the computers the code runs on."[26] Web3 innovators are replacing the business logic of traditional agreements with smart contracts, and that practice will likely spill over into the broader economy soon because users can "trustlessly encode rules for any type of transaction and even create scarce assets with specialized functionality" through smart contracts.[27]

4. Decentralized Autonomous Organizations:
How We Coordinate Assets and Action

Tokens are an essential asset class to new digitally native organizations called DAOs, through which strangers around the world can pool their resources and coordinate their skills and talent in building something of value, akin to an open-source project like Linux, but with a way for contributors to earn fair compensation. One example is Gitcoin, described on its site as a "community of builders, creators, and protocols at the center of open web ecosystems."[28] The Gitcoin platform does what Kickstarter and Indiegogo do not: it matches ideas for products and services not only with funders of grants and potential users of those products and services but also with talent to build and deliver them—*and* holders of Gitcoin tokens have a financial and governance stake in the ideas funded. Cofounder Scott Moore told us, "Gitcoin operates as a DAO now, which means that we operate as community-owned infrastructure. We're operating infrastructure aimed at creating more infrastructure. Conway's law is a governing principle," the principle that systems replicate an organization's communications structures.[29] Gitcoin advocates for its model of organizing through its funding mechanism. "That's an important piece of the way that the space works," Moore said.

He explained: In a more centralized organization, core maintainers and developers need to share context continually with a small group, only a small part of the organization. In a decentralized organization, especially an autonomous one, advocates of certain activities must share information constantly, across many different channels. "In Web3, you have your Telegram, Discord, Signal chats, Discourse forum, and Snapshot votes, and all these different governance components require attention. So, attention is still a scarce resource," said Moore. "We've been trying to figure out ways to streamline that process. That's how we've evolved the DAO over time, to streamline it."[30]

Gitcoin has executive groups in the form of work streams: members of the DAO vote in those work streams and give them budgets. External, independent members of the community known as *stewards* hold these work streams. In other words, Gitcoin has a kind of legislative body and an executive body. Moore likened it to a virtual economy with a governance structure, incentives, and individuals with distinct roles within that economy. He sees a risk of DAOs becoming very bureaucratic. He described the challenge. "In a traditional organization, we have very standard structures, very standard processes, and very standard hierarchy. People know what's happening. They know who's where. They know what they're supposed to do."[31] That's not yet true of DAOs. Moore thinks DAOs can have leadership without hierarchy. DAOs can still have structure. But people are still figuring it out.

5. Zero-Knowledge Proofs: How We Program Privacy into Web3

Zero-knowledge proofs, as the name suggests, are tools for verifying a party's knowledge of secrets without revealing those secrets.[32] "Zero-knowledge proofs are like the holy grail primitive for blockchains," Yahya said. They are "less intuitive and maybe more controversial, but just as important as smart contracts as a primitive. On top of those, people then build composite primitives that are reducible, but still fundamental, like the automated market maker or the bonding curve," two other important innovations of decentralized finance.[33]

If a government or a central bank ever wanted to re-create cash credibly in digital form (known as a CBDC), then it would need zero-knowledge proofs to support fully anonymous transactions. After all, when we pay cash for anything (that's not a controlled substance like alcohol) at the grocery store, the clerk doesn't ask us for our ID.

Yahya likened a zero-knowledge proof to a sudoku puzzle—solving it is hard, but verifying that you solved it and that your solution is correct is much easier: "That asymmetry of the amount of work solving it to the amount of work verifying the solution is the core thing." Why would we want to use such a puzzle? "Let's say I have a program I want executed. Maybe it takes a while to run. I want to outsource its execution to someone else, and I want some guarantee that this person executed it correctly. That's what a zero-knowledge proof lets me do."[34] In other words, the goal is to provide a way for one party (the prover) to prove to another party (the verifier) that they know a certain piece of information, *without revealing any information about that piece of information itself.* If people must prove that they possess certain knowledge without revealing the specifics of that knowledge, they can use this technology.

Zero-knowledge (ZK) proofs create a framework for privacy, which is foundational to financial transactions specifically and to personal freedom in general. Blockchains are immutable records of all transactions in a network. They create radical transparency for market participants. Don't trust a central authority; verify on-chain. But what if we need to verify that something happened, without sharing any of the details? Let's say an activist investor wanted to accumulate a position in a company discreetly, without the public's scrutinizing every trade on-chain. We can use ZK proofs to do that anonymously while verifying the trades. There are applications beyond money and finance. What if a government wanted to validate and verify the tally of an election conducted on a blockchain, without revealing who voted for whom? What if we wanted to build digital ID systems that allowed people to prove information about themselves without disgorging personal information?

Yahya explained: "There are two pieces to a zero-knowledge proof. There's the component that has to do with verifiable computation, and there's a component that has to do with zero knowledge, the privacy aspect. It's confusing because people use the term *zero-knowledge proofs*, but often, they're not using them for privacy; they're using them for the verifiable computation, as in ZK-rollup scalability solutions" to the current limits of platforms like Ethereum.[35] Here, Yahya is referring to the so-called Layer 2 networks, built on top of Layer 1s like Ethereum, where users can transact off the Layer 1 and then "roll up" their transactions into a round lot that others can verify on Layer 1 (which is to say, on the Ethereum blockchain). So, for transactions to occur off-chain, we need a way to verify they all occurred. ZK rollups help us to do that.

In traditional finance (called TradFi), trading firms like Goldman Sachs would not necessarily clear and settle every single transaction they engage in. They would net them all out, or "batch" them, before settling to cash. Likewise in a casino, gamblers do not go to the cashier to convert to cash every time they win a bet at blackjack before betting again. With ZK rollups, we can do provable and private batch settlements on blockchains. Rollups may act like netting with final settlement happening later, but we should not draw too close a comparison between Wall Street and Web3 transactions, said Jake Hannah, cofounder of SX Network, a popular Web3 prediction market where users can wager on the outcome of future events. SX runs on Polygon, which is similar to a Layer 2. "Ethereum isn't the Fed. Ethereum is a decentralized protocol that people can trust. It's not ten people who meet quarterly."[36]

As for ZK rollups, "The proof is very small, and so it can fit inside a blockchain, alongside the output of a computation inside a block within Ethereum, for example," Yahya explained. "That's very powerful because we've had this *scalability trilemma*—a trade-off between performance and decentralization. If we want more performance, then we have to make every node in the network more powerful. But if every node must be more powerful, then fewer people can afford to run nodes, and so the network becomes more centralized."[37] That applies only in networks like Bitcoin, where every node must do the work for every transaction. With zero-knowledge proofs, we no longer need every node do all the work; we need only one node to verify the work. That's how we break out of the trilemma. We can have what Yahya called "performance through parallelism," where every node runs one computation once and produces the proof for it for everyone else to verify, and we still have decentralization.

6. Wallets: How We Manage Our Digital Goods and Identities

What browsers were to Web1, and mobile applications and smartphones were to Web2, wallets are to Web3. Innovators have been kicking the concept of a digital wallet around for a generation. Like many of Web3's building blocks, they didn't come out of nowhere. In 1988, long before the blockchain, US Marine Corps recruits on Parris Island, South Carolina, were using a type of smart card that they called an "electronic wallet," instead of cash or credit cards.[38] In 1992, cryptographer David Chaum, who is an important forebear of Web3, described a "smart credit-card size computer" that his company DigiCash had developed that held digital identities and digital cash and could exchange the latter and verify the former.[39] It looked like a calculator the size of a thick ID card.[40]

Later, Microsoft cofounder Bill Gates shared his concept of a "wallet PC," a handheld device about the size of a traditional wallet.[41] In his 1995 book, *The Road Ahead,* Gates wrote that such a device would display messages, schedules, and email. He boldly predicted, "Rather than holding paper currency, the new wallet will store unforgeable digital money."[42] Marc Andreessen has lamented not shipping Netscape with a wallet: in his view, the Internet's original sin was the lack of a transaction layer.[43] His team was also considering a wallet as a form of early "plug-in" to the browser, something that is commonplace now with wallets like MetaMask.

Satoshi Nakamoto apparently coded the first bitcoin wallet, Bitcoin-Qt, released in February 2009.[44] Pinning down a precise definition of a digital wallet has been tough. People use a clutch of different metaphors to explain the concept. Gates likened it to a Swiss Army knife.[45] We described it as "a personal black box" in *Blockchain Revolution.*[46] Others have used such terms as *blockchain wallet, digital wallet, e-wallet, mobile wallet, online wallet,* and *web wallet* almost interchangeably. What's most important is the concept of *self-custody*: as the saying goes, "not your keys, not your coins," meaning that, if you're not in possession of your private keys, with which you move your own coins and sign transactions, then you're really not holding any tokens.[47] "The concept of 'the separation of ownership and control' has no sociological or historical meaning. Ownership *means* control. If there is no control, then there is no ownership," argued twentieth-century intellectual James Burnham, adding the central issue is the "control over access to the object in question and preferential treatment in the distribution of its products."[48]

"The collapse of FTX has crystallized my view that Web3 will coalesce around principles of transparency, self-custody, and ownership," said Sidney Powell, cofounder and CEO of Maple Finance. "Prior to this, the oft-touted refrain was that Web3 distinctly lacked speed and an elegant user experience, which meant everyone would default to using centralized financial services [such as FTX] to interact. The underlying trade-off here was taking on counterparty risk [the risk that one's trading partner will go bust]—the speed came at the expense of safety and control."[49]

Powell expects builders to rethink their design principles and emphasize rather than obfuscate the blockchain aspects of the user experience, such as connecting wallets directly and viewing transactions on Etherscan, that "demonstrate audit ability and security." In the commercial realm, he expects "an acceleration of CeFi [centralized finance like FTX] and TradFi entrants using DeFi rails" because these rails reduce their cost of capital—they won't need to pay their users as much for counterparty risk—and their users will require proof of reserves in every solution. "Overall, we're very excited by the reemphasis on self-custody and transparency because it highlights the key strengths of building in DeFi," he said.[50]

At the root of digital wallets is custody. When you hold your private keys, you hold your assets. For people looking to leave an inflationary currency or corrupted financial system, self-custody is a huge advantage, as we'll explore later. But for many who don't trust themselves to hold large amounts of wealth safely, self-custody can be overwhelming, a barrier to widespread adoption. For many would-be corporate users of tokens, self-custody can be a nonstarter: beyond the intermediary's liability if its customers' value goes missing without customer authorization, laws may require financial firms *not* to hold digital assets for their customers. However, placing all your trust in a third party to secure your digital assets is both risky and antithetical to Web3. Hester Peirce, an SEC commissioner, said in a recent speech, "Unthinking trust in centralized intermediaries is antithetical to crypto."[51] Is there another way?

Yes, multisignature and multicomputation are two related approaches to digital asset custody that could reconcile these concerns. Multisignature (multisig) requires multiple parties, such as the asset owner, custodian, or third-party administrator, or some other third party to sign off on transactions before any party can act on an asset or account. A multisig wallet could have ten different signatories— the CEO, CFO, treasurer, a third-party auditor, or other fiduciary entirely. Multisig reduces the risk of rogue actors. Because parties sign all transactions on-chain, it improves transparency in decision making. Safe (formerly Gnosis Safe) helps secure billions of dollars in cryptoassets across more than twenty thousand multisig wallets. Several leading Web3 DAOs rely on Safe for secure custody and treasury management, such as Synthetix and Aave.[52] In contrast, multicomputational systems divide responsibility for managing a single asset across several computing nodes, each having its own set of security protocols designed by a different organization, which adds redundancy and could improve transparency. Companies like Fireblocks, for example, run geographically segregated nodes that secure the asset, along with the asset owner.

Both techniques are technologically sophisticated, but those who advocate for them hope that users won't ever need to understand how the techniques work. They'll simply turn on their chosen technique with the press of a button, as they might open a car door and start the car's engine or unlock their iPhone.

Web3 Priorities

Composability

Composability in systems theory refers to the relationship of different components.[53] For Web3 users, this means applications that connect to one another seamlessly with integrated functionality. For example, a decentralized exchange for buying and selling digital assets is more composable if it can connect to a lending application for users to get a loan against assets that they hold on the exchange. With composable systems, they could use that loan for, say, buying an NFT on an NFT marketplace to play in their favorite Web3 game. This concept appeals to developers: they can click their thing onto different pieces of software instantly and seamlessly like Lego bricks, and they've got an all-new structure.

Other areas of society and business rely on such composability. For example, intermodal shipping containers are highly composable on ships and trains, and their invention was a boon to commerce and prosperity around the world. Combining businesses, entering contracts, and hiring staff are generally easier in a single jurisdiction than across countries. Laws make the business logic of contracts composable, but parties still deal with a high degree of friction, as anyone who's dealt in global trade can attest. With the high composability of Web3 applications, we can combine a near infinite number of applications—different software—into a single business Web, hastening the processes of decentralization and globalization.

In theory, composability at the software level leads to general leaps in efficiency. In practice, certain blockchains such as Bitcoin, Ethereum, and Solana are not composable (that is, not interoperable) with each other, because each has a different code base or standard, much like the alternating current and direct current standards of the early electric age, or the video home system (VHS) and Betamax standards in home entertainment. Until these different blockchains are truly composable, aspiring entrepreneurs must pick sides or hedge their bets. Andrew Young, founder of SX Network, the most popular decentralized Web3 prediction market, told us, "If you deploy your decentralized application on Ethereum or Polygon, you can actually deploy your application on something like Avalanche," which is compatible with Ethereum.[54] He contrasted this to "Solana or EOS, where you have to rebuild your whole infrastructure to deploy your application on Solana. It's like Android versus iPhone."[55] It's Web3 rhyming with Web2. As in the markets for electricity and video consumption, crypto standards wars are under way. In our electricity example, electric systems are still not composable: we need different adapters to recharge our devices in different outlets in different countries. Other times, standards that win the battles of their day often fall to disruptive innovations over time: after all, VHS, Betamax, DVDs, and other physical formats gave way to streaming.

Tokenomics

In Web3, anyone can commit code to an open-source project and earn a piece of that software via the token. Similarly, any person or group of people with an idea and talent for software development can launch their own DAO and raise their own treasury without seeking out professional investors like venture capitalists. Tokens are incentives in such economic systems in Web3. Token economics or *tokenomics* is a term used to describe the study of the economic aspects of a cryptocurrency or other digital asset. Several factors go into tokenomics: the utility of the token, the mechanisms coded into the token to attract users, the token's distribution model, the current supply and demand, and its potential to increase in value. Done with enduring public infrastructure in mind, tokenomics can power user growth for the long term. Done with short-term gains in mind, it can turn people off and divert developer attention away from building useful stuff.

By contrast, in a centrally controlled company, that coder would need to be an employee or a contractor and would receive a salary or a contract rate. If entrepreneurs wanted to start their own business, then according to the World Bank, they'd take on average 20 days to launch a business globally.[56] Some countries, like New Zealand, make it cheap and easy to do in a day, while it takes 230 days in Venezuela, 99 days in Cambodia, and 33 days in the Philippines.[57] Perhaps this high level of friction, as much owing to government inefficiency and corruption as anything else—what economists consider "unmarketed transactions"—is why all three of these countries are seeing high usage of Web3 applications and cryptoassets more generally.[58] Launching a token on a decentralized exchange like Uniswap is simple. As a result, many tokens are intrinsically worthless, and some launch from the start as a joke or a meme. Observers wrongly conclude that the low barrier to entry is an inherent flaw because any technology that allows entities to spin up any asset or organization seamlessly will lead to many failures and more than a few frauds. Without friction, entrepreneurs can more readily launch a myriad of useful and potentially quite valuable assets, even in places with corrupt or inefficient local governments that make raising capital or incorporating a business difficult.

Scalability

Like all technologies in their early days, Web3 holds immense promise and has several limitations. Internal combustion engines were unreliable, noisy, and dangerous machines, outlawed in some jurisdictions.[59] The Wright brothers flew a plane with wings made of "Pride of the West" muslin, used in ladies' undergarments; some proclaimed that the fabric was better used for its original purpose.[60]

These initial limits led some to conclude that technology like the Web would never be ready for prime time, never all things to all people. One way to express this "never ready" is the "trilemma," a heuristic for evaluating a blockchain protocol. Given the choice among network security, scalability, and decentralization, developers must "pick two." According to this framework, if developers want a secure protocol, they must give up on speed. Bitcoin is a good example of such a protocol. A fast protocol may not be as secure. Solana has plenty of users, and transactions are relatively cheap, but the Solana network has gone down multiple times.[61] That other blockchains like Bitcoin and Ethereum run 24/7/365 without downtime or hiccups is all the more remarkable. In contrast, TradFi markets shut down daily, and their systems undergo repairs and upgrades regularly; but if we are designing an immutable, secure network, then pausing the chain is a serious problem.

Perhaps we need a protocol that we can scale more easily? No, said Walden of Variant Fund. He asked us to consider the early days of the Web when many worried that the Internet protocol would not scale to accommodate all the users who wanted to get online. "That's not the way that the early Internet played out. It played out in a series of protocols that layered on top of each other, both to scale the network and add features like privacy, which came through SSL [secure sockets layer]. Email came through SMTP [simple mail transfer protocol] and IMAP [Internet message access protocol]. This specialization of protocols expanded the adjacent possibilities and gave us the rich Internet that we have today."[62] Similarly, the first automobiles did not even have steering wheels, let alone spring shocks, windshield wipers, rearview mirrors, power steering, fuel injection, and other features that became standard in a few decades. Innovation does not always progress logically, either: automakers installed the first cigarette lighters thirty years before they added seat belts.[63]

Interoperability

Despite the promise of composability, blockchains have an interoperability problem: moving assets native to one chain onto another is difficult. Rather than one standard of Lego bricks, our builders are working with a hodgepodge of materials that look similar but do not click together easily.

A casual fan of *Star Trek* knows the expression "Beam me up, Scotty." Blockchains need something akin to a *Star Trek* transporter to convert matter (in this case, on-chain assets) into a teleportable medium and then back into matter with little to no risk. The main solution—the so-called *bridge*—is more akin to Wonkavision, where transported particles must pass through the taffy pulling room to regain their size.

Consider what happened to Ronin, an Ethereum sidechain built for the popular game *Axie Infinity*. In March 2022, hackers used a vulnerability in the code to gain control of the majority of "validator keys" needed to move funds out of the Ronin bridge. That the high concentration of validator keys in the hands of Sky Mavis, the maker of *Axie*, points to the risk of *centralization* versus decentralization is cold comfort to the users affected. In all, hackers drained a staggering $600 million in ether and USDC, $400 million of it belonging to users. This was a huge setback for *Axie* and Sky Mavis.[64] This followed the hack of the Solana Wormhole bridge, which, despite what its name implies, does not transform matter (in this case, money in the form of tokens) seamlessly from one dimension (blockchain) to another. Bridges remain a huge vulnerability that undermines everyday user confidence in this technology.

The Ethereum and Bitcoin networks cannot communicate with each other, and neither can the dozens of other prominent blockchain networks functioning today. Value recorded on one network is not visible on, or transferable to, other blockchains without some kind of intermediary playing a role.

Switching to *Star Wars*, another way to achieve interoperability is through standards and protocols. Just as *Star Trek* had its universal translator, *Star Wars* had its own lingua franca, Galactic Basic, for diverse species to communicate across galaxies. Adopting common standards and protocols in blockchain can allow different networks to understand each other and exchange information.

The second problem is that, in these early days of enterprise usage, no company wants to bet on a blockchain solution that won't interoperate with its supply chain partners, its customers, or regulatory bodies using blockchain for official transactions. One way to achieve stability is to be compatible with Ethereum, the leading platform, and to run applications on top of these Ethereum-like platforms—like a "virtual world computer" that accommodates them all. That simple solution might limit innovation and force projects to conform to certain standards that don't suit their long-term needs.

"The world computer vision Ethereum and other projects are pitching, those so-called Ethereum killers, is a lot like a pre-Internet vision of talking about a world mainframe," said Ethan Buchman, cofounder of blockchain network Cosmos. "As if IBM or some other company was going to run the one computer to rule them all and no one else would need a computer, no one will need a personal computer."[65] In Buchman's telling, we would all hook up via dumb terminals to "one big supercomputer mainframe in some basement in some big company" that would scale, cover all the bases, and take care of "everyone's computing needs."[66]

The concept of interoperability falls "into two camps—the *multichain* vision and the *interchain* vision," said Sunny Aggarwal. In the multichain vision, "we'll have all these generalized blockchains, where applications deploy multiple versions of themselves on different chains. We see this on DeFi applications like SushiSwap, where SushiSwap is redeploying itself everywhere. It has instances on Ethereum, Arbitrum, Polygon, and the [BNB Chain]," he said, referring to some other popular networks. Aggarwal underscored the downside of this approach: "All these ecosystems are separate. They're splitting their liquidity across all these different chains."[67]

In the interchain vision, we have application-specific blockchains with one chain (such as Aggarwal's Osmosis) intermediating among those chains without splitting its liquidity among them or compromising on autonomy, speed, and security.[68] Aggarwal has realized this vision on the Cosmos network by using its inter-blockchain communication (IBC) protocol, which defines rules and standards for different blockchain networks to exchange data and transactions in a consistent and secure manner. For autonomy, each application can still launch its own chain. Said Aggarwal, "As an application, the only way to protect yourself from someone else's governance drama is to have your own chain." Throughput is another. Greg Osuri, cofounder of Akash Network, a decentralized cloud provider built with IBC, explained: "You have to inherit the scalability that the underlying chain provides you. That could be good because you don't have to bootstrap security. But it could be bad because you have no control over the destiny of your software."[69]

For Jelena Djuric, cofounder and CEO of Noble, a Cosmos project, Cosmos is as close as we have to the original decentralized Web pioneered by Tim Berners-Lee, Vint Cerf, and others. "In Cosmos, there's no one company, no one leader, no one founder, no single point of failure. You feel as if that's how it might have been with the original Internet—a bunch of random people all over the world who may or may not know each other, who may or may not be in business together, who are working on the same stack, developing that stack, and making that stack available to other people," she said.[70] There's that word again: *stack*. If the stack is the terroir, then this diverse group is incubating different species of organizations. Like densely planted seeds of different crops, sometimes groups within Cosmos sprout up too closely and fight for resources. But, in general, it makes for a lively ecosystem. "In the same way anyone can launch a website [on the Internet], anyone in Cosmos can launch a chain, asset, or application," said Djuric.[71]

How does Cosmos achieve security when everyone is unleashing diverse and competing creations on the Cosmos stack? According to Aggarwal, Web3 systems will not centralize security on a single supermassive platform like Ethereum. Instead, designers and architects will spread it out. "Different validators are going to opt into sharing their identity across all these different appchains," Aggarwal said. "If validators do something malicious on Osmosis," like double-spending an OSMO token, then "they're going to get slashed everywhere," referring to the process whereby stakers in a network like Cosmos lose some of what they staked for not acting in the network's best interest. In Aggarwal's view, "[t]hat's how the future of security works. It's going to be this mesh network of security where all the chains are sharing security with each other. It's not going to be a one center, like a hub-and-spoke system."[72] That's like the North Atlantic Treaty Organization (NATO) or *Star Trek*'s United Federation of Planets, bound together by a shared set of principles and shared commitment to protecting the whole galaxy—or Cosmos, if you like.

Web3 and Artificial Intelligence:
Two Unstoppable Forces on a Collision Course

Web3 is converging with artificial intelligence (AI) and machine learning, and they are combining in important ways. I am not an expert in AI, so I asked someone trained in this field to explain:

> Machine learning is a method of teaching computers to learn from data, rather than explicitly programming them. It uses algorithms to parse data, learn from it, and then make predictions or take actions based on what it has learned. The process begins by feeding the algorithm large amounts of data, which it uses to learn the relationships between the input and the desired output. The algorithm then uses what it learns to predict outcomes or act on new data. Over time, as the algorithm processes more data, its predictions grow increasingly accurate and its actions, more precise.

I asked the expert how Web3 technologies might help AI to reach its full potential without trampling the privacy and ownership rights of individuals:

> Web2 data silos limit the amount and type of data available for training everybody's AI systems. This lack of data diversity hinders the development of more advanced and sophisticated AI models for the public good.
>
> With Web3, different stakeholders can collaborate and share more data. Blockchain and peer-to-peer networks can serve as a secure and transparent infrastructure for storing and sharing data.
>
> For example, Ocean Protocol is building a decentralized marketplace for data. With this platform, individuals and organizations can securely share their data with AI developers, for creating more accurate and diverse AI models.

Another example is the Holochain project, a distributed computing platform for building decentralized applications. Scientists could use this platform to create AI systems that are more transparent and accountable as well as more secure and resilient to attacks.

I asked about the challenges to implementing AI in Web3:

The lack of scalability is a challenge: current Web3 technologies cannot yet handle the large amounts of data and computational power that AI needs. Innovators face regulatory and ethical challenges, too, such as protecting personal data and giving people fair access to AI resources.

Overall, while Web3 has the potential to support greater collaboration and data sharing to develop AI, innovators and regulators must still address significant challenges to make this a reality.[73]

Did you find that explanation helpful? I hope so. After all, ChatGPT 3 by OpenAI wrote it. If you couldn't tell that a human being didn't generate that material, then how can you be sure that AI didn't author this manuscript or anything else you might read? While those important questions are outside the scope of this book, Web2's hoarding of user-generated data and other cutting-edge technology like AI is certainly in our purview. In fact, the convergence of Web3 and AI is part of a bigger phenomenon known as decentralized science, or DeSci. Though still nascent, Web3 research firm Messari catalogued at least 85 different projects across several key verticals, such as funding (how do scientific studies and other initiatives raise money), data (how is data organized and vetted, and how are contributors fairly compensated), and even review and publishing (how do scientific findings reach their intended audience by leapfrogging legacy gatekeepers).[74] In AI specifically, large language models (LLMs) rely on reams of data, and some observers are concerned that AI practitioners are using data without the creators' knowledge, consent, or fair compensation for this use of their assets. Individuals could tokenize their data with watermarks so that every time someone uses it, its creator receives a payment. Will this throttle AI research by making data harder to access or more expensive to procure? Or will it lead to bigger and better pools of data that will accelerate this industry while protecting creators? The Ocean Protocol Foundation is stewarding a protocol with a "compute-to-data" feature comparable to other privacy-preserving technologies such as multiparty computation and homomorphic encryption.[75] Through this protocol running on the Ethereum mainnet, individuals and organizations can give AI models access to their data while safeguarding privacy and ownership.[76] This kind of solution could lead to new, more advanced AI models that we can use for a wide range of applications in important areas like healthcare and education.

Conclusion and Takeaways

As technology matures, we stop thinking about how it works. Who knows what's happening under the hood when pressing the ignition button in a twenty-first century vehicle? Until we reach that point with Web3, we need to pop the hood. Here's what we see:

1. Technology and business innovations that go back decades, sometimes centuries, and that have stood the test of time and utility. Pioneering new innovations in computer science, core primitives such as zero-knowledge proofs, DAOs, and smart contracts, with broad applicability in business and beyond.
2. Blockchains and consensus mechanisms that support distributed ledgers, digital assets, and whatever else we can dream up by combining them with smart contracts, ZK proofs, and so forth.
3. Functionalities like composability, interoperability, and scalability that are rudimentary and very much works in progress. Using tokens as incentives to build Web3 native assets and organizations has been a process of trial and error, with every failure improving the study and implementation of these tokenomic models.

4. Mechanics (that is, innovators) underneath that are harnessing these core primitives and rigging them into useful products and services.

5. Concurrent innovations, namely AI and machine learning, that we must scale responsibly in this next digital age.

All primitives are important, but some are essential. Digital assets or tokens, the subject of the next chapter, are essential to Web3.

PART II
TRANSFORMATIONS

CHAPTER 3

Assets

The assessors who compiled the Domesday Book shortly after the Norman Conquest of 1066 documented the vast wealth inequality in medieval England.[1] "The royal family directly held 20 percent of the land, the Church had 25 percent, and a dozen magnates controlled another 25 percent. . . . Effectively the country was controlled by about 250 people: the king, the great prelates (chosen by him), and about 170 barons ['tenants-in-chief'] with landed incomes of over 100 pounds per year."[2] Across Europe, a handful of people and groups often controlled all land, the most important asset class of the feudal economy.

This imbalance of asset ownership was by no means unique in history, though the detailed nationwide accounting of it was. For more than four millennia, merchants and court scribes have kept records of transactions and holdings of assets, from the inventories of King Scorpion of Egypt (3499–3200 BCE) and the Ur accounts of Mesopotamia (2112–2004 BCE) to the Ugarit tablets of Syria (1200–1185 BCE).[3] One dead giveaway of the gap between the haves and have-nots in ancient Egypt and China was the number of servants, slaves, and soldiers buried with their sovereigns, whose divine rights to property carried over to the afterlife.[4]

The industrial age shifted the balance of wealth away from landowners to capitalists. In the nineteenth century, early industrialists like Cornelius Vanderbilt harnessed new industrial technology like steam engines and the new legal invention of the limited liability company to build vast business empires and amass personal fortunes. Comparisons of our time to the Gilded Age are common, but wealth today is nowhere nearly as concentrated as during the early industrial age. On his deathbed, had Vanderbilt liquidated all his holdings, he would have removed $1 out of every $9 in existence in the United States.[5] If Elon Musk or Jeff Bezos were to liquidate all his holdings, each would take out less than $1 out of every $100 in existence.[6] Despite Vanderbilt's outsize wealth, his share was smaller than what the top medieval land barons controlled in feudal times, as the Domesday Book makes clear.

The world is still an unequal place. However, today the biggest owners of securities are not robber barons but the index funds of Vanguard and BlackRock, widely held by small and medium-sized investors. Pension funds, which invest on behalf of their plan members, are some of the biggest allocators of capital in the world. Not everyone participates equally in this expansion of the financial franchise. In the United States, 87 percent of nonwhite households had a bank account in 2013, compared with 93 percent for the country overall, and 64 percent of white Americans said they owned stock compared with 46 percent for people of color.[7] This is a legacy of America's unequal and racist past. American educator and reformer Booker T. Washington recognized very early that property was foundational to equality. During his early years of teaching Black students and watching the legislative work of Black congressmen, Washington concluded that laws and voting rights were necessary but not enough: "back of the ballot, he must have property, industry, skill, economy, intelligence, and character, and . . . no race without these elements could permanently succeed." For nearly one hundred years after Reconstruction, racist state-level Jim Crow laws made it all but impossible for blacks to employ their industry, skill, and other faculties to build wealth, revealing the need for a powerful sovereign, in this case the US government, to guarantee the rights enshrined in the Fourteenth (1868) and Fifteenth (1870) Amendments. This pattern of inequality still exists, but financial inclusion has increased significantly over the last few decades in the United States and in leaps and bounds over the centuries.

What else has changed since Vanderbilt's time? When he was amassing his fortune, Wall Street was accessible to few but the very wealthiest of individuals. Over time, markets democratized. With the inventions of open-ended mutual funds (1924), discount broker-ages (1975), exchange-traded funds (1991), zero-fee trading accounts (2019), and fractional share ownership of public equities (2010s) where an investor could theoretically buy just $1 of a $300 stock like Microsoft (instead of buying whole shares), anyone could invest in the markets. Government intervention also helped level the scales by taxing income and inheritances and expanding social insurance, which has its origins in English Poor Laws and fraternal societies like the Freemasons but was not universally implemented until the New Deal.[8] Trade unions helped guarantee more workers a living wage and military and corporate pensions helped preserve savings in retirement.

Governments have intervened to redistribute wealth in the past: Henry VIII, unable to get a divorce from the pope, seized all the Church's land—nearly one-third of all land—and sold it to private individuals, helping create a whole new class known as the "gentry," or commercialized farmers. Henry's "government intervention" may be responsible for helping kick-start modern agriculture and industri-alization, according to some scholars.[9] Back in the twentieth century, despite these transformations, we can attribute much of the gains in democratizing ownership of assets to market forces and innovation. The same will be true with Web3. Governments may intervene to break up Web2 monopolies, but more likely Web3 innovation will disrupt those business models. Ownership is a powerful incentive for adoption. Tokens give holders economic and governance rights to their digital goods, and anyone can earn them—call them *universal basic assets*.

This brings us to another long-term trend. As the economy has glo-balized, assets have become more abstract and less tactile. Land was the source of wealth in pre-industrial times when farming, logging, and mining were primary industries.[10] In the nineteenth century as industrialization picked up steam, commodities like coal and oil, as well as industrial plant and other capital assets, grew in value, as did banknotes, securities, bills of deposit, patents, and other intangible in-ventions of the human mind. With an explosion of new assets and asset classes, capitalism redefined what was possible. Biographer T. J. Stiles explained how Cornelius Vanderbilt helped usher in modern capitalism: "The imagined devices of commerce gradually abstracted the tangible into mere tokens, and then less than tokens. Money transferred from gold coin to gold-backed banknotes to legal-tender slips of paper and ledger entries in bank accounts."[11] Stiles also pointed out that the unseen architecture of modern finance that we take for granted came about in Vanderbilt's time "amid fierce debate, confusion, and intense resistance." Sound familiar? Stiles wrote, "Like a ghost, the business enterprise departed the body of the individual proprietor and became a being in itself," incorporated.[12]

Web3's killer app—rather, its *killer asset*—won't be digital versions of intangibles we already own and understand, like stocks, money, mutual funds, and other financial assets. After all, the most valuable public companies in the nineteenth century owned inventions of the mind, not fruits of the land. Property laws framed them, and new technologies embodied them, such as the securities representing interests in railroad companies, steel mills, textile manufacturers, community banks, and so forth. Likewise, the most valuable assets of Web3 will probably not be digital stocks and bonds or another legacy asset, but something native to Web3.

Of course, Web3 will help us upgrade our legacy assets. Mike Dudas, of venture capital firm 6MV, summarized industry sentiment: "a significant portion of the world's asset classes will be tokenized, starting with cryptocurrency."[13] This makes sense. Digital assets offer instant, global, and final settlement peer-to-peer between any person, business, or entity. Users stand to gain from the expanded speed, greater access, and deeper liquidity in financial assets, for example.

Most likely, Wall Street as we know it diminishes in global importance. Earlier fintechs layered their innovations on legacy infrastructure, strengthening the position of centralized intermediaries. By contrast, token issuers look to distribute control over money and assets to users. This story of creative destruction is not new: technology has more often disrupted than buttressed incumbents, with plenty of exceptions. For example, the *New York Times* transitioned from print to digital, reimagined its business model, and began reaching more people and gaining global influence, surpassing 10 million subscribers in 2022.[14] Still, the most valuable enterprises of Web1 and Web2 were not newspapers, and the most valuable entities to emerge from Web3 will not be banks. Like Vanderbilt and his industrial-age peers with their oil, steel, telegraphs, railroads, and real estate, Web3 visionaries are reconfiguring digital assets into new utility and value. Once again, history does not repeat, but it rhymes.

The Building Blocks of Web3

What makes tokens such powerful disruptors of asset ownership, wealth-making, and business? Just as shares of corporations accrued much of the industrial economy's value, much of the value in the digital economy will accumulate in the building block of Web3, namely, the tokens of decentralized networks.

Plenty of traditional corporations like Nike, Microsoft, LVMH Moët Hennessy Louis Vuitton, and others have found success in Web3, and more will come. Coinbase, the largest Web3 retail brokerage listed on Nasdaq (as COIN), is worth about $15 billion and has more users than TD Ameritrade.[15] As during the California Gold Rush, these pick-and-shovel businesses provide a service to entrepreneurs, speculators, and other pioneers. But the market capitalization of all publicly traded as well as private businesses that are directly involved in this industry, such as cryptoasset exchanges and custodians like Coinbase and Circle but excluding Nike and Microsoft, whose business are today mostly non-Web3 in nature, still pales in comparison to the $1 trillion market capitalization of tokens.[16]

How does a piece of code go from a gifted programmer's head to a value of over $1 trillion in a decade? By solving the thirty-year-old computing problem of double-spending. Tokens' value hinges on blockchains, distributed ledgers of transactions that everyone can see but no single party can alter. Blockchains act as a single source of truth for asset ownership and provenance. There are plenty of reasons for a given token's having value, but all tokens benefit from being provably scarce. Transactions in tokens are almost instantaneous, and settlement is final. Once recorded on a blockchain, these transactions are costly to reverse, and that instills trust in the tokens as well as blockchains as platforms for exchange.

Tokens have other important features. First, tokens are **programmable**: we can design them to serve nearly any purpose requiring scarcity and verifiable ownership. Individuals and enterprises are using them today to represent art, stocks, votes, songs, characters in virtual worlds, loan contracts, credit scores, identity attributes, board seats, concert tickets, credentials, financial derivatives, carbon credits, currencies, certificates of deposit for commodities, mutual fund units, and fractional ownership in buildings, to name a few.

Within a few years, compiling a kitchen-sink kind of list like that will be pointless, like the pointlessness of rattling off all the uses for websites in 1999. We can program tokens for high divisibility, when we need to fractionalize a unit of value into smaller units—as with a digital dollar as a unit of exchange or the deed to a timeshare in Aruba, but perhaps not with a vote in an election or a ticket on an airplane.

Tokens are **self-custodial**, meaning that we can choose to hold them ourselves in our own digital wallet, or entrust them to someone else (a third party). Self-custody is not without risks. If you lose your private key to your digital wallet and forget to record a backup, then you may never recover your assets.[17] According to the cryptoasset research firm Chainalysis, lost keys have stranded 17 to 23 percent of the bitcoin ever mined.[18] The percentages are probably far lower for other assets. In the early days, bitcoin was little more than a monetary experiment used by a few hobbyists. For almost two years, it had no value whatsoever, so there was not as much awareness about safely securing assets and a lot of bitcoin was lost or stranded then. Nonetheless, it is no surprise that token recovery services have sprung up to help, as have methods to recover your own tokens.[19] What appears to some as a fatal weakness may be (to some) one of Web3's greatest selling points. Self-custody in the developing world is useful when banking is accessible to the privileged few or where local institutions are unreliable.

In a few years, Web3 has gone from zero to around 320 million users, measured by people who own tokens.[20] Will self-custody prevent it from reaching mass-market penetration? Or will behaviors change? Automotive pioneer Gottlieb Daimler is reported to have said, "Global demand for motor vehicles will not exceed one million—simply due to the lack of available chauffeurs."[21] Other versions of this tale put his prediction closer to five thousand.[22] Either way, Daimler clearly did not anticipate changes in behavior. His vision for automobiles, common among early founders, was skeuomorphic: cars were motorized carriages for the wealthy who had chauffeurs. There are modern corollaries. Baby Boomers marveled at their kids, the so-called Millennials, surfing the Web in the 1990s. Today, most Americans spend at least four hours a day on their smartphones.[23] Young people are perfectly comfortable holding their own NFTs and other digital goods. Their parents may need time to catch up.

Because tokens are self-custodial, they are **permissionless and censorship resistant**, meaning we can hold and use them without interference from third parties like governments and we can program them however we like. Transactions in tokens are hard to stop or edit. Many tokens are created with open-source software; anyone can use them, like email. Digital assets have helped fund the war effort in Ukraine, finance protest movements in Belarus, Hong Kong, and Myanmar, and protect Venezuelans from the crippling effects of hyperinflation. Criminals also use tokens, as do rogue nations and probably terrorists. (See the profile of Tokens Funding Freedom Fighters below.) "The real value in a permissionless payment network is being able to support any currency," said Kain Warwick of Synthetix, a "crypto-backed synthetic asset platform."[24] "We had this idea of multicurrency stablecoins. We launched a bunch of fiat currencies. At the same time, we launched gold and silver because we thought, 'If we're going to do it, why not have gold and silver?' Weirdly, people loved gold. People were like, 'Oh my God, synthetic gold, this is what we've been waiting for.'"[25] Of course, we need not suffer under oppression to see the value of noncustodial assets: try sending a bank wire after hours. Also, in many use cases, we need quick and easy access to tokens like concert tickets, votes, and money.

Like other assets in the economy, tokens can be **fungible** or **non-fungible**. A fungible token is interchangeable with other tokens of a similar kind: for example, bitcoin is fungible. Most people would not care whether they owned one bitcoin or another: both have the same value and utility. Shares in a company like Apple are fungible. Each has the same economic stake, rights, and obligations as a share of similar class. Money is fungible. One dollar bill equals another dollar bill. By contrast, the value of an NFT is not necessarily equal to that of other NFTs. Each is unique. That's why NFTs are a popular means of expressing ownership of digital art, cultural assets, and other rare intellectual property or customized experiences. However, because we can create a near-infinite number of unique tangible and intangible assets in the world, the market for NFTs will likely grow far beyond these initial use cases.

Tokens can be **collateralized** or **uncollateralized**. The value of un-collateralized tokens freely floats against others based on the token's inherent underlying value. Money today is uncollateralized. Until fifty years ago, holders could redeem greenbacks for gold under certain conditions. Despite losing its peg, dollar bills are still very valuable: parties to the Bretton Woods Agreement of 1944 chose the US dollar as the global reserve currency. China has pushed to elevate its renminbi to global reserve status, but the dollar still represents 60 percent of central banks' holdings around the world.[26] Ethereum is the second most valuable blockchain platform in the world. It supports almost half a million developers building thousands of applications serving millions of users. Users and developers need its native token, ETH, as fuel or "gas" to run decentralized computations, applications, and transactions, rather like they would charge their cars at charging stations. This inherent usefulness makes ETH very valuable and creates demand for the token, but owning ETH does not give you a direct claim on some other asset like gold, receivables, physical plant and equipment, IP, and so on. Later, we discuss how ETH gives holders a claim on protocol revenue, a portion of which is used to reduce the total *ETH tokens outstanding*, similar to how a company might use excess earnings to buy back its own stock. Still, in the classical sense, it is uncollateralized.

By contrast, the creators of certain stablecoins, designed to hold a peg to the US dollar (USD), do make that claim. For example, the Centre Consortium backed its centrally managed USD Coin (USDC) dollar for dollar with government bonds held in US banks. Maker-DAO backed its DAI stablecoin with other tokens. Because tokens are volatile, these stablecoins maintain a reserve ratio of 2:1 or more. Either way, the holder can redeem the stablecoin at any time for the underlying asset. They are *collateralized*. Some stablecoins are notably *unstable*. In 2020, the creators of the Terra protocol, with its native token LUNA, launched an algorithmic stablecoin called US Terra (UST), programmed to hold a peg to the US dollar. The Terra algorithm calculated the relative supply or demand for UST and increased or decreased the total supply so that the value of the coin remained. However, unlike other stablecoins, it was *undercollateralized*, meaning that each UST was not backed 1:1 by USD. Insufficient collateral put the Terra LUNA protocol at risk of a bank run. That's what happened in May 2022: UST holders rushed to redeem their assets for the underlying dollars, much like the bank panics of the 1930s. UST collapsed, and the Terra protocol with it.

Tokens are transferrable **peer-to-peer**. Web3's decentralized applications (dapps) are composable, meaning that we can click them together with others like Legos, if they run on the same or compatible platforms. We can also swap any asset with any other asset within this peer-to-peer universe. As James Dale Davidson and Lord William Rees-Mogg predicted in *The Sovereign Individual*, "The odds of finding someone with exactly reciprocal desires to yours increase dramatically when you can sort instantly across the entire world rather than drawing on only those whom you might meet locally."[27]

The peer-to-peer, liquid, and composable nature of tokens inspires us to rethink fundamental concepts like money. Austrian economist Friedrich Hayek foreshadowed this: "Although we usually assume there is a sharp line of distinction between what is money and what is not—and the law generally tries to make such a distinction—so far as the causal effects of monetary events are concerned, there is no such clear difference. What we find is a continuum in which objects of various degrees of liquidity, or with values which can fluctuate independently of each other, shade into each other in the degree to which they function as money."[28] What happens when anyone can find anyone anywhere and make a market in their tokens? Some Web3 startups, like Anoma, are building private barter markets that can match buyers and sellers in any asset, peer-to-peer. Want to pay your mortgage in NFTs or use shares of Apple to buy concert tickets? Anoma founder Adrian Brink said, "The end goal of this could be the disruption of money itself, which was created to solve the problems and limitations of barter."[29] We will return to this question.

Tokens Funding Freedom Fighters

Tokens have played a high-profile role in helping fund the Ukrainian war effort against Russia. Since the conflict began, thousands of anonymous individuals as well as a few companies and public figures have sent more than $100 million in crypto donations to fight off the invasion and aid those under siege.[30] The anti-Putin art collective Pussy Riot helped launch Ukraine DAO, a decentralized virtual organization that has raised more than $6.5 million.[31]

These donations are possible only because tokens are digital bearer assets that are censorship resistant and transferrable peer-to-peer. As liquid, fungible, and self-custodied assets, holders can exchange them easily for fiat currency, goods, and services. There are countless reasons to use censorship-resistant money, and the list continues to grow. Canada's so-called Freedom Convoy protesters used cryptoassets to crowdsource their movement after GoFundMe and other intermediaries deplatformed them. Many disagreed with the actions of the protesters in Ottawa.[32] The same groups had less to say about bitcoin when it was used to fund Ukrainian freedom fighters.

Alex Wilson, founder of cryptoasset donation platform the Giving

Block, believes the permissionless nature of the asset class gels with a userbase not accustomed to asking for permission. In crypto giving, he said, "The broad category of human rights is most popular," adding that "the crypto community thinks it can do a better job than the nonprofits."[33]

Many of Ukraine's military suppliers have preferred taking payment in tokens, rather than converting it into fiat currency. According to Ukraine's deputy minister of defense, "It is easier, not complicated, transparent, and faster in comparison to a SWIFT [Society for Worldwide Interbank Financial Telecommunication] transaction, which could take more than a day."[34]

That tokens are helping fund the war effort highlights how Web3 and Web2 differ. Imagine if this conflict erupted ten years ago. In the Web2 version of events, impassioned citizens could donate to the Red Cross and post an encouraging message on a centrally controlled social media platform like Facebook, where others could deride them for their "slacktivism." If they violated terms of use or service, then they might get censored or even deplatformed without due process. In the Web3 era, we can use digital assets to arm those fighting for their freedom, answering Ukrainian president Volodymyr Zelenskyy's call: "I need ammunition, not a ride."[35]

Tokens Are to Web3 What the Website Was to Web1

Tokens are the defining tools of Web3, animating its varied applications, just as websites defined Web1. What the standard shipping container did for the global movement of goods, tokens can do for the peer-to-peer movement of value. They can lower costs, improve speed, reduce friction, and boost economic productivity. Just as we can fill a shipping container with a wide diversity of goods, we can program a token with a near-infinite number of attributes. Programmable money is a good example. Let's say you're sending money to your kid studying in college. Programmable money would work only at certain retailers like Walmart and Whole Foods, not at liquor stores.

If the website containerized information, then tokens containerize value or assets. Chris Dixon of Andreessen Horowitz told us, "I think of a website as a container. It's a container that can hold code and images and text. It's a container that holds hyperlinks to other websites. People could fill their containers with whatever they wanted."[36] However, the websites were only a piece of the puzzle. The original World Wide Web allowed us to piece our websites—these containers—together.

The choice of metaphor is intentional. The modern shipping container radically improved the speed and efficiency of the transportation industry so that organizations could globalize their supply chains. By one estimate, the adoption of containerization increased trade by 790 percent over twenty years, far outstripping the benefits of free-trade agreements in the same time span.[37] Similarly, the design of the original World Wide Web had a system for connecting these containers with each other, "and that's how we got this beautiful bottom-up, emerging system—all these little worlds within worlds that link with each other."[38]

Just as you can put anything in a shipping container or website, you can put anything in a digital asset and ascribe ownership to it. Said Dixon, "The key property here is, instead of being a delivery container, it can be an ownership container."[39] Despite the infinite possibilities, most people assume all tokens are a variation of bitcoin, a cryptocurrency, or some other financial asset. Partly, the confusion stems from semantic ambiguity with words like *token* and *cryptoasset* and phrases like "digital asset" and "virtual asset" used interchangeably. The industry and the media that cover it do not help by using crypto*currency* as an umbrella term. Most tokens have nothing to do with currency as a use case. Is an NFT credential a currency? What about a piece of art? Or a token that gives you governance over a decentralized organization? Or an avatar you play in a Web3 video-game? What about an NFT containing the terms of a bespoke financial contract between two parties?

More likely, the early discussion around Web3 focused on bitcoin, and thus money and other existing financial assets. The focus on money, stocks, and so forth is comforting and easy to grasp because these assets already exist. We often describe bitcoin as "digital gold" and emphasize their similarities, like the fixed supply, limited production, and high energy use, much as we compared early websites to magazines, newspapers, and classified ads. It was skeuomorphic.

Chris Dixon thinks Steve Jobs popularized the word *skeuomorphic*. That makes sense, because Jobs was always designing in the future, then pulling his audience into it. There are two meanings relevant to Web3. The first is the challenge of marketing disruptive technology. It often makes too jarring a mental leap from existing technology so that its potential users can't see how to use it, can't see how it relates to the technology they're already using. Why would they want a phone with email, a camera, music, and geospatial positioning? Jobs had to make metaphorical transitions with visual cues: hence, the email icon is an unopened envelope, the phone icon is an old-school handset, the browser is a compass, and the notes app is a paper notebook. Most obvious of all, he called his invention a phone, the iPhone, even though it was far more than that. This was a deliberate technique for making the jarringly new feel more familiar. Jobs was the master.

The second meaning is the challenge of seeing the potential of a jarringly innovation *only* in terms of today's technology, where metaphors like paper and publishing—or like digital cash and distributed ledgers of transactions—grossly limit the legislator's or business leader's imagination. That's Dixon's concern. "In technology, one of the key mistakes people make is confusing the initial instantiation of a new technology with the technology itself." Bitcoin launched and dominated the early "crypto" industry and the analysis of it, long before Web3 entered the vernacular.

Consider the evolution of major new creative media, where creators tend to import behaviors from prior media. Early motion pictures looked a lot like pantomime, no more than stage plays set to music. Perhaps that was a function of fundraising: how to pitch a breakthrough idea without sounding crazy. Over time, directors and producers added sound, establishing shots, close-ups, and zoom shots. They used editing, visual and sound effects, animation. As Dixon said, the industry took two or three decades "to develop what we now think of as native grammar, vocabulary" for making movies—rather, for creating immersive experiences that were sweeping and cinematic rather than resembling stage plays.[40]

What is the analogue for the Web in the predigital world? Historian and novelist Irene Vallejo, whose towering work *Papyrus* charts the dawn of books, made an astute observation about the Internet, pointing out that Tim Berners-Lee "found inspiration in the orderly, flexible space of public libraries." The Web's unique locators, known as URLs, were "the exact equivalent of a library catalog number," and the Web's hypertext transfer protocol, known as HTTP, "works like the request cards we use to ask a librarian to find the books we want to read." The Internet, she said, "emerged—multiplied, vast and ethereal—libraries."[41] To wit, Berners-Lee founded the World Wide Web Virtual Library, which continues to function today.

Dixon agreed. "You could say the Web in 1993 was like a magazine. But if you look at its essence, you'll see it was a way to link code, images, and text together through this tapestry of hyperlinks. Fast forward to today, and you have Sigma, a full graphic design suite in a website.[42] You have all these rich [software-as-a-service] apps." In other words, saying the Web was like a magazine is like saying a novel was like a library. The first library we would recognize was established in Alexandria, Egypt, by Ptolemy, one of Alexander the Great's generals. It took nearly two thousands more years for the modern library to be born of Medici patronage in Florence, Italy, in the fifteenth century.[43] Sometimes, good things take time. Dixon again: "So, people took ten, twenty years to figure out what they could do with this new primitive, the website."[44] Kind of like what people were able to figure out how to express with books as the medium over the millennia. They may have started as a way to tell the stories of kingly conquests or gods' glories, but they evolved in infinite variations. What does the future of the digital asset, or token, hold?

Though some early apps are skeuomorphic, often they end up as niche products rather than powerful disruptors. Sunny Aggarwal, founder of Osmosis, a decentralized exchange for tokens, said, "There will be a transition process of getting legacy assets to be digital native."[45]

Ethereum core developer Tim Beiko captured the vibe when he told us, "When mobile phones came out, Excel on your iPhone was not the killer app. The killer app was Instagram because it leveraged the camera or Uber because it leveraged GPS. The app developers asked, 'What are the computational capabilities of the device? How do we leverage those?' People want the apps that are uniquely possible with a blockchain, and a lot of those are around censorship resistance. That people own their NFTs is huge. There was not a Bored Ape Yacht Club or CryptoPunks before Ethereum," citing two popular NFT projects.[46]

What Will Be Web3's Killer Asset?

In the paperback edition of *Blockchain Revolution*, we introduced a taxonomy to understand the burgeoning world of digital assets. Since then, we have expanded the list to eleven types:

1. **Cryptocurrencies** like bitcoin are attempts at building Internet-native money that can act as a store of value, unit of account, and peer-to-peer medium of exchange. Money, one of humanity's greatest and most enduring creations, is undergoing an epochal revolution. Money, which has evolved through the millennia from cowrie shells to clay tablets to precious metals, banknotes, and bank balances, is taking another great leap forward. Money is becoming digital. The next decade of innovation will prove decisive as state powers, global corporations, and an increasingly assertive digital civil society vie for control over the lifeblood of our economic lives. If you want to understand our collective future, follow the money. Bitcoin is the dominant cryptocurrency, with a market value of approximately $400 billion US dollars. Bitcoin also represents nearly 40 percent of the total market value of all tokens.

2. **Protocol tokens** like ETH, which powers the "Layer 1" smart contracting platforms like Ethereum, are foundational to the development of Web3 applications. Think of Ethereum as a Web3 utility. In this analogy, Ethereum is the power grid and ETH is the electricity. To heat our homes and charge our cars, we need electricity. To run applications

and transact on the Ethereum network, we need ETH. The more applications that people build on Ethereum, the more value that accrues to its native token because of the greater demand for ETH. A power utility makes more money when it has more customers. Similar smart contracting platforms include Solana and Avalanche. Some of these platforms are backward compatible with Ethereum, such as Avalanche, while others, like Solana, are separate self-contained networks. John Wu, president of Ava Labs, likened Ethereum compatibility to a past technology standard. "Look at the history of technology. For example, Betamax or VHS. Once you have a minimum number of people using a certain standard, you have critical mass for liftoff. Ethereum got there. Why not make that compatible but better?" he argued.[47] A separate category of protocol tokens powers the Layer 2 networks on top of Layer 1 networks like Ethereum. Layer 2s act like substations, pumping power through grids to make them run more smoothly and quickly, while also benefiting from the underlying security of the "mainchain." These are also known as execution blockchains. The more demand for the substation to regulate the flow of transactions (like "peak hours" in a grid), the more demand for that token. Transactions on L2s are peer-to-peer. But if there's a dispute, then it can be escalated to the Ethereum L2. In this way, you can think of L2 transactions as private contracts and ETH as a court system that mediates a dispute on-chain. Layer 2 chains such as Arbitrum and Optimism have their own token and so fall into this category.

3. **Governance and utility tokens** give holders an economic stake and a say in how a protocol, service, or product is operated. Adopters of the product or service can earn or buy these tokens in the open market. In this respect, they are powerful incentives to join a network early. We can issue governance tokens on top of a smart contracting platform. For example, holders of UNI have a vote on decisions affecting the Uniswap decentralized exchange, which runs on Ethereum.[48] Or we can base governance tokens on stand-alone blockchains. In the Cosmos ecosystem, for example, every application has its own chain. Other projects, such as Filecoin, have their own dedicated blockchains. Imagine if the early adopters of Facebook participated

in the economic upside of the platform simply by using it? They'd earn Facebook tokens for posting pictures and engaging with friends. Eventually, they'd have a vote on how the company managed the platform, in such decisions as selling the personal data of Facebook users to third parties.

4. **Oracle tokens:** Blockchains are immutable records of transactions in a network. Information recorded to blockchains is trustworthy, searchable, and auditable. This is one of their great benefits. However, they are self-contained systems, meaning they do not have "access" to data that happens in the real world. Let's say you had a smart contract tied to the Federal Reserve's benchmark interest rate, the price of Apple shares, the outcome of a sporting event, an AI data feed, health records, population numbers, GDP figures, inflation, home prices, or any of the other infinite "off-chain" data sources. How do we bring that data into a blockchain so the contract can execute? This is known as the "oracle problem," something we will address more in the chapter on financial services. One solution is to use a single source of authority, but that runs the risk of centralization. Protocols like Chainlink and UMA seek to decentralize the oracle process while ensuring reliable data. Their native token is paid out to network nodes that provide accurate data. If our Web3 thesis is correct, then there will be much greater need to bring off-chain data on-chain, driving demand for Oracle networks, and thus the underlying token.

5. **Interoperability tokens:** These are the native tokens of protocols like Cosmos and Polygon, which help to connect different blockchains. Earlier I described the challenge of composability and interoperability between chains. To overcome this challenge, we need ways to connect disparate networks, roughly as TCP/IP connects Web networks. These tokens defy easy categorization. For example, many applications built in the Cosmos ecosystem do not "sit" on Cosmos as they do on Ethereum. As a result, application development does not necessarily drive demand for ATOM, Cosmos's native token. However, developers benefit from the "shared security" of validators shared with the mainchain, making Cosmos more valuable because it is the biggest. Perhaps the easiest way to think of them is as the unit of

account for canals and other arteries of blockchain commerce. The more intercontinental or interblockchain commerce there is, the more these platforms prosper.

6. **Securities tokens** are tokens that represent a claim on a security like a stock or bond. A securities token could be a share in a company, bond, derivative contract, mutual fund unit, and so on. DeFi index funds like Index Co-op, a DAO launched by Set, functions like a decentralized token ETF, with around $400 million. Because securities are a regulated market, this is one area where legacy firms have done a lot of work. Blockchains enable instant clearing, settlement, and record-keeping for assets, including securities. However, securities tokens are not without challenges. Legacy attitudes are resistant to change. Switching to a "crypto-native" format is challenging when your whole workflow is analog. Customers are used to the old ways and may not want to switch over. Despite these challenges, dozens of securities tokens offerings have succeeded, from entities like Santander, Société Générale, the World Bank, Banco Bilbao Vizcaya Argentaria, Bank of Montreal, Union Bank, and others. While the potential is enormous, securities tokens remain a niche, largely because laws don't widely recognize them yet.

7. **Corporate tokens** are issued by centralized businesses, often cryptoasset exchanges. In a way, they are hybrids of loyalty points and governance tokens. We can earn them by using a platform and redeem them for special rebates, rewards, promotional offers, and so forth on centralized exchanges. But they do not always come with economic and governance rights, like a governance token (or equity, for that matter). However, they are typically more useful than traditional loyalty points, and they are fungible. I cannot trade my Starwood rewards points for cash on the popular exchanges Binance and Coinbase; I can redeem them only at the hotel chain. But I can easily swap my corporate tokens for cash. People can also misuse and abuse tokens. Now-bankrupt FTX created its own token called FTT purportedly as a useful asset that it deployed on its platform for many of the above reasons, but then manipulated the trading in the asset to inflate its value artificially and used the inflated FTT as collateral

to do risky trading and perhaps illegal fund transfers to its sister firm, Alameda Research. To build trust, an organization will need to distribute its corporate coin in a fair and equitable way. Done correctly, corporate tokens could be the template for loyalty rewards programs for companies in Web3.

8. **Natural asset tokens** are backed by assets like carbon, water, or air. Earlier we described the difference between collateralized and uncollateralized assets. Both have found product/market fit. Uncollateralized assets like bitcoin have found millions of eager investors who consider it digital gold. Stablecoins, backed by dollars in the bank, have proven an easier, faster, and cheaper form of digital money than what financial intermediaries offer. Natural asset tokens are a form of collateralized asset, such as the carbon credit. Carbon offsets can help fight climate change. A decentralized global registry to buy, sell, and retire credits could expand the industry materially.

9. **Stablecoins** are digital assets pegged to another asset with stable value, such as the US dollar. Stablecoins are the primary medium of exchange in Web3 and have grown twenty times in a few years to $135 billion.[49] Right now, there are two kinds of stablecoins: *centralized* and *decentralized*. Centralized stablecoins are issued by companies and backed by reserves held in TradFi institutions. Centre's USDC surpassed $45 billion in circulating supply and handled about $12 billion a day in volume in 2022—more than ten times that of Venmo, the most popular payment app in the United States.[50] The second category is decentralized stablecoins, which are backed by cryptoassets locked in smart contracts, effectively software controlling money. DAI, the original decentralized stablecoin, launched on Ethereum and maintained by MakerDAO, has about $4.7 billion in circulation and at its peak had $500 million a day in volume.[51] AngelList, a leading platform for VC investment, now accepts stablecoins for eligible investments.[52] Mastercard announced plans to integrate stablecoins into its network. Visa now supports transaction settlement with the USDC stablecoin. The list goes on.

10. **Non-fungible tokens** (NFTs) are unique and non-interchangeable digital goods.[53] There are as many use cases for NFTs as there are

unique assets in the world. The idea of programming digital goods dates back a decade, with so-called "colored coins" on the Bitcoin network. They failed to take off because that network supported transactions, not programs. Not until Ethereum came along with a quirky token standard called ERC-721 did NFTs take off. Rather than storing all token IDs as a single balance, "each [ERC-721] unit has its own unique ID that can be linked to additional metadata (such as data, texts, images and so forth), which differentiate it from other tokens stemming from the same contract."[54] A good example is a piece of digital art. The metadata is the art itself. The ERC-721 NFT is akin to a signature and stamp of provenance.

11. **Central bank digital currencies** (CBDCs) are digital assets issued by governments and central banks. The *Economist* in 2021 ran on its cover "Govcoins: The Digital Currencies That Will Transform Finance."[55] The hype is palpable. However, as of this writing, few, if any, projects are live and operating at scale. Theoretically, CBDCs could improve the efficiency, reach, and responsiveness of central banks. Its advocates argue that it could accommodate unbanked people, reduce costs, and expose financial risks earlier. The Communist Party of China views its digital yuan as complementary to its social credit score, a means of nudging citizen behavior. The *Economist* recommended treating CBDCs "with optimism and humility."[56] We add "skepticism" to such treatment. As Chris Giancarlo, former chairman of the Commodity Futures Trading Commission (CFTC), told us, "Money is too important to be left to the central bankers."[57]

Collectively these eleven types make up nearly 100 percent of all digital asset market value. But market value may be an incomplete measurement if we look at Web3 assets in their totality. Consider one Web3 asset under development—*soulbound tokens*—a term of art used to describe a nontransferable and non-fungible token tied to an individual, like a smart Social Security number with its own digital wallet.[58] Perhaps the government issues us one at birth, like a birth certificate. Perhaps it becomes core to our identity—a secure, private, and evolving repository of data that we can access and use freely, say, to get a driver's license, open a bank account, prove our identity without divulging personal information, perhaps via a zero-knowledge implementation. When you order a drink at a bar, the server needs to know only whether you're at or above the legal drinking age, period—not your name, where you live, whether you're an organ donor, or other personal information.

This raises some interesting questions about tokens. What is the "market value" of soulbound tokens if we can never create a market in them? What about votes in an election? We know people spend money to sway elections, but can we quantify the value of a voting token that has no other utility (like, say, a governance token that allows holders to vote and perhaps earn protocol revenue)? Furthermore, this is not an exhaustive list. There will be dozens, perhaps hundreds, of different token types in the taxonomy. Perhaps the concept of market value will become a less useful measure as more tokens represent valuable things like identity that, by law or code, we cannot buy or sell.

While we feel confident that these categories of digital assets will endure and grow, we have less confidence in what individual assets will survive in the long term. If the token is the fundamental building block of Web3, just as the website was the fundamental building block of Web1, then many of today's digital assets will end up like the early dot-com websites—in the dustbin of history. Some assets may become the basis of multitrillion-dollar platforms supporting the new Internet of ownership, just as early dot-coms like Amazon became leviathans of Web2. However, Web3's killer asset has just as likely not yet emerged.

What should we look for in the next crop of Web3 projects? History gives us a guide: new technologies not only make the difficult easier to do, but they also make the *impossible* possible to do. Still, in the early innings of a new technology, emerging innovations tend to be skeuomorphic, mimicking what already exists: Web1's early websites looked like magazines, catalogs, and classified ads, but the real power of the Internet was as a platform for communication and collaboration online. Web3's early assets look like assets in the real world and even use the same language—crypto*currencies*, crypto*collectibles* (what we now call NFTs), stable*coins*, and so forth. The same was true with Web1's killer apps of the web *page* and e*mail*.

How Should Policymakers Think About Digital Assets?

Web3 is a greater shock to the status quo for regulators and policy-makers than any information technology that preceded it. Of course, the computer, Internet, and smartphone raised tough questions for regulators and forced them to challenge their assumptions and established laws. One of the early building blocks of the Web was a security protocol known as SSL, or secure sockets layer, replaced by transport layer security. It was hugely important to the early development of the Web, as it dealt with encrypting information like credit card or Social Security numbers securely across the Internet. It also used 128-bit encryption, considered weapons-grade cryptography and illegal for commercial use. Overzealous regulators could have killed the Web but decriminalized it instead, giving the commercial Web a big boost.

Today, regulators face even tougher choices. Some consider all digital goods to be securities because they have a price or value and can be bought or sold, which is like calling all blogs newspapers because they use words that can be read, quoted, and plagiarized. Yes, tokenized stocks and bonds of companies are securities, as are many other financial assets. But what about digital art, tokens that grant access to licensed IP, and fungible virtual goods in videogames? What about soulbound tokens associated with our identities? Whether these asset classes have *precedent* depends on how legislators, regulators, and courts interpret them under existing laws and where they think those laws apply, case by case, jurisdiction by jurisdiction. The industry must help to educate regulators, and regulators must prioritize educating themselves, tread lightly, and put innovation and experimentation first. Those jurisdictions that establish the ground rules and the guardrails will attract the innovators, jobs, and the spotlight. We revisit these in chapters nine and ten.

Tokens: The Building Blocks for
Internet-Native Organizations

Joint stock companies in England and Netherlands were a huge innovation: they pooled risk and pursued large undertakings like transatlantic voyages. Industrialization kicked the company into high gear
with the invention of the first limited liability company (LLC), where
individual investors not only pooled their resources but were limited
in liability to their initial investment. When you buy a share of Apple
for $100 and the company goes bankrupt, you stand to lose $100. You
have no additional liability if the company, say, owes creditors billions
or must settle a class-action lawsuit.

"Prior to limited liability and the Delaware C-corp, if you were a
railroad company and somebody died on your railroad, then you'd
go to jail or get sued. As a result, people formed companies, partnerships, only with their family members, people they trusted deeply,"
said Chris Dixon of Andreessen Horowitz.[59] Even if you didn't kill
someone, you could end up in debtors' prison for going bust.[60] LLCs
changed all that. Shareholders incorporated the Merchants Bank as
the first LLC in 1811 at the dawn of a golden age of American
industrial expansion.[61] The C-corporation went one step further, sep-
arating the assets, income, and tax liability of owners or shareholders
from those of the company. This distanced the proprietors of businesses further from the corporations themselves.[62] Corporations became separate living entities, gaining personhood under the law and
outliving their founders and early shareholders by generations.

The corporation fully aligned with the business undertakings of the
industrial age. Technically complex and capital-intensive undertakings, like building a railroad or launching a car company, steel mill,
oil refinery, or gold mine, were impossible for families to finance, and
far too risky. Corporations helped to spread the risk and gave investors a road map for how the company and its business would survive
its founders. It also helped individuals take a modest first step toward
owning capital themselves. But does the corporate form of ownership

work for building and launching networks? Launching a new corporation to compete with today's Web2 giants would be very capital intensive indeed. Absent any alternative, would-be rivals have assumed that corporations were the best vehicle for forming and sustaining new networks, and "tried to graft on a structure invented for high-capex [capital expenditure] industrial companies." As a result, these big networks are behaving more like industrial age trusts, trying to hoard all the resources to become monopolies.[63]

"What happened in Web2 is somewhat predictable. To design a better system, we need to rethink the asset class on first principles. That wasn't Satoshi's original intention, and it probably wasn't even Vitalik's," Dixon continued, referring to the pseudonymous inventor of Bitcoin, Satoshi Nakamoto, and to the visionary behind Ethereum, Vitalik Buterin. "But I think this new native asset class of information networks emerged collectively from all the community efforts. It's purely digital. It's global," he said.[64] Tokens are the building blocks of Web3. They are a new toolset that will mirror human ingenuity and perhaps our lesser impulses into a dizzying array of new networked and global organizations. The endgame for tokens may be to disrupt the corporation itself.

Conclusion and Takeaways

Digital assets are a new elemental capability, or technical primitive, that we use to program virtually anything of value online. Until blockchains, we had no way to engineer digital scarcity, meaning that no one could copy valuable digital goods over and over, and no way to express ownership online without trusting a third party. Here are some takeaways:

1. We can understand tokens in two contexts:
   i. While the "Matthew Effect," a biblical parable, states that wealth accumulates to the wealthy, in the long arc of history, wealth has become more evenly distributed: today, index funds often held by small investors are the biggest shareholders of American indus-

try.[65] Pension plans, which invest on behalf of working people, are some of the biggest allocators of capital in financial markets. Web3 tools will accelerate this democratization of wealth.

ii. As the economy grows more complex, assets became more abstract. In feudal times, land was the most important asset class in the economy, and gold was the medium of exchange when barter was not an option. Industrialization accelerated asset innovation, with the advent of securities like stock certificates, bonds, bills of lading, and depository receipts. The digitization of assets and the invention of new Web3 native digital goods are part of that historical arc.

2. We have several categories of tokens today, such as cryptocurrencies, protocol tokens, stablecoins, governance tokens, and NFTs. They represent most of the market capitalization, but that taxonomy will change as we advance on this journey.

3. Tokens have some core principles that make them different from legacy assets. They are peer-to-peer, censorship resistant, self-custodial, and existent on immutable public databases. Beyond that, they are infinitely varied—fungible or non-fungible, collateralized or uncollateralized, and issued by a corporation, government, NGO, or Internet native entity like a DAO.

4. For the above reasons, savers in the developing world are adopting tokens such a bitcoin to hedge against currency devaluation, fund protest movements, or move money peer-to-peer without using cash. The ability to earn value in Web3 for what you contribute to networks, regardless of where or who you are, benefits everyone, especially you.

As we will see, Web3 empowers creators and Internet users to earn more from their contributions online, changing the dynamic among platforms, creators, and consumers.

CHAPTER 4

People

Everyone a Creator and a Patron

For millennia, wealthy rulers and patrons have supported many of history's greatest artists. In medieval times, for example, society was far too desperate to support broad-based individual education, let alone professional art and higher forms of culture. Wealthy individuals and institutions had different reasons for championing the arts. For the Medici banking family of Florence, art and architecture were useful in projecting wealth and power. After all, building monuments to the family would outlast any individual (aka the edifice complex). For the Catholic Church, huge artistic undertakings inspired awe in the masses—surely, only a hand guided by divine power could have created such beauty! That and vivid scenes of damned souls descending into hell kept the peasantry in their grip.[1] For the monarchs, commissioning plays and performances helped stoke nationalism. Whatever the reasons, we wouldn't have Shakespeare if we didn't have Queen Elizabeth I, or Botticelli without Lorenzo Medici, or Michelangelo without Pope Paul III. Religious art and iconography specifically flourished when the Church was one of the wealthiest stakeholders in the economy. People still expressed themselves creatively through folk art, crafts, dance, and music, not for monetary compensation but for the joy of performance.

In the nineteenth century, this began to change. The lithograph made it possible to mass-produce visual art that the professional classes could afford. Rising literacy combined with industrial printing techniques made books and newspapers affordable and accessible to most, a boon to writers. In the late nineteenth century, Thomas Edison invented the phonograph, his favorite creation. He produced discs that, when struck by a needle, could play back music. Initially a luxury item, phonographs became a set piece in the parlors of Gilded Age America. In the 1920s, radio and film further democratized access to culture, but not so much the creation of it. It broadened the base of people who paid for it and ushered in an age of mass media.[2]

Historians may recall the twentieth century as a first golden age of creative industries, when different kinds of artists could earn a decent living from their craft—when, for example, vinyl record and compact disc sales generated a steady stream of royalties so that recording artists, studio musicians, songwriters, lyricists, and others behind the curtain all earned a decent share. Studios and other intermediaries controlled production and distribution, and so compensation did not equal control or power.[3] Often these go-betweens extracted more than they deserved.[4] Artists hoped that the Internet would help to disintermediate gatekeepers and middlemen—and it did that, to a degree and for a time. But it also made earning a living as a creator more difficult, especially for musicians. So new intermediaries stepped in. Now, with NFTs and other digital goods, we have a new toolset for content creators to monetize their work in a way that harks back to the patronage of old. In the Web2 economy, creators are "paid in likes," said Tyler Winklevoss, cofounder and CEO of Gemini, a regulated cryptocurrency exchange, wallet, and custodian. "Likes are abstracted as a form of money, the extracted layer between getting paid and the influence you've built up," he explained. Web3 users get "paid in tokens, which is fairer and rewards people in proportion to the value they put in."[5]

The twentieth century's model for creative production was industrial in nature, very one-size-fits-all. The model for Web3 will be more bespoke: creators will be able to tailor their relationships with superfans who spend more than casual fans. It also removes gatekeepers from many steps of the creative process. Superfans become like the patrons of old, spending more than the average admirer, and stakeholders in undertakings they support. Creators and their fans together own the value they generate.

How Does Web2 Fail Creators?

"For the longest time, especially working in animation, I felt like a small cog in a big machine, always executing on somebody else's vision," said the artist known as pplpleasr.[6] "I grew up watching [Hayao] Miyazaki films, anime, Pixar movies, and everything that involves good storytelling in the form of animation and live action." That's what pplpleasr wanted to do: tell stories in digital media. But there were multiple barriers in the way. First was gender disparity. "The visual effects computer graphics industry is a male-dominated one," pplpleasr said. The last traditional job pplpleasr had was not as a staff employee but as a contractor, and the department that pplpleasr worked in at Blizzard had never hired a female staff employee. Second was culture. "Brought up in an Asian environment, you're not taught to speak up for yourself, to fight for yourself, or to climb social ladders. It's more the concepts of being humble and letting your work speak for itself," pplpleasr recalled. "Being a quiet factory worker in a visual effects studio seemed to make a lot more sense to me" as the main path to stability.

But making sense was less important than making the art pplpleasr wanted to make. "I realized that all these DeFi protocols had all this money but were promoting themselves using very lo-fi memes, made by non-artists using Microsoft Paint and other platforms. I started making these little animations for promoting various DeFi protocols, capturing the specific spirit and culture of crypto Twitter. That's what people loved so much about my work back then . . . so I pinballed one by one. I bounced around and did a video for one protocol, and then another one would hit me up. Just like that, I did one for every DeFi protocol. It was through word of mouth."

Pplpleasr is a self-starter—a self-taught animator, a self-made DeFi artist, a person who spots opportunities to engage with the crypto community and seizes them. "I did the animation for the Uniswap V3 announcement," she said, referring to one of decentralized finance's more popular applications, adding, "I knew there would be a lot of eyeballs on this specific animation. I worked harder on it than on any other animation because I knew it was a big deal. Around that time, NFTs started picking up. I had dabbled in NFTs in 2020, but they weren't that crazy at the time. I was thinking about how I could combine these two areas. When the Uniswap video came together, I auctioned it off as an NFT [for $525,000], which I hadn't done with my previous DeFi videos. It became my magnum opus. The PleasrDAO helped propel my name in the space."[7]

The meteoric rise of NFTs has inspired clickbait headlines, mostly focused on the eye-watering prices commanded by popular and sometimes controversial NFT projects. Sotheby's sold the now-famous digital artist Beeple's piece *Everydays: The First 5,000 Days* for $69 million. NFTs for so-called "generative art projects" like Crypto-Punks, which are simple renderings resembling eight-bit videogame characters, have become popular for their rarity and cultural cachet, and have sold for hundreds of thousands of dollars or more. This kind of conspicuous consumption by those with money to burn has led to an NFT backlash. Below the headlines, at a more modest scale, NFTs are empowering artists and other creators to earn decent money for their craft. Culture needed a new business model. NFTs are part of the solution. Not everyone will be an artist now, but all artists now have a tool to support doing what they love.

Pplpleasr's "ultimate dream was making artwork for myself. I had all the ingredients, but I didn't know how to put together the sandwich." Pplpleasr created an Instagram account for brushing up on skills: "I'll make little 3D digital art." But it became a platform for self-expression: "I had not been encouraged to do this during my career in visual effects. Those years were necessary for me to learn the skill sets to target my visions better now."[8]

Instagram is a Web2 platform that tried integrating NFTs. "You get fifty percent of what they sell or something like that. But that's compromising because the work itself is animated, so then you have to choose one specific frame." Pplpleasr discovered that the traditional art market was not much different from digital art and animation. It was "so much about liaising with the right people, networking with the right people, going to shows and galleries, getting picked up by curators. There are so many gatekeepers, too many mountains to climb, for somebody taught to be quiet and humble. I was interviewing. Waiting to hear back from interviews, I'd get really anxious."

When NFTs came along and pplpleasr sold that first NFT of digital art, "[m]y mind was blown. A person just bought the thing in its digital form, and I get ten percent of this, every time it sells in the future. That was a game-changer moment for me. It was the first time that we had a way to monetize our work, other than farming 'likes' or trying to get shown in a gallery."[9]

Pplpleasr pays almost hyperclose attention to audiences. "Even though people thought my animations were really cool, what was getting even more traction were my behind-the-scenes video. When you watch Pixar movies, the DVDs have these special featurettes, where [the creators] tour the studio and tell you how they made it. I found that people just loved that stuff. When I put my face in front of a camera, recording myself talking about my work on my webcam at low quality, that drew attention as well."[10]

From User Generated to User Owned and Monetized

Hollywood screenwriter Jessie Nickson-Lopez has brought some of modern TV's most indelible characters to life. As a founding member of the writing team on *Stranger Things*, she developed the story line for the character Eleven and has written for *The Outsiders*, *Narcos: Mexico*, and other hit shows. In 2022, Apple green-lit Nickson-Lopez's show *Lucia*, to be directed by Damien Chazelle, the Academy Award–winning director of *La La Land* and *Whiplash*, with Nickson-Lopez as showrunner. She has established herself in the Hollywood firmament. At age thirty-five, she has a résumé most writers aspire to. Despite her success, she considers screenwriting her day job. She revealed her true passion as cofounder of Web3 startup MV3. At the intersection of storytelling and technology, it promises to disrupt TV, film, and the Hollywood business model itself. Nickson-Lopez's story reminds us of the profound breadth and diversity of backgrounds of the builders in this space.

MV3 is a collection of 6,500 NFTs of different characters, the building blocks for what will be a richly rendered narrative "universe," created by Nickson-Lopez and the MV3 team. Owners will participate in the IP, have a say in their character's arc, and even co-create the story with the MV3 team. These different character assets could ultimately appear in film, TV, and other storytelling media. They could be playable characters in videogames or avatars in the metaverse. Imagine buying a Star Wars character in 1976 before the first film's release and then sharing that character's journey over dozens of films, adaptations, and licensing deals—that's the ambition of MV3. From the initial mint, the "creation event," MV3 has raised about $2 million to fund the development.

We spoke to Nickson-Lopez by Zoom from her home in Los Angeles, where she lives with her husband and MV3 cofounder, Torey Kohara, a director. She explained how her brother and third cofounder, Roberto Nickson, convinced her, finally, to pay attention to NFTs in 2021. According to Nickson-Lopez, "I came into this space with a vengeance. I was throwing money into Ethereum, and I got it. I understood not just the highs from gambling, which is part of it, but also the opportunity that existed for ownership—ownership of a property." It wasn't long before she started to connect the dots to her own world. "The writer in me instantly went 'I know how Hollywood works.' In the next couple of months, NFT projects are going to come across my email, and they're going to say, 'Hey, we're looking for a writer to adapt this NFT.' It's just going to happen. Hollywood adapts absolutely everything. I knew that I wouldn't be able to do it."[11]

Why? Because most NFT projects had no story. Creating these character assets to exist in a film is so antithetical to how content creation works today, where studios own the IP and decide how to use it, that the early pioneers did not even consider trying it out. Early NFTs were more like Pokémon cards than anything radically new. In other words, they were skeuomorphic.

For example, the scarcity and programmability of NFTs spawned hundreds of gimmicky "profile picture" (pfp) projects, each with a few hundred or thousand variations on a common theme: a penguin, ape, gorilla, pixelated eight-bit character, a gray rock, and so forth. The logic is, the more unique the character, the more valuable. In the heady days of the bull market, these "extremely rare" NFTs fetched prices in the hundreds of thousands or even millions of dollars, though only a few of these initiatives retain much value.

Consider Bored Ape Yacht Club (BAYC), created by Yuga Labs. BAYC began as a collection of gaudily rendered cartoon apes, popular as online pfps for influential Internet personalities and celebrities. If you own a Bored Ape, then you can resell it, fractionalize it, sell the parts, and even get a loan with the NFT as collateral. In other words, they are digital assets with many of the rights commonplace for nondigital assets. Yuga Labs parlayed the success of the initial pfp craze into other avenues, including narrative storytelling and a massive multiplayer online role-playing game called *Otherside*, which is in development following a massive fundraising round where Yuga sold $1 billion of virtual assets in *Otherside* to would-be users, called Voyagers, of the still-undeveloped game.[12] Bored Apes also entitles the holder to license the IP. That's exactly what actor and producer Seth Green had planned with his Bored Ape named Fred Simian before a "Mr. Cheese" stole Fred; Green decided to pay the ape-napper's ransom of roughly $297,000 to resecure his IP rights, surely a first in this brave new Web3 world.[13]

Green is a creative person who may do something inventive with his ape Fred, but to Nickson-Lopez, "most writers I know wouldn't be able to adapt an NFT project because there's no story inherent in most of them. They're just variations of the same photos."[14] These early NFT projects are valuable for their scarcity and what they signal to the world, making them more like rare collectible luxury goods than characters to adapt into a movie or TV show. They may prove very valuable for their scarcity but adapting a pfp for a story makes about as much sense as casting a rare Gucci handbag to star in its own miniseries, putting aside the horror genre of killer inanimate objects. To paraphrase the great philosophical axiom, one thousand bored apes working for one thousand years will *not* be able to write the next Hollywood blockbuster (though that won't stop Seth Green from trying).

The MV3 story is "a collision between Silicon Valley and Gotham City, where tech entrepreneurs have usurped politicians and sentient androids roam the streets in search of liberation."[15] Set in the "dystopian cyberpunk society" of 2081, after the "climate has gone to hell," MV3 focuses on "a ragtag group of idealistic" rebels struggling to "take power from the corporation that owns the city."[16] Nickson-Lopez's brother Roberto thinks MV3 has the potential to be the "next great franchise, birthed from an NFT collection, where holders can directly participate in the upside of the IP." Nickson-Lopez said, "In Hollywood, you live or die by your fans. No matter how good your project is, if the fans aren't watching, if they don't show up for your film or your TV project, you won't get anywhere. You won't get picked up for a second season, your show won't get picked up." Knowing that fans will support a project is key for firing up the Hollywood machine to spend $100 million or more on a film or TV show. Nickson-Lopez said, "So we reverse-engineered it, and I created the world of Eluna City and the characters that reside in it." It is ambitious, and the MV3 team knows it.

Though Nickson-Lopez architected this world and crafted story lines for main characters, she and the team alone will not decide the direction of the story. "For me, what's been most exciting is seeing how much creativity we're inspiring in people who have never created before but are consumers of dystopian worlds and of fiction. There's this hunger to play. Our fans are our community and our co-creators. Because they're invested in the world and in the characters, they're really excited to build it up with us. It's been so inspiring for me."

MV3 now offers creative workshops for holders of their NFTs to help them develop their characters' backstories. Fan fiction, where fans write alternative endings and new chapters to existing IP, has been a big part of popular franchises like Harry Potter but is rarely integrated into the official story lines in any way. As MV3 cofounder Kohara said, "I think fan fiction has always been considered this stepchild of the franchise."[17] But now, by owning their characters, fans can write in their stories and participate economically in that upside. I was curious, and so I bought one of the NFTs. Now I'm a stakeholder, and I get to see if a business writer can credibly do sci-fi.

The studio system would never allow fans to co-create and co-own content, according to Nickson-Lopez. When first presented, fan fiction struck some industry mainstays as a radical idea—possibly even copyright infringement. "As my lawyers say, 'It's like you're ripping off pieces of value and just giving it to people.' And we're like, 'Exactly! That's exactly what we're doing.' People can't really wrap their head around it. What's so exciting to me about it is being able to change."[18]

Regarding copyright, the World Intellectual Property Organization and other legal experts have offered their analysis of its potential application to NFTs, but we generally get more clarity through each legal dispute and court ruling.[19] That said, NFT artists and other creators who are familiar with IP laws often specify how they want the market to treat their NFTs in a specific jurisdiction. As with Creative Commons licenses, they have the option to pick and choose which standard IP rights they want to reserve, if any, and which they want to license to NFT buyers.[20] "If NFTs are all about enabling ownership, then why would creators choose to give away intellectual property rights through Creative Commons licensing (CC0)?" asked Harvard Business School professor Scott Duke Kominers, rhetorically, on Twitter in August 2022.[21]

In a blog post that followed, Kominers and coauthor Flashrekt, a pseudonymous NFT influencer, attempted to answer that question. Their argument sounded reminiscent of Lawrence Lessig's book *Free Culture: How Big Media Uses Technology and the Law to Lock Down Culture and Control Creativity.*[22] In that 2004 book, Lessig—a Harvard Law School professor and cofounder of the Creative Commons—explained the "social dimension of creativity: how creative work builds on the past and how society encourages or inhibits that building with laws and technologies." Lessig described how "cultural monopolists" of big tech have "[shrunk] the domain of public ideas."[23] His point: it should be the creator's choice, not a corporation's, to release a work into the commons, and creators have many options to do so under CC licenses. Likewise, Kominers and Flashrekt described how art lives and dies by its cultural relevance, such that allowing everyone to copy, iterate, and riff off an original work from time to time can diffuse it more widely and make it more culturally relevant. They advocated for creators to "seize the memes of production," but add that their options are now programmable in NFTs.[24]

Returning to MV3, the model of giving away or selling IP at the beginning is backward in other ways. MV3's road map—raising funds by selling characters, writing stories for them, and creating IP around them—resembles that of Web3 gaming. Ria Lu, a Web3 gaming executive in the Philippines, explained the difference between NFT games and traditional games: "In traditional gaming, you make the game, you put it out there, and then slowly you bring in the money. Slowly you build the community. Whereas in NFT gaming, you build the community, you make the money, and then you create the game."[25] Community comes first. MV3 is taking a similar approach.

In the end, projects like MV3 will work not only because they engage their fans in the economic upside but also because they hand some control to fans to shape how a story unfolds. Handing over control and economics to fans is antithetical to the Hollywood model, and Nickson-Lopez recognizes that. "I am now a writer for money, for hire, out of necessity," she said. "And I hate it. I genuinely hate it because I'm like, 'Oh, wow, now instead of writing for the people I love and care about, and for myself, I'm writing to make money. So, I'm writing for the shareholders at Apple right now. I need to make them happy.'" Engaging fans in the creative process, for love of the characters and not just for money, is what clearly drives these creators and gives their respective projects purpose and meaning.

People might write fan fiction for the love of the characters, but the ones whose stories build audiences might as well get compensated. In the case of MV3, the best writers will write their characters into the narrative in an organic and substantive way.

How are Nickson-Lopez and her team making their MV3 vision a reality? What challenges do they face? For starters, for people's IP to appear in a videogame, someone needs to design the game in such a way that people can introduce their characters and story lines into the larger narrative. In terms of risks, studios may never agree to option IP that they can never exclusively control, and so creators of any film or TV properties may need to self-fund. If they do self-fund a project, then they will need to consider carefully how to calculate the value these people create and then compensate them fairly for it. Other questions to answer include, what are the laws and international treaties governing this kind of co-created intellectual property? Like the business maxim, no matter how well you hire, more talent will always be outside your organization than inside. The same is true in these communities. How do you sift through all the talent to find the gems who will enrich this universe? Once you have adopted this content, how will different jurisdictions rule on disputes? Will co-creators based in the Philippines have standing to sue for their rights in the US district court in California? Can the builders and visionaries at MV3 and other NFT projects really disrupt Hollywood? And, of course, will Hollywood wake up and create its own version, where studios remain in control?

Warner Bros. has already announced a limited-edition series of NFTs related to the Lord of the Rings franchise, and countless celebrities have piled in to NFTs to burnish their tech credentials or boost their brand. But we are a long way from people being able to buy an elf, an orc, or a hobbit. The most innovative Hollywood studios may struggle with the innovator's dilemma and innovate only on the margin of this technology. Nevertheless, the risk from incumbents' co-opting this technology or else suing the innovators out of their seed funding is real. Can a bunch of upstart creators armed with these new tools take on Tinseltown? It is a tall order. Then again, stranger things have happened.

From Corporate to Community Control

Pplpleasr has launched a different experiment in NFT-enabled storytelling called Shibuya. In a blog post announcing the project, the artist identified some of the constraints on storytelling today: "Many of us still dedicate our undivided attention to watching long-form content, whether it be a short film, movie, or TV series. The problem is, this type of content is extremely expensive and time consuming to create." As a result, only big companies like movie studios can afford to make them. But what if creators had another way to crowdsource a film or other big undertaking and raise the funds needed to make it into a reality? The blog post continued, "The technology behind NFTs can be used for much more [than pfp projects]! A desire formed within me for a space for long-form content on the blockchain. This is where the idea of Shibuya came about, a Web3 experiment where long-form content is free to watch but monetized on the blockchain to allow viewer participation on the creative process and also shared ownership."[26]

Pplpleasr gave us the elevator pitch for Shibuya: "'a decentralized Netflix-meets-Kickstarter platform,' where you're crowdsourcing not only information, but also funding, and it's simultaneously doing both." Shibuya uses "methods of interacting with the actual medium, to make the process of crowdfunding feel more interesting than something like a Kickstarter," where people give money and then wait.[27]

In traditional filmmaking, Hollywood studios make all these intellectual properties in a mysterious black box; nobody knows what happens in there except for those in the industry. The industry's top-down hierarchical structure promotes "sure bets" over unproven but potentially great works by new artists. As such, we end up with multiple sequels instead of new IP. Hollywood has adapted some fan fiction when it could get 100 percent control over the project. But it is reluctant to engage with fans on an economic or creative level. In other words, it doesn't know how to coordinate a group of people who don't know and don't necessarily trust each other. Pplpleasr thinks that "blockchain is a good step forward, because there's a bunch of people who don't trust each other, but they all agree that blockchain is something that they can trust."[28]

Governance of the creative process is the challenge. Taking any idea and letting the community run with it completely in a flat structure, including people who have no expertise or knowledge of the process, could result in "nothing or something not good," pplpleasr said. Shibuya is among those initiatives trying to address this challenge now, finding the fine line between how much control to give people in general and how much to give people like creative directors who know what they're doing in a project, which MV3 and probably countless other future Web3 creative projects will struggle with. "Finding the right balance will give us the best product." Pplpleasr pointed to the wisdom of the crowd on Rotten Tomatoes or Yelp, where users "trust the opinion of a generalized sum of people." Shibuya seeks to harness this aggregate mentality and apply it to IP creation. "I think it's good to involve the superfans or the community on an early stage, instead of doing everything in a writer's room in a black box Hollywood-style, not showing anything to anybody," pplpleasr said. "There's definitely value in looping in the community from early stages, but you'll find that people don't actually want to do as much work as they say they do."[29]

One project, *White Rabbit*, has a skeleton of a plot with two alternate endings. Whichever ending receives more votes will determine whether the film's main protagonist is a good or a bad character. Creators seeking funding must identify those points in the process where they want crowd input, where such input won't sacrifice the quality of the story or the artwork. "Why not let people in on this good content, instead of saving it for a few gatekeepers who are monopolizing the traditional film industry?" pplpleasr said.

"I don't think I would've stood a chance without this new technology or this paradigm shift. Trying to climb my way into traditional Hollywood, in a pre-crypto or Web3 world, would just be fighting an uphill battle that I'd most likely lose."[30]

In December 2022, Shibuya announced that it had raised $6.9 million from Andreessen Horowitz and Variant Fund, with celebrities like Kevin Durant and Paris Hilton rounding out the financing. In a press interview at the time of the round, pplpleasr said she wanted Shibuya to be the "A24 of Web3," referring to the Hollywood studio known for its indie hits like *Moonlight*, *Lady Bird*, and *Everything*

Everywhere All at Once.[31] The ultimate irony will be when Universal Pictures options *White Rabbit* and pplpleasr becomes a Hollywood bigwig, but perhaps we are peering through the looking glass.

From Platform-Based to Portable Communities

Roneil Rumburg loves music. He cares about music as an art. He supports artists and is an avid member and advocate of the music community, and so he was concerned to see all his favorite creators fleeing SoundCloud en masse. "SoundCloud was where that community was at the time, and that's where we spent all of our time at that time," he told us.[32] "We started to ask ourselves, 'Why are they leaving?'"

It came down to SoundCloud's making decisions that weren't in the best interest of the early community. "They changed how discovery worked, that folks felt was penalizing community content in favor of more institutionally owned and managed content. They also adopted a bunch of different community policies that didn't align well with the user base." As a result of those poor decisions, "a lot of artists left the platform," Rumburg said.

It was the latest in a series of disappointments for artists who had transitioned from one music distribution platform to another. "From Myspace early on, to YouTube, to SoundCloud, they would lose their following each time, and they had no sovereignty or control over the data, and no ability to reach those folks," he said. "If you're a huge YouTuber, and you start a new TikTok, there's no way to carry over your existing fan base to TikTok. You're starting from scratch." It's a means of locking in the best creators to a platform—and, to a certain extent, it works. "Very rarely do folks transition successfully from one media platform to another, but a big part of that is not being able to carry the fan base over." As a result of this creator lock-in, it appears rightly or wrongly that "new forms of media favor different forms of creativity. A new class of creators rises with every new media platform."

What's more, each new platform owns the relationships with fans in the form of their data. Artists don't know who their fans are or how they're using content, so that they can develop new content accordingly. It gets worse. To upload music to Spotify, independent artists must go through third-party distributors. The royalty payments flow in reverse, going first to these third parties, then to the artists, "with a lot of friction along the way."

Rumburg boiled the problem down to "the misalignment of incentives between what's good for the company and what's good for the creators and consumers of those assets." Web2 media properties eventually form "parasitic relationships" with the people who make their content networks valuable. "YouTube would have no value or utility if no one was uploading videos to it. Same with Spotify. But the network effects of these platforms have been durable. That's what keeps people coming." He has watched the pattern play out with each new media property: "Typically, content is free and great, and the platforms work well as the networks are small and growing. Once they achieve some network effect, the dynamic of the relationship shifts" to one of extraction.

Rumburg wondered whether a platform that helped "artists connect with their fans directly and build relationships with those fans would be more durable to these types of pressures over time," alluding to SoundCloud's pressure to turn a corporate profit.[33]

Rumburg cofounded Audius, a community and discovery platform for music that puts the artist in control.[34] "Not that Audius is not about helping artists make money, but there was a level of time pressure at SoundCloud that forced it to make a series of poor decisions," he said. Audius is built on Ethereum and Solana. Its cofounders believed that "if artists actually owned, operated, and controlled the means of distribution, Audius could be resilient to these errors in decision making. Also, through enfranchising artists in the upward trajectory of the network, we could create a system that would live forever."[35] An artist's ability to import or export data would be a key distinguishing feature.

That's incredibly important. "If the culture is everything, then communities are what defines part of that culture," Aleksander Larsen told us.[36] He is cofounder and chief operating officer of Sky Mavis and its game *Axie Infinity.* "Web3 is so nascent, it depends on where you are fraternizing or spending your time. Like, the DeFi side is very different from the NFT side with artists, musicians, and gamers," he said. "The plot is more about these other tribes that are using crypto as well. Like the *Axie* community is a very set culture compared to what you might find in a DeFi protocols community. But, on the broader scale, people want ownership of assets. They want freedom. They value transparency."

Internet platforms are valuable because users are also publishers of content, creators online. Perhaps you enjoy posting comments on Twitter, participating in discussions on Reddit, or uploading your own photos and videos to Facebook, Instagram, or TikTok. Your user-generated content and the social graph you maintain through your participation are both essential to the success of those platforms. Facebook's value directly relates to network effects, which are a function of user engagement on the platform. Despite Web2's failing grades in some areas, the democratization of publishing is broadly a positive outcome.

To be sure, Web3 is not without its platforms that extract value for offering convenience and a useful service. Consider OpenSea, which launched as the dominant platform for listing and trading NFTs. OpenSea takes a fee or "royalty" from the sale of NFTs on the platform, not unlike an art dealer or other legacy middleman. However, following a bout of early success, OpenSea quickly faced several competitors. As Web3 research firm The Block notes, "NFT marketplaces had been fiercely competing for liquidity by circumventing creator royalties, allowing competitors to siphon liquidity from OpenSea and spawning zero-fee marketplaces such as Sudoswap, X2Y2, and Magic Eden." As a result, "zero-royalty trading volume jumped from 2.8 percent of total trading volume in January to 30 percent at November end" of 2022, a significant increase. With open platforms, users and creators can take their assets elsewhere, if they'd like. No lock-in. This kind of vigorous competition can lead to more innovation and more money in the pockets of creators.[37]

If Web2 enabled users to generate content, then Web3 enables communities to generate *and own* that content as a collective. What does that mean exactly? In the case of MV3, users own the assets they create *and* can shape the arcs of their characters' stories and the future direction—the community-owned content—of the MV3 universe.

In building Shibuya, pplpleasr viewed these Web2 and Web3 tools and platforms as complementary. "So many people in Web3 make the mistake of thinking they need to disassociate completely from Web2." Shibuya could be the place where users crowdfund and create intellectual property, but Shibuya may not be that IP's final destination, or only distribution method. For example, people could make a short film on Shibuya and distribute it through YouTube. "It's the same idea as Right Click Save is not a bad thing, because it's free advertising for the thing that you're making in Web3.[38] Web3 is just the new avenue to monetize it, but right now, we're nowhere near getting as many eyeballs on anything in Web3. So, we still need traffic from Web2 to complement what we're building in Web3. It's the natural evolution of the Internet. Web3 is now providing us with solutions for certain problems with Web2."[39]

This community ownership is important for creators: through NFTs and smart contracts, creators can codify their claims to revenues and automate payments of those revenues. Musicians, artists, and other creative people are harnessing the tools for Web3 to reimagine their craft. These capabilities affect everyone, all the creators and users of Internet platforms, which means all of us. Web2 gave us social networks with social graphs.

As venture capitalist Jesse Walden argued, Web3 is giving us socioeconomic networks with socioeconomic graphs: "What ties people together here are necessarily personal relationships, instead of economic relationships or interest-based relationships."[40] Web3 will not replace Facebook with some look-alike social network with Web3 characteristics. It will likely replace Facebook with some different, new, and previously impossible alternative.

NFTs and other tokens are already the key to unlocking "token-gated communities" where participants have provable ownership of some asset that gives them access to services and other benefits and perquisites—like a country club membership where the token is the ticket in. Only the imagination limits what those token-gated communities can offer in terms of products or services. Some might be interactive stories and world-building projects like MV3 or Shibuya, or they could be token-gated collectives like Friends With Benefits for digital art creators, or they could be a social network for friends and family, or a fantasy football league, or a guild of players who join forces to play in a role-playing game, or a DAO for art collectors like Flamingo DAO, or Trends.vc where holders get early access to trend reports, or countless other social, business, or community constructs.[41]

Whatever content and creative energy you put into these socioeconomic networks will make you economic participants in the upside. Said Walden, cofounder and general partner at Variant Fund, "The model that we're starting to see play out in Web3 is not that of a creator streaming on Twitch TV, creating content for an audience of one to many. Instead, it's a model where creators are working directly with the community of fans who are owners of the actual creative product they're generating, to build stories and entertainment together."[42] You won't join these communities for the financial payout alone, but you'll be grateful to have it.

The New Medium Is the New Message

"If bitcoin is a store of value, NFTs are a store of culture," said Yat Siu, cofounder of Animoca Brands, a Web3 game studio, adding that culture is the "deepest economic sink ever," a gaming term that refers to how value is created and where it flows (like water in a sink). Siu believes culture is an asset that has been undervalued and now we have a mechanism to store that value digitally.

In 1964, media theorist Marshall McLuhan quipped, "The medium is the message."[43] At the time, print, radio, and TV were the dominant media. This was the age of broadcast, when media went one way—from producer to consumer. Fast-forward to the Web2 era. With the printing press that was the Internet of information, anyone could create content and publish it online, but only powerful platforms with strong network effects like Spotify could monetize music. Individual artists had to bow to streamers or risk the wilderness where users shared and copied their art without recourse or compensation. Digital visual artists had it worse: they had no tools to monetize and protect their craft from infringement.

While big Web2 platforms were consolidating and commodifying creative media, simultaneously those platforms were making creators of everyone, giving us tools to act as citizen journalists, photobloggers, and micro-influencers in our social circles and online communities. Algorithms controlled by a handful of large companies herded early communities of like-minded individuals into self-reinforcing echo chambers, where the purpose was not to inform or entertain but to stroke egos and confirm existing biases and opinions. McLuhan's aphorism was targeted at broadcast media, specifically TV, but it applies to other eras. Social media is the primary medium for information today and often the medium itself has become the center of the discourse, whether it is the role of Facebook in spreading disinformation or amplifying extreme voices during the 2016 election and subsequent campaigns, or the ongoing soap opera of Elon Musk's Twitter acquisition.

In 1996, Bill Gates posted an essay, "Content Is King," where he predicted the impact the Web would have in its second era as a platform for users to publish content: "One of the exciting things about the Internet is that anyone with a PC and a modem can publish whatever content they can create."[44] Gates defined content broadly as "ideas, experiences, and products." Web2 users did create plenty of content, and some did very well—especially the makers of software. But software platforms controlled distribution and extracted most of the value, much like television networks before the commercial Internet.

"In Web2, information is a commodity. Information is infinite," said Lex Sokolin of ConsenSys. "Therefore, information is worth nothing, but the attention on top of the information is productized and packaged via advertising." For those who spent a career in the Web2 paradigm, using ownership to put limits on distribution feels wrong (even if it means creators get peanuts). "NFTs are super-icky to Web2 entrepreneurs who are there to liberate information and democratize access," Sokolin added.[45]

While platforms dominate distribution today, Yat Siu has bet his business, Animoca Brands, on this dynamic power changing. One of Animoca's central theses is that digital property rights transform "consumable" content into an "asset" with tremendous value. As a result, the content becomes the platform. Creators capture value at the *content* level, not at the *distribution* level controlled by a handful of companies. So far, this intuitively makes sense: the combined value of all NFTs minted on OpenSea is greater than the market value of OpenSea itself. The value of all tokens is much greater than the exchanges and wallet providers that give us access to them.[46]

McLuhan's observation feels more prescient than ever.[47] If broadcast media and its skeuomorphic imitators are synonymous with Web1, and social media with Web2, then digital goods like NFTs will help to define Web3. When an artist sells an NFT, the artist is wrapping the message (the art) up with the medium (the digital good) into a single thing.

We Are All Creators

These stories highlight the novel ways creators are harnessing the Web3 tools to engage with fans on a different level while opening more commercial avenues to make money and participate as *owners*. But most people are not artists or screenwriters or living fully Web3 lives where they are earning tokens and speculating on the value of NFTs and other cultural artifacts. Are most people destined to play the role of spectator in this renaissance of creativity? No, said Yat Siu of Animoca Brands, and one of the most influential investors in Web3.

Siu has always been comfortable straddling different cultures, languages, and economic systems, a by-product of his atypical upbringing. Ethnically Chinese, the entrepreneur was born in Vienna, Austria, to two classically trained and accomplished musicians. He grew up speaking German with his mostly white classmates and friends. As a child, Siu spent time with his mother in East Berlin, where he saw authoritarian communism up close. On his return to Vienna, he would log onto CompuServe, where he found a community of people from many different countries. He studied music in school but gravitated to computers. As a teenager, he got his first job at Atari in Germany. In his professional odyssey, he has started Internet businesses in all three eras of the Web. He was buying and selling virtual assets in the 1980s. By the early 2010s, his firm was pioneering mobile games before Apple deplatformed his apps.[48]

In 2017, Yat Siu stumbled into Web3, grasping its significance immediately and reorienting Animoca Brands to this brave new world. Animoca Brands soon became one of the most influential builders and investors in the industry, especially in Web3 gaming. His decades of experience and unique upbringing have given him insight into the world that many of his contemporaries lack.

First of all, Siu's parents embraced technology. They were the first family on the block with satellite TV so that they could watch world news.[49] That gave Yat a global perspective. They also bought him an Atari ST personal computer. "I discovered online communities in the pre-Internet service" where "it didn't matter that I was Asian."

Founded in Silicon Valley in the 1970s, Atari was an industry juggernaut at the time, famous for the games *Pong* and *Space Invaders*. That the company would hire an Austrian teenager with a music degree sight unseen might seem unusual. But the firm was notoriously unconventional. Walter Isaacson wrote in his book *The Innovators*, "Every Friday there would be a beer bash and pot-smoking party, sometimes capped by skinny dipping, especially if the week's numbers had been made." One of the founders held staff meetings in the hot tub as a matter of routine.[50] I'm guessing the German office had better beer.

Siu may have been among the first people to buy a virtual asset in an early computer game. "There was no payment system, there was no PayPal. I literally had to send in a check and wait for it to cash." The seller could have disappeared once he got Yat's money, but he honored the deal: "We met in the equivalent of a seedy bar inside this multi-user dungeon, and we swapped items."

As the child of musicians, Siu knew that making a living as an artist was hard. "My mom never really understood much about business per se." Those who ran the industry took advantage of musicians like his mother and her peers, "basically because they lacked knowledge of financial systems, business systems, and contracts," he explained.[51] Siu acknowledged that not everyone will benefit equally from ownership online, but everyone can participate. "We think Web3 can deliver, not universal basic income, but *universal basic equity*, the concept that we are all creators of some form of data." There are active creators such as artists, software developers, and game makers; and there are "passive creators who are contributing to the network effect and are rewarded for it."[52] Siu described the economics of the gaming industry, which we expand upon in the next chapter. In free-to-play gaming, users can download and play games for free; but if they want more game features, they need to pay. Siu said that only 1 to 3 percent of people ever pay. "The $100 billion of revenue generated in free-to-play gaming comes from a single-digit subset of the total gaming audience." The other 97 to 99 percent are still important because they are contributing to the game's network effect. Some may help bring in five or a hundred people who pay a little, or one person who pays a lot. If the free riders didn't show up and play, then the players who were willing to pay wouldn't pay up. "It is a value shift," said Siu. Those playing for frees are "contributing to the network effect and, therefore, should be rewarded."[53] It is their data and time, after all.

In referring to how we might apply this model to a traditional network like Facebook, Siu said, "Maybe most of the users are worth only hundreds or thousands of dollars. That's okay, right? But we're also building equity. We're not saying that we're all the same. We're saying that we all now have a stake in this."[54]

Jesse Walden agreed. Not just professional creators can benefit from digital ownership. In his view, Web3 empowers fans of creators and communities more generally. In November 2021, a loosely affiliated group of crypto enthusiasts and history buffs got together online to raise money for buying the last copy of the US Constitution in private hands.

To raise the millions necessary for a credible bid, the group formed the ConstitutionDAO.[55] It quicky morphed into an online phenomenon. By auction time, the DAO had a war chest of $40 million from thousands of contributors who saw an opportunity for "We, the People" to control an important artifact. Benjamin Franklin would have been proud. In the end, ConstitutionDAO didn't win, but it was a watershed moment: it showed us how individuals can use Web3 tools to organize spontaneously around a cause, raise money, and build something with utility or economic value.

Walden raised his own hypothetical. Taylor Swift lost control of her master recordings to Scooter Braun, a record executive. As payback, she rerecorded whole albums, undermining the value of his catalog. She did not try to buy them back. "Maybe there's a price that Taylor's not willing to pay, but maybe her fans are willing to pay collectively. Because they don't value just the royalties; they value the experience of being an owner," said Walden. "The thesis is, the next generation of the Internet is going to turn all the users of products and services into owners."[56]

Variant is a seed investor, which often means that it invests in ventures before they have a product/market fit or even a product. Sometimes, startups need an outsider's perspective to see what insiders cannot, which explains Walden's unlikely path to becoming one of the industry's most well-regarded investors.

Walden said that tokens are products that fulfill certain needs and desires of users, including the need for financial security, to be heard, and to participate. For some holders, tokens provide social belonging and community, and they satisfy the need for control over how we work.[57] They also add a level of privacy: token holders can shield their ownership of digital goods behind a wall of pseudo anonymity, if they choose.

In 2016, Ida Auken, a member of Danish parliament, caused a stir when she penned an opinion piece for the World Economic Forum titled, "Welcome to 2030. I Own Nothing, Have No Privacy, and Life Has Never Been Better."[58] The article became a lightning rod for criticism online, especially among certain right-wing groups who were already deeply suspicious of the World Economic Forum. Today the piece feels like a time capsule of the mid-2010s, when so-called "sharing economy" companies were making it easier to ride-share, rent vacation homes, and so forth. Millennials, kneecapped by the financial crisis and unable to afford much, gladly used these services, getting an extra boost from venture capitalists who were subsidizing the growth of these Web2 startups, making them affordable to many. Auken's thesis that "everything you considered a product, has now become a service" feels naïve with the benefit of hindsight, given the struggles of many of these businesses to turn a profit when faced with heightened competition and without the financial backstop of VCs. If anything, Web3 inverts her language. Auken said all products become services. Web3 posits that all services become assets through ownership online.[59]

In these so-called sharing economy companies like Uber and Airbnb, those who create the value (such as the drivers, renters, and users) don't share the wealth equally. These platforms are natural monopolies that aggregate and resell surplus labor, cars, vacant rooms, and so forth. Research has shown that such monopolies have not delivered commensurate value for workers, customers, and society. Imagine instead Web3 platforms owned by no one and governed by users where they accrue the value they create.

But Auken was farsighted in some respects, anticipating the trade-offs we make in Web2 when we become reliant on platforms. In her 2030 piece, she noted, "Once in a while I get annoyed about the fact that I have no real privacy. Nowhere I can go and not be registered. I know that, somewhere, everything I do, think and dream of is recorded. I just hope that nobody will use it against me."[60]

Two big behavioral shifts have happened since Auken wrote this piece. First, more Internet users are wary of how their data is used and are taking steps to protect it. Second, and perhaps more profound, ownership is making a comeback. It turns out Millennials do want to own stuff that they could not afford until recently. Today they comprise 43 percent of home buyers, by far the largest of any generation, and they are the biggest purchasers of cars and other staples previous generations took for granted.[61] The dual conditions of Web2's "renter" economy, where we have no ownership and no rights, combined with the pendulum swinging toward ownership more generally create perfect conditions to test whether an ownership Web can become ubiquitous.

John Locke, the giant of the Enlightenment, said, "Every man has a property in his own person: this nobody has any right to but himself. The labor of his body, and the work of his hands, we may say, are properly his." Locke rooted his argument in the idea that a person's labor and actions earned the person property. "For this labor being the unquestionable property of the laborer, no man but he can have a right to what that is once joined to."[62] Locke, it should be noted, was perfectly comfortable compromising those rights when it suited him, as his contemporaries did to advance colonialism or slavery, which endured in the British Empire until 1833. Still, the idea that when people put time and effort into creating something of value, they ought to have some right to it, is sound. Yet online, that is not how things work for creators, including everyday Internet users.

Decentralized finance has demonstrated that user-owned networks can grow quickly by incentivizing early adoption. Uniswap, a decentralized exchange, is a good example of this: exchanges become more valuable the more liquidity they have, so Uniswap incentivized users to provide liquidity early on with its native token UNI. The more liquidity an exchange has, the better. A win-win for platform and user/creator alike. Now imagine a Web3 social network that is just starting out. The startup costs of launching a new service are high, so to offset that the project incentivizes early adopters with a governance token giving economic rights and a say in the platform. It turns out tokens serve as an immensely powerful incentive for mass collaboration and adoption by turning early adopters and users into economic participants in the network.

Chris Dixon said, "In the Web2 era, overcoming the bootstrapping problem meant heroic entrepreneurial efforts, plus in many cases spending lots of money on sales and marketing."[63] This difficult and costly process led to only a few networks reaching global scale. Once they were firmly entrenched, it became difficult for new networks targeting similar users to compete (think Facebook). Dixon continued: "Web3 introduces a powerful new tool for bootstrapping networks: token incentives. . . . The basic idea is, early on during the bootstrapping phase when network effects haven't kicked in, provide users with financial utility via token rewards to make up for the lack of native utility."[64] Users have no barriers to launching a token and trying their hand at network building. More projects might fail than in previous technology cycles, since the denominator of total projects will be so much higher, underscoring tokens' role in incentivizing mass collaboration, coordination, and value creation.

Sanity Check: Could Token Incentives Make for Bad Application Experiences?

In 2004, I was a freshman at Amherst College when I first heard a girl in my class talk about a new website called "The Facebook." Since I had a crush on this girl, I eagerly took her suggestion to set up an account, despite my initial skepticism. I knew people who used Myspace and Friendster, and I'd concluded that anyone with real friends and interests didn't spend all their time online. Alas, the girl and I were never meant to be but I became an avid Facebook user and, like the million or so other "early adopters" of the social network at the time, I quickly grew a social graph with hundreds of connections. The early Facebook was ad-free and kind of charming: we were glad to trade our time and social capital for access to a free communications service better than email.

For any new network, early adopters are enormously valuable. All our connections helped to create the network effects that solidified Facebook's position as market leader. Despite this fact, we did not share any financial upside from our contributions. Initially, that seemed okay because The Facebook was a fun and useful diversion.

Later, we all fell into Web2's Faustian bargain, forfeiting our data, privacy, and autonomy online for hypertargeted ads.

Now imagine a Web3 version of a social network. From the beginning, everyone's interests are more aligned: we still use this service to connect with friends, share photos, and create communities, but we retain full rights to our photos if we so choose, we earn a stake in the network, and we have some say in strategic decisions and technical changes. The more we use it, recommend it, and upload to it, the more we earn. With such powerful incentives, others join, participate, and drive new users to the network. Despite stiff competition from entrenched and well-capitalized incumbents, the user-owned social network steadily chips away at their base. New users benefit with the rise in value of the new network's native token. Founders and early adopters both do well. Where is the fault in this concept?

Unfortunately, some creators have designed their Web3-based models so poorly that early users show up only to exploit the token rewards, indifferent to the underlying service. Once those incentives dry up, they move to the next exploitable platform, and remaining token holders fight for scraps of ownership. This behavior turns off regular users who fear hyperfinancialization of their Internet experience.

The introduction of financial rewards could lead to other unintended consequences. Jimmy Wales, cofounder of Wikipedia, told me why he thinks Web3 incentives are a "terrible idea for Wikipedia."[65] His chief concern was that money would corrupt what he described as the intellectual purity of Wikipedia, where contributors edit because of the love of knowledge, not because somebody is willing to pay them. "If you're talking about an article on, say, the Exxon *Valdez*, there's probably only one player with any money who cares, and that's Exxon." Taking payments from subjects of articles was "probably not what we really want from a high-quality neutral encyclopedia," he said.[66] His second concern was, How or why do contributors get paid? If they received money for page views, then they would have incentive to sensationalize articles at the expense of context and accuracy. Third, he thought that some blockchains like Bitcoin had unacceptable ecological footprints, and that's why

Wikipedia stopped accepting donations in cryptocurrencies.[67] Finally, Wales was skeptical of raising funds with tokens to support volunteers: "It's not something that anybody in the community is asking for or demanding." An innovator like Wikipedia could design a system to address these concerns, but for Wales the risks were disqualifying.[68]

Despite these reservations, Wales was enthusiastic about user-owned platforms for other purposes, such as music and video streaming, where creators could get paid better and have more access to their data. In our discussion, he viewed the creation of easy ways for contributors to earn a piece of the platforms they use as a broadly positive aspiration. Like pplpleasr, Nickson-Lopez, and many other creators who are harnessing these tools, Wales saw DAOs specifically as simple Internet-native tools to organize like-minded people around a creative idea. "We're not going to do all this hard work and give it away for free. We're going to do all this hard work, then try to get it on Netflix, sell it on Amazon Prime, and we're going to try to get it released in theaters," Wales said, intuiting the mindset of DAO members. "We're going to make it online, as a community, we're all going to vote, and we're going to get shares, according to our contribution. We're going to figure out how to make that fair." Most importantly, everyone becomes an owner and shares in the success. "If you work for a studio and you get a smash hit," added Wales, that's great for your résumé and great for the studio, but you don't get a cut of ticket sales, merchandise, streaming and video on demand, overseas licenses, and other revenues because "you didn't become an owner."[69]

Despite these clear benefits, user-owned networks are not inherently more just or sustainable models. For example, a user-owned network could voluntarily create an ad-driven model rather than generating enough profit to sustain the network's ongoing development, security, and user experience. In this example, a majority of token holders would vote for a model that most users opposed. Is Web3's version of nineteen-year-old Mark Zuckerberg a token-obsessed entrepreneur set on launching a viral token distribution model, the value of which spikes, plummets, and peters out?

Smart entrepreneurs with good intentions have initially stumbled in their execution. For example, *Axie Infinity* kicked off the play-to-earn category, but the incentives weren't quite right. Early users extracted huge value. Those late to the game borrowed money to play, only to find out that the rewards had dried up, leaving them in debt. Sky Mavis, maker of *Axie Infinity*, went back, focused on great gameplay, and engaged players to help improve on its own work. Aleksander Larsen, founder of Sky Mavis, wanted gameplay to drive the next stage of growth. He said, "If you can match existing games, especially mobile games, in terms of quality, and then sprinkle on top Web3 ownership of game items, that would be a killer recipe."[70]

Others like Uniswap have remained popular after those earning easy money (through native tokens) have come and gone. How do they do it? First, they create an equitable and sustainable token distribution model that incentivizes long-term adoption. Second, they don't rely solely on token incentives to drive adoption. Issuing too many tokens could dilute the value of each token, even when growing the network short-term. This might work as a growth strategy, but if ownership in the network is part of the user experience, then owners will want their assets to hold value, not leach it into oblivion like Weimar deutschmarks. Third, they make the underlying application or service inherently useful. People join for the community, culture, and functionality, not just for the token reward. Finally, they make ownership part of the user experience, not the only user experience. Too often, Web3 entrepreneurs have developed applications to justify earning a token and little else. With an ownership stake, users participate in wealth creation and have a say in how the platform runs.

The Virtual You

The concept of the "individual" has played a starring role in society and the economy since the Enlightenment. Martin Luther encouraged a private interpretation of the Bible, disintermediating priests and the pope. In *The Wealth of Nations*, Adam Smith advocated for individuals to pursue their self-interests for the benefit of the whole.

Hedonism invites individuals to find higher purposes in their personal pleasures. Democracy puts the individual, with "one person, one vote," at the center of the narrative.[71] In this rubric, the individual is sovereign and has rights. Individuals have agency and ownership over themselves. Yet, in Web2, we have lost some agency and control over our own selves, starting online. One example of this loss is reputation.

Reputations are foundational to all economic activity. "Whenever there is an interaction, an economic transaction between two parties, these two parties want to establish trust," said Stepan Gershuni, cofounder of Gyde One and an authority on Web3 reputation systems.[72] The cost of establishing trust is one of the main friction points Ronald Coase identified in his seminal work, "The Nature of the Firm."[73] "It could be a bank or a protocol giving out loans and making sure that they will be paid back. It could be a gaming company looking for power users. It could be an employer who wants to hire a solidity developer," said Gershuni. "They can do five rounds of interviews, or they can look at someone's on-chain professional reputation and make this hire much quicker, because they can be sure that this person knows all the hard skills, and then reduce it from five to one round of a cultural interview."[74]

Governing and controlling our own identities will simplify our online lives, enhance our privacy, and help us manage and benefit from our data assets.[75] With Web3 services like Braintrust for credentialing, we could verify a candidate's bona fides more easily, changing the role of recruiter, job seeker, and human resources manager. There is no consensus in industry and government on how to move on-chain identity forward. A digital identity could be an asset every individual has and controls starting with a birth certificate, or it could be relevant only at the wallet level as a means of storing and managing digital assets, certificates, and accounts. Ryan Selkis, founder of Messari, said, "Tie a number of different attributes to wallets, and those wallets can own different attributes or different NFTs or credentials that you can selectively showcase. As an individual, you might have ten different wallets or one wallet that holds all of your assets, all of your IP."[76]

Another building block in use to secure self-sovereign digital identity is the Ethereum Name Service (ENS), a decentralized version of the domain naming system that individuals and businesses can use to create a unique on-chain identity associated with an Ethereum address on the Ethereum blockchain. They could use this name rather than share private data to send and receive payments and access services and applications. Businesses could use ENS to authenticate customers, provide access to services, and store customer data securely.[77]

ENS is a building block for other projects. For example, Unstoppable Domains is developing applications for users to create and manage their own Web domains tied to their ENS name. Other projects, such as Name Bazaar, are developing marketplaces where users can buy, sell, and trade their ENS names. Finally, projects like Universal Login are creating apps for users to access dapps with their ENS name—no more remembering long and complex addresses associated with blockchains. For individuals, a censor-proof domain could be the linchpin of their digital identity. Imagine a group of dissidents who could maintain a web page on ENS, running on a decentralized cloud under an authoritarian regime that could not take it down.

For his part, Gershuni identified dozens of companies building decentralized reputation systems, and all are looking at different use cases. Credit scoring is one of the bigger ones, with players like kycDAO, Violet, and Spectral.[78]

What's different about these on-chain systems? Gershuni explained: in Web3, we don't need a single source of trust like Equifax. In fact, we don't even have to see the data. We can use what Gershuni called "zero-knowledge badges," which prove that private or secret information is true without revealing it. He pointed out that Sismo, another player in the space, is using zero-knowledge badge technology to do exactly that.[79]

In early 2023, we saw an explosion of on-chain identity solutions such as the widely used Gitcoin Passport. It gives Web3 users a way to build out a decentralized record of their credentials. The system allows users to gather "stamps," which are like receipts for on-chain activity. With a portfolio of stamps, passport holders can unlock new Web3 experiences and benefits from platforms like Gitcoin Grants: "The more you verify your identity, the more opportunities you will have to vote and participate across the Web3."[80] Web3 reputation systems like Gitcoin Grants are composable: they allow users themselves—not the sites visited or the platforms used—to aggregate all kinds of Web3 activities into a single sovereign identity. In Web3, you actually own your virtual self, with its reputation, assets, transaction history, data, and more.

Conclusion and Takeaways

Web1 and Web2 democratized the ability for creators to share their content, ideas, and talent to a global audience. Web3 gives them the tools finally to monetize it properly. And, it turns out, we are all creators, and each has a role and an opportunity in this new creator economy. Key takeaways for this chapter are:

1. Web2 failed creators. Artists such as musicians were used to selling physical copies of their work. Digital technologies turned that asset into a free commodity pushed through the printing press of the Web until its value hit zero. This vacuum created opportunities for platforms to reintermediate the value chain. The upshot was creators received even less money than before.

2. User-generated content is becoming user-proprietary content, not content automatically captured for free by social media platforms. Fans and other patrons who contribute time and energy to communities, artists, and creators online will get rewards for it. Fans act out of love, fun, and passion; if their actions create value, then they should get a cut. With Web3, they will.

3. Web3 will invert the ownership model for IP, if projects like Shibuya and MV3 succeed. Giving away part of the franchise on day zero is anathema to old-paradigm bigwigs, but it may be how creators launch new projects while maintaining creator or community control. Also, communities will be portable and composable, not relying on a single platform, because users control their own assets, data, and identity.

4. The medium is still the message. Web3 is a digital medium for value, not only information. When Yat Siu said NFTs are a store of culture, he was channeling Marshall McLuhan. Tokens are the medium and, therefore, the message.

5. Tokens do not guarantee a more equitable or sustainable model. Bad token models can stunt the growth of otherwise promising projects by misaligning interests and incentives. Designed correctly, however, tokens and their ecosystems can foster new breeds of Internet-native organizations.

6. In Web2, the virtual you exists in fragments owned by dozens of companies, government agencies, and other third parties. In Web3, we control and own all the pieces of our virtual selves.

7. Culture needs a new business model: Web3 tools can help ensure creators get paid promptly and fairly and partiticpate more fully in the value they create.

CHAPTER 5

Organizations

Introducing Stake*hodler* Capitalism

As the cofounder of Variant Fund, a leading Web3 venture capital firm, Jesse Walden has backed some of the best-known decentralized organizations, such as the exchange Uniswap or the Ethereum scaling solution Polygon, today worth $5 billion and $8 billion, respectively. An American-born graduate of Canada's McGill University, Walden started his career in Montreal as a manager for emerging indie musicians like Solange Knowles and Blood Orange—the "types of artists you read about in Pitchfork," he quipped.[1] "Music is one of the most Luddite industries, when it comes to new technologies," he told me. Walden saw an opportunity to help the artists he managed leverage technology platforms, "to reach their fans directly and monetize, independent of any major label third party."[2] Applying what he knew from his time in the music industry as an agent, Walden founded Mediachain, a blockchain data solution to help creators get paid for their work online. "Bitcoin was the best-known thing going in the crypto space in 2014. We were interested in what blockchains could do for different kinds of digital assets. We did all media assets like images, videos, songs," Walden explained.[3] Mediachain was a good idea, and many of its core concepts are now commonplace in the NFT market. In 2014, Mediachain's time had not yet come, partly due to the lack of a good technology platform to make it work. "This was pre-Ethereum launch," he said. "So, a little bit too early, frankly."[4]

Still, Walden's time as artist manager and media entrepreneur helped sharpen his thesis for Variant, which he started in 2018 after a stint at Andreessen Horowitz, where he helped launch its first Web3 fund. He said, "We're all creators online of one kind or another. It doesn't have to be music. It could be code or could be content on social media. Web3 has this potential to make all of the creators online, all of the users of these products and services, into owners."[5] If Variant's thesis is correct, and if all *five billion* Internet users worldwide become owners of the services they consume, with all the rights and responsibilities that ownership entails, then we are on the precipice of one of the greatest economic and social upheavals in living memory. We must therefore try to answer the many pressing questions about what this means for businesses and how today's leaders should respond.

Let's start with what to call these new user-owners. Commonplace in corporate circles is "stakeholder capitalism," the notion that companies should act not only in their shareholders' interest, but also in the interests of their customers, supply chain partners, employees, and the communities in which they operate—and that includes the environment and the companies' impact on climate and social inequality. While stakeholder capitalism has its flaws—after all, does society want corporate leaders deciding what's best for society rather than the citizens themselves through their elected representatives?—by and large, stakeholder capitalism has made better corporate citizens of many a capitalist enterprise. But for user-owned networks, let's coin a new term, *stakehodler*. It combines *hodler*—derived from the typo *HODLING*, meaning hanging on to one's tokens for the long run and expecting future value worth the pain of riding out market volatility—with the word *stake*, to mean an Internet user with ownership of a digital self and digital assets, who earns a fair share from whatever the user creates online.[6] A stakehodler has both a voice and a vote, an economic interest in how each network stewards important global resources. Like hodlers, stakehodlers own tokens, not solely as long-term investments but as day-to-day experiences as Internet users.

What should we call these global, decentralized, and Internet-native organizations, built on a model of token ownership, where users get a slice of the pie? *Decentralized autonomous organization* (or DAO) is the common term used. Granted, that's a bit of a mouthful. But, as it turns out, the term is both accurate and appropriate. While DAOs are novel, they share a common economic thread with Silicon Valley startups, which are rooted in the human response to incentives.

"If you want to get the best talent in the world to come and work on your moonshot project, you've got to compensate them with ownership in it," Walden said, articulating a key Silicon Valley maxim.[7] *Owners care more.* They take pride in what they do and work hard to make it succeed, because they have a stake in its future. Web3 applies the concept of ownership, normally reserved for founders, VCs, and key early employees, to entire networks. "Going all the way back to Bitcoin, where the earliest developers and technologists who built and operated the Bitcoin network were rewarded with ownership for their contributions," said Walden. So, as an investor, Variant views itself very much as a partner not only of the teams it backs, but of the user-owners of these platforms. "What really struck me and captured my attention early in my journey into crypto was, the earliest networks in the crypto world were not built in Silicon Valley. Yet, they were using the same model of ownership to attract the talent to build and operate the networks."[8]

Jimmy Wales raised the hypothetical of a peer-produced film, suggesting that, through a DAO, people in dozens of countries could participate and earn an interest in some undertaking on equal terms. Such an initiative would be nearly impossible in a Web2 world, said Wales, because "doing contracts that are legal in all those countries and then paying people is super complicated," indeed prohibitively complicated. Instead, said Wales, "We're going to do it as a DAO."[9] Sure, these kinds of early-stage ventures are risky, Wales acknowledged, but the experience of Silicon Valley tells us that plenty of knowledgeable people will accept risk in the short term for a long-term reward.

This model departs from the past. In the same way that the Hollywood studio model demands creative control of IP, traditionally VCs want control over their investments or, at least, a big say in how entrepreneurs run their operations. After all, backing early-stage ventures can be risky and comes with opportunity costs. In Web3 networks, VCs (and founders, for that matter) often make up a small minority of token holders, with users owning the rest.

The emergence of these token-based Internet-native organizations

(DAOs) represents the biggest disruption to business and the firm since the invention of the limited liability company two hundred years ago. New technologies and innovations compel business leaders into tough choices about how they move forward. At the early stages, where we are today, there are often more questions than answers, and leaders reveal themselves by the quality of their questions.

What does it mean for organizations, and companies specifically, when the ownership table includes millions of individual users? How can a management team effectively "lead" a firm when customers have an economic stake in its success and a vote on how executives run it? From the user or customer perspective, how does ownership change the user experience? Does it make users more loyal to a brand or more willing to move on when offered greater financial upside elsewhere? For technology platforms like social networks that benefit from network effects, does the potential for greater economic ties make the network more resilient and better positioned to grow? Or does it hamstring it with distractions? Will users fixate on the ups and downs of their investment like fickle investors? "Turning users into owners means that your users are investors, and investors are subject to the whims of the market," said Jesse Walden. A great user experience is insufficient. "To keep them engaged as users, I need to provide a great *owner* experience" (emphasis added).[10] Perhaps ownership online solves for that elusive problem of Internet-based organizations like Wikipedia or the Internet Archive (or nonprofits in general, for that matter), which is that users have no incentive to maintain and improve these digital commons other than their passion for the work and their advocacy of the underlying missions.

Yochai Benkler, author of *The Wealth of Networks*, a seminal book about the early days of Web2, said, "Individuals can do more in loose affiliation with others, rather than requiring stable, long-term relations, like co-worker relations or participation in formal organizations, to underwrite effective cooperation."[11] But the reality of Web2 was that formal organizations ruled supreme and loose affiliations got marginalized. Perhaps Kevin Owocki and the Gitcoin team have it right: that ownership via tokens makes it easier to match talent with the problem to be solved and allows us to apply the open-source model to the corporation's realm of coordinating complexity and delivering services.

From Joint-Stock Companies to User-Owned Networks

Though the first joint-stock companies date to eleventh-century China, with a smattering of other examples in Europe around the same time, it was the age of exploration in the fifteenth to seventeenth centuries that brought them into the mainstream. The concept was a simple one necessitated by the era's newest business model: global trade. Several investors could pool their capital to pursue a large undertaking like building a mine or, more often, outfitting ships to conduct trade.

Joint-stock companies were an important innovation in the history of capitalism that popularized a couple of new concepts. First, they enabled complex business undertakings that individuals couldn't pursue on their own. Second, owners could trade shares with no impact to the company's continuing operations.

In the mercantile age, few people had the money to fit out several ships for a transatlantic journey. Besides, these early ventures were highly risky. As Matthew Campbell and Kit Chellel wrote in their book *Dead in the Water*, the oldest surviving marine insurance policy, dating from 1613, "pledged to bear the financial impacts from 'men of warr, fyer, enemyes, piratts, rovers, theeves, Jettezons, letters of marte and countermarte, arests, restreynts & deteynments of Kings and princes and all other persons, barratry of the Master and mariners, and of all other perils, losses and misfortune whatsoever they may be.'"[12] No single person would be foolish enough to risk it all with so much that could go wrong. Better to gather a few aristocrats and city merchants looking for a bit of fun, incorporate them into a new company, and then set sail as quickly as possible in search of treasure. The colorful names of these enterprises, like "The Company of Adventurers of England trading into Hudson Bay" (later, the Hudson's Bay Company), give us a sense of the shareholders, inspired as much by bragging rights as by the economic upside.

Still, early joint-stock companies took care to minimize risk where they could, by securing exclusive monopolies in the form of royal charters on the advice of the Privy Council in England, or parliamentary charters under the States-General in the Netherlands, with the explicit or implicit guarantee that a nation's ruling body would intervene on behalf of the company (and sometimes the other way around).[13] As Locke was writing his *Two Treatises*, and the Dutch East India Company and Hudson's Bay Company were plying the ocean trade, the modern insurance industry was born in Lloyd's Coffee House.[14]

Joint-stock companies gained in popularity in global trade but did not initially extend to other industries. The notorious South Sea Bubble, the financial calamity caused by the speculation in and collapse of the joint-stock South Sea Company, led to the creation of the Bubble Act of 1720, which forbade the incorporation of joint-stock companies without a royal charter. Over the next century, the Crown granted charters to only two other companies.

In the early 1800s, the demands of modern capitalism and industrial production necessitated a change to laws to make it easier to incorporate businesses to pursue manufacturing, railroad construction, and other high capital-expenditure (capex) businesses. Enter the limited liability company. "I think of the limited liability company as the native asset class for high-capex industrial companies," said Chris Dixon of Andreessen Horowitz. By law, a limited liability company separates the assets and income of owners or shareholders from those of the company. Investors can lose only what they have invested in the company, and so their financial liability is limited.[15] They can invest or divest over time, and the company can outlive them and outlive generations beyond them.

When steam engine technology and rail standards came along, entrepreneurs who wanted to build railroads could not raise enough money from their families. Ditto for building out the hardware needed for electrical grids. They needed a new mechanism for raising capital from people they didn't know. The limited liability company was a vehicle for doing that. That helped to grow stock markets and all the other financial infrastructure we have today.

The limited liability company is now widely regarded as a foundational innovation to modern capitalism, along with the steam engine and railroad locomotive. In 1926, the *Economist* wrote that the "nameless person" who invented the concept of limited liability deserved "a place of honour with Watt, Stephenson, and other pioneers of the industrial revolution."[16] The asset class of the joint-stock company, stocks and bonds, fully aligned with this new category of business.

But have the limited liability company and the C-corp reached the end of their useful lives in a digital age? When computer networks came along, "we tried to graft on a structure invented for high-capex industrial companies. Now we have these big networks behaving like railroad companies, trying to hoard all the resources," said Chris Dixon.[17] Railroad magnates understood the need for different networks to interoperate with the use of common gauges, but Dixon is correct that they zealously tried to consolidate monopolies in various parts of the country. "When weapons or tools of production can be effectively hoarded or monopolized, they tend to centralize power," James Dale Davidson and Lord William Rees-Mogg argued in *The Sovereign Individual*.[18] The conduct of the early Internet giants suggests that companies leave something to be desired. If chartered companies were foundational to the mercantile age, and limited liability companies to the industrial age, then user-owned networks may come to define the next era of the digital age.

LLCs and DAOs share similarities. Both types of organizations allow individuals to share the risk and potential reward in a commercial undertaking. But LLCs are creatures of our legal system, usually single legal entities managed by a limited number of individuals and subject to the laws and regulations of their jurisdictions. DAOs, on the other hand, are not (yet) bound by any legal framework and often operate without government restrictions, though that will almost certainly change. Last, LLCs often require significant capital to set up and begin operating, while DAOs can form and launch with minimal capital.

The industrial revolution marginalized the landowning elite who had dominated society, though the process took a very long time.

To pursue vast undertakings, Cornelius Vanderbilt set in motion his model of using giant capital-intensive and legally complex corporations in the middle of the nineteenth century, but it took decades to become the dominant model. Albert Wenger, cofounder of Union Square Ventures and author of the book *The World After Capital*, told us, "When we went from being foragers to agrarians and land became the scarcity, the people who ultimately had power were the people who controlled land."[19] When the Enlightenment kicked off an era of science, technology, and eventually industry, the people in power "didn't think, 'Here comes the industrial age! We should be enabling the industrial age!' They went, 'We can have tanks and battleships so we can have *more land*'" (emphasis added).[20] The ascent of capital over land is usually cited as occurring in the late nineteenth century, but Wenger said old habits died very hard, with disastrous consequences: "Hitler's whole program was *lebensraum*, and the people who approved it were the aristocrats, and they controlled land. This made total and complete sense to them." (*Lebensraum*, literally "living space," was a Nazi policy to clear tracts of Europe for German settlement, whatever the cost to human life.) Sometimes the transition is more pernicious, said Wenger, with those in power concluding, "I'm going to use this new tool to cement my existing power."[21] By the middle of the twentieth century, agrarian elites no longer controlled the most productive or lucrative assets in the economy. Land gave way to capital, aristocrats to plutocrats. What, then, should leaders of today's dominant paradigm—corporations—do to prepare for wholesale change?

The Innovator's Dilemma Revisited

Web3 will surely disrupt many companies, as Web1 and Web2 disrupted the mail-order catalog business, talent recruiting, and the shopping mall as a popular teen hangout. For example, decentralized exchanges like Uniswap have pioneered a frictionless peer-to-peer way of transacting in nearly any asset. Users will apply the core innovation, known as an automated market maker (AMM), to stocks and bonds, upending the businesses of traditional exchanges. Creator-owned platforms for sharing music, such as Audius, will challenge the business model of Spotify. Stablecoins could replace the traditional banking networks we rely on for international remittances.

However, despite the long-term impact of Web3 technologies on various industries, such as gaming, and the risks to incumbents—chief among them disintermediation from new upstarts, loss of control over data, transaction and customer assets, and the increased competition from new models and how that forces them to confront the old way of doing things—today the risks are somewhat muted. Thus, the opportunities for many incumbents to embrace this technology are still emerging. As a result, they have mostly chosen a wait-and-see approach with tinkering on the margin. Brands embracing NFTs as token collectibles come to mind, as does the push from some financial firms to offer bitcoin investing specifically to clients without considering the broader impact of DeFi and digital assets more generally on their business. Some incumbents struggle to see the opportunity. SEC commissioner Hester Peirce echoed Clayton Christensen when she implored her peers to be patient with Web3: "Technology takes time to develop and often must combine with innovative developments in other fields to realize its full potential. In the interim, it can appear, particularly to outsiders looking in, awkward, useless, or downright harmful."[22]

This paradox, that we see the disruptiveness of a technology but not its place in our business today, defines the challenge for many business leaders. Successful companies, especially well-run ones, often discount new technologies because management focuses on delivering value to their best customers, not to a fringe minority, often the least profitable potential customers. In 1997, Christensen wrote, "Generally, disruptive technologies underperform established products in mainstream markets. But they have other features that work for marginal customers or non-customers."[23] This is true for Web3: emerging markets such as the Philippines have the highest adoption of Web3 play-to-earn gaming apps.

"This 'telephone' has too many shortcomings to be seriously considered as a means of communication," wrote a committee appointed by the president of the Telegraph Company (precursor to Western Union) to analyze Alexander Graham Bell's patent for a telephone, which Bell was offering to sell.[24] The tools we use to measure our most successful products and services often fail us when we're confronted with something new. "Markets that do not exist cannot be analyzed," Christensen observed.[25] "Not only are the market applications for disruptive technology *unknown* at the time of their development—they are *unknowable*."[26] Therein lies the challenge for incumbents. But not for venture capitalists. Said Chris Dixon of Andreessen Horowitz, "We don't rely too much on market sizes for much at all, because really powerful tech tends to create new markets and new use cases. If you looked at Airbnb in terms of the hotel market, then you'd have missed the real scale of the opportunity."[27]

Likewise, how do we gauge the potential impact on incumbents' revenue from this type of disruption? Dixon said it was impossible to quantify because of the many variables, including new business models. "IBM is still around. HP is still around. I don't think they're particularly relevant in the world. I don't think they're growing that fast. But big tech incumbents tend to stick around in some way. People still use Microsoft Office. People will probably be using some form of Google Search thirty years from now," he observed. "But will they be as fast growing, as profitable? Will they be as culturally relevant, as economically relevant? Will creators need to depend on them, on Facebook's or TikTok's ranking algorithm? I don't know. I don't have a strong view. Frankly, I don't care how those companies do."[28] Many incumbents will fail to transition to Web3, but history includes many examples of companies that have successfully leapt from one computing paradigm to another, such as IBM, which dominated the category from the turn of the twentieth century until the dawn of the PC age. This time around, companies like Microsoft have positioned themselves in Web3, artificial intelligence, and other emerging areas—and so they might be okay.

Dixon explained: "In tech, we have these layers. If a company wins, if it succeeds, then it keeps doing its thing for a very long time. Then we have these breakthroughs, these next waves. That's how I think about Web3. Let's win the next wave." He referred to the greenfield/brownfield go-to-market phrase in enterprise software, "where *greenfield* means going after new opportunities, and *brownfield* means trying to win the previous ones. With new technologies, going after new ones is easier. The crypto aspect of Web3 is very important, and I think Facebook has made some real efforts there. Outside of Facebook, tech incumbents have basically ignored it. That's good because that's an opportunity for all of us in startups."[29]

When the technology is so nascent that the market opportunity is poorly defined, business leaders are challenged to marshal resources and corporate willpower to enter these markets. This has been true in Web3 until recently: companies have shied away from the most cutting-edge Web3 areas and retreated to their comfort zone, doubling down on existing technologies and tinkering on the margin in what Donald Sull of the Massachusetts Institute of Technology called "active inertia," "responding to the most disruptive changes by accelerating activities that succeeded in the past."[30]

Or they have joined consortia to compare notes with their peers, to promote their own point of view, and to attempt to influence the development of blockchain in their industry. In a chapter aptly titled "Consorting with the Enemy," David Furlonger and Christophe Uzureau of Gartner shared their findings on why companies partnered with their competitors in blockchain-focused consortia: to learn, to discuss ideas openly so as not to run afoul of antitrust laws, and perhaps most important, to manage risk by developing and promoting industry-wide standards for business, technology, and vendor validation.[31] Then Furlonger and Uzureau snap us out of it with a reminder: "Businesses that compete directly with each other in an industry don't have a strong history of playing nicely." The number one reason for consortium failure? Information hoarding. "The issue comes down to trust," they wrote, without irony.[32] They found that "narrowly focused consortia with clear goals are more effective than broad ones with ill-defined intentions."[33]

For Yat Siu of Animoca Brands, enterprise blockchains failed to grasp what makes these networks so powerful: their openness and composability. "Generally speaking, enterprises like to keep things fairly private . . . when we look at the benefits of digital property rights, it's that we can compose freely on top . . . constructing network effects. Digital ownership gives us the ability to create limitless network effects, on top of the work of others, in the way that physical property rights have enabled as well."[34]

The potentially *limitless* network effects are also *shared* network effects, not captured by any single company or entity. "Because of open composability—and this informs how we think about investing in this space—we can't try to monopolize and accrue the network effects."[35] Communist countries tried that model, and it failed; "the people" weren't really the owners of the means of production, and those systems were closed. The same is true of enterprise blockchains. "When you create an enterprise blockchain, you are limiting the ability to compose on top of it," said Siu. "With your enterprise network of one hundred or maybe even one thousand clients or customers and vendors, it can still work. But when you talk about aggregating millions of customers and people then . . . the public ledger starts to be of advantage."

For example, a startup can look at anyone who traded on OpenSea in the last six months based on on-chain data and incentivize them to switch with token rewards. Since users own their own art and digital collectibles, the cost to them is trivial. As a result, OpenSea has not retained its monopoly position for more than a few months. Siu asked us to consider a hypothetical: "Imagine if everyone could access Amazon's database and say, 'Oh, every customer who bought a Razer computer monitor, we have a special monitor for you that you can try. Or we'll give you ten percent off if you come to us. [This openness] flips the whole model upside down, and that's what we love about this space."[36]

Yorke E. Rhodes III, cofounder of blockchain at Microsoft, has a slightly different take. "I'm not saying there aren't successful consortiums. We're running a successful supply chain consortium within the high-tech ecosystem, that we should have fully deployed to production within the next six-plus months. Today it's a Web3 stack, running Quorum," he said. "My point is, consortiums may work, but they're tiny compared to the world. How could you have enough consortiums to satisfy all the needs of a FedEx, which is doing commerce with everyone? That's the scale problem of consortiums."[37]

In Rhodes's view, enterprise decision makers started to question the feasibility of these closed networks that, by their nature, could not bridge to public infrastructure. By contrast, "if you're doing Ethereum-based chains like Quorum, then yes, you can. You can take your platform and do something public with it because it's ninety-nine percent compatible." He described a project he has launched at Microsoft, focused on supply chains: "I'm taking a very small team, a peer and a mentor researcher, and validating the hypothesis that I can take this application stack, with very minimal changes from a code perspective and an infrastructural perspective, and deploy it on a combination of mainchain and Layer 2s in an EVM-compatible space," referring to blockchains that easily interoperate with Ethereum. "That will validate my thesis about the technology stack's being essentially the same."[38]

Under Satya Nadella, Microsoft has completely shifted to a software-as-a-service model, a cloud model. It's moved to new markets successfully, unlike HP and IBM. It's the second-largest company in the world. Dixon agreed. "Microsoft has done a good job. It's essentially an enterprise software company at this point. The enterprise software market has different competitive dynamics. The switching costs in enterprise software are very, very high. Microsoft didn't win the Internet. It was late to cloud, and it obviously really missed mobile, but it did a very good job catching up, and it did so through effective bundling," Dixon said. He described how the consumer Internet and consumer markets in general tended to be more subject to total disruption than enterprise and government markets. "The fate of Blockbuster was far more dramatic than the fate of IBM and enterprise software companies. Each market has its own characteristics. Consumer software can be quite tough, if you don't stay modern and ahead of the trends."[39] Web3 disruptors focused on business-to-business markets may take longer to dislodge Web2 enterprise service providers; but if they succeed, then they may have slightly more time to navigate future disruption.

Rhodes works in a computer company founded well before the Web whose cofounders had enough vision in the early 1990s to recognize the value of David Chaum's digital payment system, eCash, and want to integrate it into Windows 95.[40] Microsoft transitioned into a diversified technology company, focusing on converting their downloadable software to enterprise software as a service (SaaS), rather than on advertising revenue. We should note LinkedIn is a social network that monetizes user data, but most of its revenue comes from paid subscriptions, not targeted ads.

Rhodes had a firsthand view of this opening of the corporate mind. Referring to himself as "an enterprise guy," he said, "there was a recognition that public blockchain versus enterprise blockchain was very similar to Internet versus intranet in terms of a protocol stack." When the commercial web burst onto the scene in the early 1990s, many companies saw its potential but had concerns. It was "not secure," "not robust," and "used only by criminals." Sound familiar? Instead, they built their own Internets. These were proprietary, permissioned networks using Internet protocols. They were called intranets. Over time, however, as the public infrastructure became robust and global, they dropped these closed systems and embraced the public Internet. Rhodes argued that something similar is happening today with blockchains. As blockchain technologies evolve into Web3, enterprise leaders are beginning to understand that they can build robust applications on public networks that are far more powerful than private ones, just as the shift from intranets to the Internet brought new capabilities to companies decades ago.

Rhodes described the early days of enterprise blockchain, where people who had an enterprise focused on their digital wheelhouse—their cloud, their technology, their desire for patents—"ran off and tried to re-create the magic of public blockchains at scale, but with incentives for 'the enterprise.' That resulted in products like Hyperledger Fabric, a glorified database. Or Corda. The problem with those was, they didn't have the public tool. In terms of our resourcing, we always stayed close to what had viability on the Internet as a public tool."[41]

As companies like Accenture, IBM, and others got into the enterprise blockchain space, they realized that the concept of blockchains as distributed systems that coordinated governance across multiple parties was interesting. "But it's actually quite hard to get people on board," said Rhodes. IBM did have some success in attracting big-name participants—Carrefour, Dole, Driscoll's, Golden State Foods, Kroger, McCormick, McLane, Merck, Nestlé, Tyson Foods, Unilever, and Walmart—in early pilots of its private blockchain solution for food and drug provenance and in partnering with the Danish shipping giant Maersk to develop a platform for container logistics.[42] "IBM is poster child for permissioned blockchain," said Gennaro "Jerry" Cuomo, who was a leader and a spokesperson of IBM's blockchain efforts early on. In that role, he said, "I studied the bitcoin and blockchain. I studied them, but I never touched them with my own hands." Then he got hold of Ethereum, grokked Vitalik Buterin's vision of it as a virtual world computer—and "fell in love."[43]

Cuomo was excited, sharing one revelation after another as he explored public blockchains more fully. Take reputation, for example. IBM has devoted well over a hundred years to understanding the "computing, tabulating, and recording" needs of businesses, with acquired patents dating back to the 1880s and its first major government contract in 1890, for tallying and analyzing the US Census that year.[44] IBM's reputation has grown with the growth of its industry and the electrical grid. Yet, Cuomo observed, "with these blockchain networks, you can build trust and reputation *with algorithms*," not generations of service.[45] You can also destroy reputations with algorithms pretty quickly, too. Think of the Terra ecosystem, with its native token LUNA backing its algorithmic stablecoin, Terra USD. The algorithm worked as designed, but when holders started chucking their Terra USDs, LUNA couldn't steady the stablecoin's value.[46]

Rhodes of Microsoft shared his own experience, likening Ethereum and other public blockchains as substrates (or base layers) to the public Internet as a substrate, a default. "If you say, 'We're building on this, and we can provide secure connections to it,' then you don't have to argue about the substrate. Instead, you decide whether to join this little group or that little group. Ethereum recognized that and was very public about it early in its journey, saying, 'We have this existing substrate. It's the public Internet version of blockchains. We're doubling down on that. It's the substrate. It's there. If you want to participate, then let's figure out how, whether it's mainchain, Layer 2, or what have you.' That's actually an easier choice for enterprise *because it's a nonchoice*. It's a choice to be on a global substrate or not. If I want a bigger target audience, then I go toward this public substrate rather than pull people into a center of excellence or a consortium network."[47]

For a company nearly fifty years old, Microsoft has positioned itself to lead in three foundational technologies of the future: Web3, artificial intelligence, and the metaverse. Microsoft's enterprise customers who want to experiment with Web3 tools call Rhodes's team because of its rare institutional knowledge of the technology. The greening of Ethereum following "the merge," its move to a proof-of-stake consensus algorithm, has removed any environmental, social, and corporate governance (ESG) concerns about using public blockchains, something consumer-facing businesses and indeed all companies should care about. As we will discuss, new and easy-to-use Web3 tools like NFTs significantly lower the barriers for adoption.

On the AI front, Microsoft is also leading. To fund AI research, it invested $1 billion in OpenAI, which released the user-friendly web application ChatGPT (for "generative pretrained transformer") in November 2022.[48] ChatGPT demonstrated that it could answer complex questions, write poetry, debug code, tell jokes, and more. We may still be a ways off from what Ray Kurzweil called "the singularity," when AI exceeds human intelligence, but AI and machine learning will clearly be a dominant force in our lives. Microsoft not only backed OpenAI but secured an exclusive cloud agreement with the AI startup. Now, Microsoft is widely deploying OpenAI's tech across its suite of software.[49]

Finally, Microsoft's aggressive growth in videogames and virtual worlds presages its metaverse ambitions. When Bill Gates and the Rock (Dwayne Johnson) announced the first Xbox at the Consumer Electronics Show in 2001, the company probably did not anticipate that two decades later the platform would help it leap into the metaverse, but here we are.[50] In 2014, the company paid $2.5 billion for *Minecraft*, the popular virtual world videogame where users can create their own built environments with blocks. *Minecraft* is more than a game. *Minecraft* users have collaborated to build virtual cities as big as Los Angeles (500 square miles), for example, and in 2020, Reporters Sans Frontières, aka Reporters Without Borders, "commissioned the construction of a museum within *Minecraft*," called the Uncensored Library, where people in Russia, Saudi Arabia, and Egypt could read banned literature and the work of censored journalists.[51] By the end of 2022, more than 170 million people were using *Minecraft* each month.[52] The Federal Trade Commission (FTC) has filed a complaint against Microsoft to block its acquisition of videogame publisher Activision Blizzard.[53] The FTC is worried about the company's "suppressing competitors to its Xbox gaming consoles."[54] There are limits to how open-minded Microsoft has been to Web3. For example, the company recently announced a ban on bitcoin mining through its Azure cloud service.[55] However, taken together, its openness to Web3, investments in AI, and long-standing history in videogames and virtual worlds position the company better than most for the next era of computing, entertainment, and business.

Impact of NFTs on Enterprise Awareness

Thanks to the growing popularity of NFTs, a brand like Gucci and even Taco Bell can launch a Web3 project, for relatively little cost and with low technical capability, that can have an outsize impact. For example, Nike has made more than $150 million from its NFT sales.[56] To be sure, some of these are publicity stunts, but others, like Starbucks's NFT rewards program, are meaningful innovations to the core business. All these companies had their managerial approach in common. As Christensen wrote, "They planned to fail early and *inexpensively* in the search for the market for a disruptive technology."[57]

Yorke Rhodes of Microsoft described the effect of non-fungible tokens on the space. "This funny little token called the ERC-721, or NFTs, captured the mindshare of creators and anybody who was dealing with digital assets outside cryptocurrencies." Rhodes is an adjunct instructor of marketing and public relations at New York University, where he teaches a course on e-commerce marketing.[58] "Any business that's a digital-first business, whether it's software licensing, gaming, advertising, and so on, is doing digital marketing. NFTs have very defined properties that you can associate with brands and consumer products goods, in the form of Nike, Adidas, and others." He explained how the enterprise narrative shifted: "All of a sudden, all companies found relevance in this technology called 'public blockchain,' and the cryptocurrency substrate that it lives on." Even companies like pharmaceuticals, which didn't lean in initially, found relevant applications like supply chain traceability.

"We're hearing from brands that we never heard from before," said Rhodes. "So that changes the necessity for people across all of Microsoft, all divisions including our executives, to say, 'There's something here. Our brands are asking us for help. How do we respond to that?' So, we're on a journey internally as many other large technology enterprises are. We have consumer-facing products, to professional user-facing products, to back-end products, all the Office products, to cloud. There's so much landscape for Web3 implementations."

In 2018, Microsoft acquired the popular code repository hosting service GitHub, using the open-source distributed version control system Git.[59] Rhodes thought that GitHub had embraced elements "like verifiable claims or soulbound NFTs as tools for verifications of community and participation in developer [repositories]. That's kind of a GitHub decision. Should LinkedIn embrace soulbound tokens, claims, or anything else? That's a LinkedIn decision. So, I'd have to say the strategy is, there's something relevant happening here." The individual teams must figure out what makes sense for them, how to educate themselves enough so that they can make informed decisions.

"While people view Microsoft as a Web2 company, we are better positioned to take advantage of verifiable claims, decentralized identity, because it's not core from a revenue perspective, whereas ninety-seven percent of Facebook's revenue comes from apps monetizing consumer data. That is abhorrent to us. While we do have a Bing search engine where some of that happens, we firmly believe that sovereignty of consumer data and privacy is really important. The assets that we do have, where we hold data about professionals or businesses or consumers, we don't want to hold it. We would rather not have it. It's a honeypot risk for hackers, and so there's a very big value case to think about."

A Framework for User-Owned Networks

If users are going to own networks, we need to create a new model for how we will organize this peer production online. We must solve for decentralized resource governance: decision making, directing funds to new initiatives, hiring and firing contributors, suing counterparties for wrongdoing, buying property across different jurisdictions, lobbying governments, entering into contracts, and so forth. What will our motivation be? To maximize profit for token holders or to improve the user experience. Will we pay distributions when the network earns revenue, or reinvest it into new products and services?

In *The Wealth of Networks*, Yochai Benkler argued that "the term *peer production* characterizes a subset of commons-based production practices. It refers to production systems that depend on individual action that is self-selected and decentralized, rather than hierarchically assigned." Many early DAOs have had many well-intentioned people who have self-selected to contribute but occasionally we need some coordinating mechanism. Benkler maintained that "[c]entralization is a particular response to the problem of how to make the behavior of many individual agents cohere into an effective patter or achieve an effective result."[60]

To overcome these issues, user-owners can organize their user-owned networks as DAOs with a leadership or management team and can also be optimized for different outcomes. Jesse Walden said, "Shareholder-owned companies have one optimization function, which is the maximization of shareholder profits, whereas user-owned networks can optimize for whatever the users want. What the users might want is for the network or product or service to remain minimally extracted. Meaning don't charge fees that you don't need to charge. Only charge the fees that are necessary to operate the service at cost."[61] In the 1970 book *Future Shock*, Alvin Toffler anticipated this more flexible and dynamic form of governance and decision making, dubbing it *adhocracy*, "the fast-moving, information-rich, kinetic organization of the future, filled with transient cells and extremely mobile individuals."[62]

If corporations were the embodiment of industrial-age production, then DAOs are the embodiment of what Benkler called "networked intelligence." Despite their name including the word *autonomous*, DAOs are very much a human-made construct, like corporations. They mirror human ingenuity (and our worst impulses) in an array of new networked and global organizations. DAOs can give structure to Benkler's peer production networks. Benkler wrote in the mid-2000s, at a time when open-source software was producing hugely important new resources: "Free software projects do not rely on markets or on managerial hierarchies to organize production. Programmers generally participate in a project because . . . their boss told them to. . . . They do not generally participate in a project because someone offers them a price to do so, though some participants do focus on long-term appropriation through money-oriented activities, like consulting or service contracts."[63] DAOs are mechanisms for users to earn a share of the products and services they use but also become a convenient and easy way to pay contributors of code and other value to the network.

What are some of the specific characteristics of DAOs? First, they often have a shared wallet—like the community fund in the board game Monopoly—controlled by its users and stakeholders. Anyone can become an owner of a DAO by earning or buying into the native token, which can be a governance token or NFT. This token facilitates the governance and economic coordination of the funds in the wallet.

Token holders also vote how to disburse funds, allocate budgets, hire and fire contributors, and so forth. DAOs already coordinate the economic resources of DeFi projects like Uniswap. DeFi protocols typically have lots of transactions—think about an exchange with people buying and selling assets all the time. The protocols divert fees from that business activity to the common wallet. But we can also fund DAO treasuries in many of the same ways companies access capital—from external investment, revenue earned from users, or the appreciation of their native tokens.

DAOs have other characteristics. As their name suggests, they are decentralized, meaning they often pull in contributors and users from around the world. They are generally open and permissionless, which means anyone can engage with them, though if you want to participate in the economic upside or governance, you typically must be an owner. DAOs are also customizable. They are a blank slate for experimenting in community ownership, governance, and novel business models. That means they can be complex or simple. DAOs are already widely employed in Web3 for a range of tasks, from organizing a small collective of people with some shared wallet to being the organizational structure for a Web3 protocol with millions in its treasury. They can re-create functions of complex corporations or simple and even temporary tasks such as forming a guild in a virtual world/videogame or starting a charity to fund a pressing humanitarian need, as Ukraine DAO did in the wake of the Russian invasion.

If DAOs are human constructs to organize assets and people toward a common cause with a shared treasury and periodic voting on important matters, then are they really corporations with *token holders* instead of *shareholders*? No. Vitalik Buterin, cofounder of Ethereum, wrote that the early days of DAOs have led to calls for DAOs to resemble companies more closely: "The argument is always similar: highly decentralized governance is inefficient, and traditional corporate governance structures with boards, CEOs and the like evolved over hundreds of years to optimize for the goal of making good decisions and delivering value to shareholders in a changing world."[64]

Buterin wrote that critics of DAOs see their proponents as idealists whose belief in an egalitarian and decentralized model over a hierarchical one is naïve. He pushed back, making the case that DAOs are not only superior to companies but are the only workable model in three circumstances. The first is what Buterin called "concave environments," by which he meant situations where there is no either/or answer and require a compromise or partial solution. Centralization may lend itself to polarizing responses to a divisive question. Decentralization is more deliberative, and the wisdom of the crowd beats one central decision maker. In the second scenario, the network requires decentralization for censorship resistance. Sometimes applications must keep running "while resisting attacks from powerful external actors," including large corporations or state powers. Ukraine DAO helped raise money for the Ukrainian military when payment processors shut down other efforts for violating their terms of service. In the final area, DAOs must maintain credible fairness, where DAOs are "taking on nation-state-like functions like basic infrastructure provision, and so traits like predictability, robustness and neutrality are valued above efficiency."[65] There are plenty of other reasons DAOs might be a good fit—lower cost to organize, greater ability to tap global talent, more input from owners, and ease of generating and distributing ownership rewards in the form of tokens, to name a few. Let us explore a few areas of DAO experimentation and implementation.

DAOs for Business, Culture, and Gaming

Other DAOs strive to make Web3 tools easier for many kinds of businesses to use. For example, the Web3 startup Aragon helps different organizations to coordinate and collaborate, but companies could also use DAOs to create and manage decentralized teams or departments, allowing for greater internal collaboration and flexibility. Aragon provides open-source infrastructure and governance plug-ins to more than 3,800 DAOs looking to leverage decentralized decision-making processes. With Aragon's suite of applications and services, anyone can easily launch a DAO. Holders of Aragon's native token ANT can participate in the governance of the Aragon Network DAO and the

Aragon Court dispute resolution system. Since launching in 2016, Aragon has cultivated a globally distributed community of 300,000+ members.[66]

Why would non-Web3 firms embrace these tools? There are several reasons to explore. First, companies could use DAOs to manage relationships with external partners, suppliers, or customers.[67] Public DAOs provide a transparent and decentralized means of managing the data that constitute these relationships. DAOstack and Boardroom are trying to do something similar.

Web3 gaming is another frontier where innovators are deploying DAOs like DGaming, *Axie Infinity*, *The Sandbox*, ChainGuardians, and *CryptoSpaceX*. In a Web3 game, DAO creators could use the DAO to govern certain aspects of the game, such as the distribution of in-game assets, the management of a game's virtual economy, or its native currency, as in the case of *Axie*. All transactions in DAOs are on-chain, transparent, and immutable. If the process is open and public, where the game's community can see proposals for change, contribute to the debate, and see the vote tallies regardless of whether they're voting themselves, then they will have more confidence in the decision to make changes.

Innovators are also using DAOs to govern resources in the shared Web3-based metaverse. For example, Decentraland is a decentralized 3D reality platform collectively owned by its users who share a vision for "determining the future of the virtual world." In this virtual world, users can explore LANDs, create unique experiences, and trade digital assets among themselves. They can also monetize content and applications via two tokens on the network: MANA (cryptocurrency) and LAND (NFT). Founded in 2017 by Ari Meilich and Esteban Ordano, Decentraland raised $25.5 million in investment to incentivize a global network of users to collaborate in operating this virtual world. It claimed to have 8,000 daily active users (DAUs) as of October 11, 2022, but by December it changed the estimate to 60,000 *monthly* active users.[68] Using four different tools, CoinDesk came up with figures ranging from 526 to 810 DAUs.[69] Decentraland's DAO structure puts MANA and LAND holders in control of the world's behavior, as they set policies through governance community votes. As of this writing, it had a market capitalization of around $1.3 billion with a total of $17.4 million in its treasury, the vast majority of which is its MANA token.[70]

Community organizers can use DAOs to mobilize around a set of interests, principles, or values with a few rules to govern the behavior of the group. This is becoming increasingly popular in creative and activist fields. Friends With Benefits, mentioned earlier, is a DAO whose creators and token holders seek to shape Web3's future with collaboration from a wide array of unique individuals, especially artists. This community collectively fundraises and allocates resources toward projects relating to the decentralization of web services as voted by holders of FWB, the native token. Founded in 2020 by Trevor McFedries to "merge culture and crypto," this social DAO is ever growing, with 3,000 members such as artists, entrepreneurs, and enthusiasts in the crypto and culture spaces. In November 2021, it received a $100 million valuation and a $10 million investment to help build out its team and scale its footprint via real-life events in so-called FWB Cities.[71] FWB is a "token gated community," meaning that members must hold FWB tokens to participate in governance. It's also exclusive in the traditional sense that people who want to join must submit applications to the FWB community for approval and buy a minimum of seventy-five FWBs.[72] The platform validates the participation of official FWB members in governance.[73]

DAOs for Global Problem Solving and Global Solutions

Web3 tools can also help us address global problems like climate change. Using DAOs and digital assets, broad groups of stakeholders—companies of all sizes, NGOs, academics, and governments at all levels—can collaborate and mobilize with a goal of accelerating the transition to clean energy. We can now represent carbon credits with tokens, for example. Earlier, we described how Ukraine DAO raised funds for the Ukraine war effort when other payment rails failed. Climate change is another area that some DAOs seek to tackle, with projects like Regen Network, KlimaDAO, Aragon, Flowcarbon, and others.

Gregory Landua, cofounder and chief regeneration officer of Regen Network, told us, "Climate change is a failure of markets, policy, and coordination."[74] Issues like the collapse of biodiversity, the spread of microplastics, and threats to the biosphere were caused by market failures, he said. But he also sees a path to planetary health in markets: "One hundred percent of wealth and one hundred percent of business requires a healthy planet." Carbon markets try to place a cost on carbon. Because there is a cost, we will sequester it or use less or trade it. But there are challenges: How do you reach consensus that a party has authentically sequestered its carbon? "This is an odorless, tasteless invisible gas," said Landua.[75] Regen Network seeks to embed the social and scientific process of monitoring ecological health into the economic process on-chain.

There are various implementations of this concept. Generally, the idea is that your "carbon market" smart contract integrates with existing carbon credit registries or constitutes a new registry on a blockchain, perhaps Ethereum. These smart contracts enforce the rules of the carbon trading market, such as compliance with regulations and limits on the total number of carbon credits that any party can trade. Participants in the carbon trading market can interact with the DAO's smart contracts by buying and selling carbon credits, like an AMM, but for carbon offsets. The smart contracts automatically execute these transactions atomically (that is, peer-to-peer via the contract) and update the carbon credit registry accordingly. Because the DAO runs on-chain, it provides a transparent and immutable record of all carbon credit transactions. In some versions, DAO members who use the system could earn a governance token for voting on proposals to change market rules or allocating funds for carbon offset projects. But that is not a requirement.

We could employ DAOs longer term as the organizing entities for new countries. Far-fetched as that may sound, a growing movement wants to use Internet tooling to start a so-called "network state," defined by author Balaji Srinivasan as a "highly aligned online community with a capacity for collective action that crowdfunds territory around the world and eventually gains diplomatic recognition from pre-existing states."[76] It would start as a "cloud first" state, entirely online. Then it would bootstrap all the functions of a state, eventually funding a treasury and physical land.

Srinivasan has been mulling these concepts for a long time. He described a DAO to me, in 2014, when governance tokens were known as "appcoins." He mused that, if I wanted to build a new version of Tor, I could prefund its development by issuing a "Tor coin" and using the proceeds to "develop the software open source and use it to pay nodes who run servers on the network." He added, "Now we've created a way to monetize open source in a way that was never possible before."[77]

If we can use the Internet toolset to build decentralized products and services, why not bootstrap a state? CityDAO is one project borrowing from this playbook. It offers "citizenship" to members, with rights to vote on proposals or make their own. CityDAO also has guilds organized around solving problems. It even owns some land in Wyoming.[78] Srinivasan pointed out in his book that achieving statehood is a multistep process. Only after forming a community, acquiring land, connecting nodes, and developing an economy and culture can such a community seek to gain actual statehood.[79] Compared to war or revolution, a gradual and peaceful approach, harnessing these tools, is appealing.

DAOs in Artificial Intelligence

Another area of DAO innovation intersects with AI. For AI and machine learning, some of the leading DAOs are SingularityNET, Ocean Protocol, DAOstack, the TensorFlow Governance DAO, and the AI Ethereum DAO. We already asked OpenAI to explain Ocean Protocol, where data owners can pool their data in a commons for use in machine learning algorithms, while owners retain privacy and control. With such a decentralized marketplace, individuals can discover, contribute to, and consume data on initiatives they care about, such as scientific research on diseases and treatments. To purchase data and participate in community governance, users must hold the native OCEAN token. Founded in 2017 by Bruce Pon, Ocean Protocol has raised a total of $33.1 million from investors to safeguard open access, govern data, and drive network growth. By staking OCEAN tokens on datasets, individuals become liquidity providers and earn a percentage of the pool's generated transaction fees. Ocean Protocol has a market value of approximately $158 million and a fully diluted market value of $514 million.[80] So despite the promise of Ocean Protocol and others, valued by market size, we would consider these microcap companies if they were publicly traded.[81]

SingularityNET is another promising project, a "decentralized AI marketplace, running on blockchain."[82] The platform allows different AI programs to work together and share information, becoming smarter and more useful so that they can solve problems too difficult for any single AI program to solve on its own. For example, one AI program might recognize faces in pictures, while another might understand natural language. By collaborating on SingularityNET, these two AI programs can help each other. In a way, we can say that SingularityNET is trying to make AI algorithms composable in a trustless and on-chain way.

Life After Companies?

DAOs are a promising means of organizing capability in the economy and could transform business and the world in profound ways. They liberate us to rethink everything—from the role of the firm in the economy and the nature of work to how we collectively govern public goods and how we build and sustain open-source technology. DAOs are digital petri dishes for new models and metrics of governance with applications beyond business and technology. They create mechanisms for Internet users to exercise ownership of the platforms and other shared resources they use. By lowering the cost to collaborate, transact, and establish trust, they could come to replace the corporation in many instances.

DAOs also come with tremendous risk and uncertainty. As with digital assets, DAOs lack legal and regulatory frameworks for operating within traditional legal systems. An entity without legal standing may struggle to hire or fire salaried employees, make payroll, and enter and enforce traditional legal contracts. Smart contracts can automate these functions but lack legal enforceability. This remains a point of friction. DAOs are built on public blockchains and employ software like bridges, which make them vulnerable to cyberattack. Of course, traditional corporations get hacked regularly with disastrous results. Governance by users is a nice idea in theory, but for the system to work as intended, users must engage in decisions and take actions. Passive and inert users do not make for a vibrant community. The track record of voters in similar systems (such as corporate governance) should give us pause that DAOs will solve governance matters in the economy. Today Web3 entrepreneurs use DAOs to launch new products and services. However, the technology will evolve, and the industry will overcome implementation challenges while exporting its vision to the rest of the world, making it likely we will see more and more industries adopt and benefit from DAOs.

Conclusion and Takeaways

If Web3's promise to transform creators into owners of the products and services they use is true, then we can expect many new user-owned networks. Some of Web3's innovations will come from companies, but Internet-native DAOs will perform a greater role in our digital economy. Here are the takeaways:

1. Stakehodler capitalism will spread. Internet users will care more about the platforms they use and own. They are not passive, inert, or powerless users. They are stakehodlers in Web3-enabled communities.
2. DAOs as networked organisms may be a better fit than corporations when the goal is not only profit but also network health and utility. As experiments in governance and economic coordination, DAOs are pioneering new models that we can apply beyond business.

3. Enterprises face the innovator's dilemma. The market opportunity of Web3 is ill-defined for most firms. Do they embrace this technology or wait? They could try and fail (or succeed) inexpensively. NFTs have lowered the barrier to experimentation. For most firms, especially those selling to consumers, this is a good place to start.

4. DAOs face many implementation challenges. We need a framework to govern, manage, and grow this new breed of organization. DAOs also lack legal standing, limiting their ability to enter contracts, hire and fire, and so on. Every DAO is also different. They can be complex or simple, global or local, manage online assets or physical assets.

5. DAOs have succeeded in DeFi, but we expect to see DAOs in many areas, such as physical infrastructure, culture, gaming and the metaverse, and AI.

In the next chapter, we dive deeper into Web3 transformations in three key industries, exploring how DAOs, token incentives, NFTs, and other Web3 primitives are poised to transform big aspects of our economy, for the better.

CHAPTER 6

Decentralizing Finance and Digitizing Money

By 2005, the dot-com bubble was receding into history and as the techlash ebbed, it was clear that the Internet was not some passing fad or a technology with limited and unexciting scope, as alleged by many mainstream critics like Paul Krugman, who said the Internet would prove no more impactful than the fax machine.[1]

Instead, the Internet was about to become a far more powerful tool for transforming business and culture than expected even in the heady days of the late 1990s. In its first era, the Web had democratized information to those who had access to it. Then it democratized access to publishing: instead of merely being inert and passive recipients of information, we, the users, could join the conversation and even program the Web itself by uploading photos, music, files, and our own writings. We could all be citizen journalists, amateur scientists, at-home digital artists, armchair financial analysts, and more.

Blogging, short for Web logging, was an important early Web2 application that made the Web writable to laypeople. Yochai Benkler said of blogs, "They can be modified from anywhere with a networked computer, and the results of writing onto the Webpage are immediately available to anyone who accesses the blog to read."[2] From blogs grew the potential for "large-scale conversations."[3] The impact of a writable Web was to enable, in Benkler's view, "large-scale, collaborative-content production systems available on the Web . . . they are intended for, and used by, very large groups. . . . They are intrinsically group communication media."[4]

The Wealth of Networks is filled with a sincere hope that people would engage in large-scale cooperation online and that we would enter a new golden age of collaboration and innovation. After all, look at Wikipedia: by 2006, it had become the largest and most authoritative source of information ever compiled, made up entirely by volunteers using the Internet.

The excitement around the potential of this new digital toolset is understandable. The Read-Write Web reimagined how we produce value, collaborate, and coordinate our activities. It could therefore reframe the role of the corporation, governments, and our other institutions. "Effective large scale cooperative efforts," now known as the open-source software movement, would challenge business and political dogma. To Benkler, the notion that people would gather online voluntarily without clear monetary reward to build and maintain worldwide communities, resources, technologies, and cultural value ran "against the grain of some of our most basic Economics 101 intuitions, intuitions homed in the industrial economy."[5]

A Report Card for Web2 Innovators

A sober analysis of Web2 results gives innovators a mixed report card. On the one hand, they created tremendous economic value for stockholders and founders. They accelerated Internet adoption and connected the world in ways many of us could not have imagined a few decades ago. They created space for previously marginalized voices, with platforms like Twitter leveling the playing field and giving scientists, entrepreneurs, athletes, investors, and others a platform to reach new audiences. Platforms gave like-minded people tools to self-organize, often with positive outcomes, sometimes not. However, overall, use of the technology has not lived up to its early and lofty aspirations and has created new problems that Web3 innovators seek to solve.

Once dynamic upstarts themselves, many of these companies have ossified into a form of managerial capitalism as defined by James Burnham in his book *The Managerial Revolution*. Except for Facebook, none are founder-led. They operate as oligopolies or monopolies in many areas. And owners are detached from decision making. And they are deeply intertwined with the state, especially in China, where they often operate hand in glove with the Communist Party.[6]

Said Chris Dixon, "Web2 has been very good at excellent user interfaces, bringing very slick free services to billions of people and making them very usable. In an ideal world, we could design a system, where we combined the best of both those worlds, the advanced, sleek functionality of Web2 with the open-ecosystem, community-driven development of Web1. That would be the best version of the Internet."[7]

How did Web2 fall short? First, in the absence of an Internet-native ownership and transaction layer, advertising became the primary revenue model. Many platforms that began as more open-ended converted to ad-friendly models and then worked hard to keep users engaged to harvest their data. "Advertisers want a controlled experience," Dixon said. "They want their ads to show up next to certain content. For a bunch of reasons, the advertising model led Twitter to shut down its open ecosystem, to close the service off. The same happened at Facebook. They became these monolithic, siloed services built around optimizing engagement and advertising dollars."[8]

Second, Web2 enriched financial intermediaries: they did not need to innovate to stay relevant because Web2 did not change their role as intermediaries. As we have shown, most fintech innovations proved to be digital wallpaper on the old edifice of finance.

Third, as the Web went mostly mobile, two companies—Apple and Google—controlled the primary gateway to the Internet via the Android and Apple ecosystems and began to charge exorbitant monopoly (or duopoly) rents for developers on their platforms. Mobile app stores have become bottlenecks for new development. Not only are they gatekeepers, but they extract rents for almost all economic activity in apps themselves.[9] For example, Apple exacts its 30 percent on the apps it sells and their in-app sales.[10] These fees have come to represent a tax or toll on doing business for most tech developers. The centralized custodial service Coinbase alleged that Apple wanted users of the Coinbase Wallet app to pay "gas" fees through Apple's in-app purchase system so that Apple could take its cut of that, too.[11] Coinbase said it was technically impossible to do and likened it to putting a tax on email protocols; so Apple blocked Coinbase's latest app release, thereby blocking users from sending NFTs through the Coinbase Wallet.[12] Mobile computing also further entrenched the ad model. Facebook has its eyes on the next frontier of computing and wants to extend this model to its closed metaverse but ratchet its take to 50 percent.[13]

Fourth, users have no control over platforms and, in some cases, no visibility into how they are run. Platforms could also change without community input: some Web2 businesses that began as open-ended networks became closed-ended platforms in pursuit of greater ad revenue.

Fifth, Web2 became a winner-take-all model that created monopolies stifling competition. Bootstrapping a competitor network in the Web2 economy became too costly and risky—a Sisyphean task destined to struggle for eternity. Web2 giants have dual classes of shares that empower executives and reduce accountability from shareholders and the board, exacerbating this dynamic. Elon Musk's willy-nilly decision making at Twitter has driven away users, advertisers, and corporate value.

Sixth, Internet users were hooked by recommendation engines that, while often useful in helping people find what they were looking for, also pushed them into self-reinforcing echo chambers. Web2 algorithms learned that extremism increased engagement, as did misinformation. The fragmentation of public discourse and the growing extremism in our politics can be attributed in part to this phenomenon.[14]

Seventh, these large platforms became chokepoints for the Internet and targets for government pressure to track citizens. In China, the state co-opted its Web2 giants, turning them into an extension of the state's surveillance system, and then moved quickly to co-opt Web3 innovation.

How will Web3 transform industries? In the next section, we explore the biggest ones: financial services and money.

Reimagining Finance and Money

Banks emerged not long after the first large civilizations appeared in Sumerian Mesopotamia. Originally, banking was a function of temples, which were central to political, economic, religious, and cultural life. These proto banks were a secure place to store and exchange goods. They also pioneered systems of accounting and record-keeping, so that they could track transactions and manage accounts. Clemens Reichel, professor of Mesopotamian archaeology at the University of Toronto, joined me on a panel discussion hosted by the Royal Ontario Museum in Toronto in November 2022.[15] Reichel described how banks in Sumerian times evolved "from storing physical money," loosely defined as physical goods of value like grain, "to storing information about money." He added that the earliest form of writing, cuneiform, emerged concurrently with money not only to transmit information over long distances but also to keep records of accounts.[16] This early form of record-keeping gave money value as a means of storage and unit of account before the emergence of coinage. In a sense, from the earliest trade, money was always virtual—an etching in cuneiform on a clay tablet, not a physical commodity like gold or cowrie shells. Eventually, banking outgrew temples and specialized in services, but each specialty institution still maintained ledgers as records of value, and they serve a similar function today.

The financial services industry is the heart and cardiovascular system of global commerce. But, like Frankenstein, its body is a kludge of disparate parts well past their sell-by date. On average, it takes days and costs 6 percent to move money cross-border, according to the World Bank.[17] It excludes about 1.4 billion people.[18] It is entrenched: as Web2 moved more transactions online, financial intermediaries have enriched themselves without commensurate innovation. It is opaque, which makes for counterparty risk. It is centralized, giving it greater influence over governments than big tech, pharma, or oil and gas. It is siloed, operating on different systems, under different regulatory regimes, and in different marketplaces, all of which limit its global composability and liquidity. No surprise, it is bracing itself for one of the larger transformations in history. Web3's DeFi innovators are decentralizing many of these services and forcing us to rethink the meaning of money itself.

Digital Money

Money emerged to solve the barter problem—in transactions, parties needed a medium of exchange that was fungible, liquid, divisible (spendable in increments), and verifiable (of a certifiable substance, like gold and silver) or backed by a powerful institution.[19] Often, the more inherently useless the commodity, the better placeholder it was for money. John Locke said that money was merely something that one "by mutual consent would take in exchange for the truly useful, but perishable supports of life."[20] It is a form of collective delusion. Gold works as money because it is not *truly useful*. Above all else, trust was foundational to many forms of money, making governments a natural fit as currency issuers.

Governments could also innovate. The Spanish eight-piece became popular in the sixteenth century in part because its craftsmen—Indigenous peoples in Mexico, Peru, and other Spanish colonies—used new-world silver, the purest in the world and the lightest to carry. These craftsmen cast them individually or hand-cut them so that users could easily break them into eight pieces to make change (hence the name). The eight-piece was used in Spain's colonies and later was adopted by the fledgling United States of America after the thirteen colonies broke ties with England.[21] They also stamped the coins with the Spanish coat of arms on one side and the Catholic cross on the reverse side, to underscore their sovereign power.

Before the Spanish crossed the Atlantic, Kublai Khan, founder of the Yuan dynasty in the thirteenth century, enforced the use of paper banknotes that were difficult to forge: Kublai employed an ingenious production technique integrating the bark of a rare tree, a technology that endures to this day. On his visit to the Middle Kingdom, Marco Polo found that merchants and citizens readily accepted these paper banknotes. Why? Kublai threatened violence to those trading in his empire if they abused or refused to use his banknotes, punishing the forgers and killing the disobedient.[22] This was money by *fiat*, or government decree. Kublai's use of centralized state power to enforce adoption and prop up his monetary system proved the winning model. Today, fiat money reigns supreme.

Web3 is ushering in a new era of money—a digital bearer asset, which we can use to move and store value, transact, and do business, like cash but with instant settlement, immutability, and global liquidity. The next decade of innovation will prove decisive as state powers, global corporations, and an increasingly assertive digital civil society vie for control over the future of money.

Three innovations, all anchored by blockchains, will contend for the future of money. The first are public *cryptocurrencies* like bitcoin, which we have discussed. The second are privately issued digital dollars, backed by collateral. These so-called "stablecoins," are mainly backed 1:1 to the US dollar in a bank, but that may prove to be just a skeuomorphic first kick at the can. A basket of various assets will likely back future stablecoins, as in Facebook's ill-fated Libra project. The third are CBDCs, digital currencies minted and managed by central banks.

Will bitcoin reign supreme? Don't count it out. Bitcoin has succeeded in some ways and fallen short in others. As of this writing, Bitcoin's market cap is $400 billion, more than Mastercard's $335 billion.[23] People all around the world use bitcoin as a store of value and a medium of exchange. It is a lifeline to the world's unbanked. Freedom fighters on the left and the right favor its censorship resistance. Advocates say bitcoin and other forms of permissionless money are essential to defending freedom of speech, arguing there is no freedom of speech without freedom to transact. "Freedom of speech is hollow if you can't pay the print costs for your magazine. Freedom of religion is hollow if you can't pay the rent on your church. The freedom to protest is hollow if you can't pay bus fare to the protest site," said technology writer Scott Alexander.[24]

Founded in 2007, the Human Rights Foundation (HRF) supports civil society and democratic movements in authoritarian countries. As part of its mandate, it gives voice to dissidents and other prodemocracy leaders from countries such as Russia, Venezuela, and Lebanon. Chess grand master and Putin critic Garry Kasparov chairs HRF. The arrival of bitcoin gave HRF another arrow in its quiver to empower oppressed people. "In the human rights and politics camp, finance and money are rarely discussed but they are very important," said Alex Gladstein, chief strategy officer of HRF. "Most of the people we work with live under regimes that have a terrible fiat currency, one that is typically collapsing at a much faster rate than the US dollar." These regimes exploit their people through money and banking services. They restrict connections to the global financial system, confiscate funds, freeze bank accounts, and limit or criminalize access to the US dollar. "You can even be arrested for having dollars, where citizen attempts to get assets like gold are restricted," he said.[25] Gabriel Abed, a Web3 entrepreneur and Barbados's ambassador to the United Arab Emirates countries, said Bitcoin doesn't judge users based on creed, race, religion, or income. He knows from personal experience. "I didn't get a proper bank account until I became an ambassador. Bitcoin saved me. It gave me sovereignty over my financial control."[26]

Gladstein told me how the "financial privilege" of the "golden billion" people living in the United States, Europe, Canada, Japan, and a few other countries blinds them to the harsh reality of the seven billion other people on the planet. Bitcoin has its faults, but one of its strongest selling points in Africa and elsewhere is that it helps free people from local dictators and former colonial powers, whose legacy of financial domination casts a long shadow to this day: 80 percent of inter-African finance flows through an American and European company, according to Gladstein.[27]

But bitcoin is also energy intensive, slow, and volatile, much like gold and other commodities. What's more, it faces a skeptical audience: central bankers. What do these bankers suggest as an alternative? CBDCs. Governments tout CBDCs as better alternatives to public cryptocurrencies like bitcoin. CBDCs, they argue, can make the economy more inclusive, reduce volatility, and improve the responsiveness of central banks to crises by increasing transparency.

However, CBDCs raise concerns about human rights. For example, how exactly do we protect privacy rights when the government can see in real time how users spend every digital dollar in the economy? Governments must protect these civil liberties if they want citizens and visitors to adopt their CBDCs. Some industry commentators think that we won't get a choice: "Governments have a powerful incentive to require exclusive usage of crypto fiat. It makes tax enforcement easy, lets governments 'turn off' the money of criminals and political dissidents, and central banks love it for the real-time transparency and tighter monetary control," said Web3 investor Ari Paul. "They will first roll out crypto fiat, and then quickly thereafter to ban anything that competes with it: cash, non-crypto fiat, and if they enjoy significant usage, gold and public cryptocurrencies like bitcoin."[28]

This brings us to the final category, stablecoins. The leading versions, USD Coin (USDC) and USD Tether (USDT), are worth more than $100 billion combined.[29] Facebook attempted its own stablecoin, initially called Libra and based on a basket of assets. But the US government viewed it as a threat to the US dollar system and national security, revealing the risks to any company trying to reinvent money.[30] "I am deeply torn about stablecoins," said Gladstein. "We have to acknowledge and maybe even celebrate stablecoins. They have given tens, if not hundreds, of millions of people a US dollar instrument—and they don't need a bank account to do it." But he worries about how stablecoins will calcify the existing power imbalance wrought by the US dollar system. "Stablecoins expand the US dollar's network effect, which is contra to bitcoin's intended effect."[31] A subcategory of synthetic decentralized stablecoins, like MakerDAO's Ethereum-based DAI, are backed by assets held in smart contracts, operating like pieces of software with bank accounts. However, DAI is somewhat centralized as it holds a lot of USDC and US government debt as collateral. The addition of real-world assets to Maker may help it scale much as USDC scaled, but it is trading some of its censorship resistance as a result.

If bitcoin (digital gold) and CBDCs (digital fiat money) are skeuomorphic iterations of money for Web3, then perhaps decentralized stablecoins backed by a basket of assets held on-chain, free from censorship, will eventually win out. Perhaps the idea of "digitizing money" is itself skeuomorphic. What if Web3 allows us to return to a form of private, digital barter? In 1997, James Dale Davidson and William Rees-Mogg anticipated this idea, arguing that "the odds of finding someone with exactly reciprocal desires to yours increase dramatically when you can sort instantly across the entire world rather than drawing on only those whom you might meet locally."[32] They added, "Digital money on global computer networks will make every object on Hayek's continuum of liquidity more liquid, except government paper."[33] They may prove prophetic except for one small change: one of Web3's first killer apps—US-dollar-backed stablecoins—have increased the liquidity and usefulness of government paper (in this case, the US dollar).

Global digital barter is itself a form of composability. Web3 entrepreneur Adrian Brink is building his project Anoma so that "any asset [can] function as means of exchange or payment, which—all things being equal—can create greater liquidity, less slippage, and more privacy in transactions. The end goal of this could be the disruption of money itself, which was created to solve the problems and limitations of barter."[34]

Spotlight on USDC

When Jeremy Allaire founded the Internet payments company Circle in 2013, he and his cofounders had a thesis for an "HTTP of money," a protocol that could work for money as the protocols of information exchange worked on the Internet, where "anyone could connect to the protocol and exchange value just like anyone can connect a web browser and a web server and exchange information."[35]

Originally, Allaire wanted to build his company on the Bitcoin network. The prevailing thinking was that developers could program Bitcoin to handle different kinds of applications like smart contracts and other assets like dollars, yen, stocks, NFTs, and more. Before Bitcoin, innovators had no public utility to move value around the world, as they moved information over the Internet. Bitcoin solved this problem. So, like Chris Dixon and other longtime Web3 builders we spoke to, Allaire thought (reasonably) to build his business on top of the thing that worked. But as time passed, Allaire found the technology limiting and the community hostile to issuing new code, largely for what he called political and ideological reasons.[36] So, in 2017, four years after launching, they made what, at the time, felt like a momentous decision: scrapping their plans to build on Bitcoin and instead building on Ethereum, the upstart protocol that had turned heads with its novel and programmable architecture and more open-minded culture.

We interviewed Allaire for *Blockchain Revolution* in 2015. He remains focused on the goal of building simple public tools for moving and storing value. He hoped then that in several years "a person should be able to download an app, store value in whatever currency they want—dollars, euro, yen, renminbi, as well as digital currency—and be able to make payments instantly," globally, privately, and securely.[37] How has Circle fared several years later? Quite well.

Today, Circle's flagship stablecoin USDC has a circulating supply of more than $45 billion and is theoretically available to anyone with a digital asset wallet, estimated to be at least 100 million people.[38] USDC runs on public protocols like Ethereum, Solana, and Cosmos. USDC facilitated $4.5 trillion in transactions on the Ethereum network alone in 2022, and 60 percent of all transactions in DeFi and Web3 gaming, highlighting the importance of USDC to the Web3 economy.[39] In its 2022 annual report, Circle notes that of the 2 million USDC-enabled wallets on Ethereum alone, "over 75 percent of these wallets hold balances of less than $100, which is less than typical minimum balance requirements of banking accounts and attests to a prerequisite for addressing financial inclusion challenges."[40] In 2015, Allaire told us that he wanted the protocol for money to be free, like the Internet. Circle has made great progress to that goal: average fees to spend USDC range from less than a penny to about fifty cents, with transaction times ranging from one second to three minutes.[41]

Circle was successful by leaning into the developer community in Web3. Allaire said in DeFi there "were all these people building new protocols for composable, programmable money and [we] got them

excited and got Coinbase excited, got the leading crypto retail platform to do it, and we were off to the races. Obviously, the ultimate
growth and monetization we didn't know, but we knew that we were
building the right thing that eventually could get a lot of traction."
Today USDC is issued across eighteen different blockchains, integrated into two hundred different protocols, and has been adopted by
Visa, Mastercard, Twitter, and Stripe.[42]

Circle is a US-domiciled company building a product on top of
public blockchain infrastructure. We need more hybrid approaches
like it for Web3 to succeed, said Allaire. "I think if you set the bar at,
everyone has to adopt a non-government-issued, non-sovereign commodity money of some sort, I think that's a bridge too far. So, we're
going to live in a hybrid world of government debt obligation money
expressed in digital currency form but built on open, decentralized infrastructure, built on protocols that are open and programmable and
composable."[43] He cites other examples where a hybrid approach is
warranted, such as digital identity, which will combine government
and other traditional attestations with on-chain information, or the
tokenization of real-world assets, or DAOs, which need some legal
standing to enter into contracts, hire and fire, and compete with corporations. But all these new Web3 services will be built on open, programmable infrastructure, just like USDC.

Circle has found a business model that works for right now. USDC
is fully backed dollar for dollar, meaning that Circle has invested
the $45 billion-plus in collateral it holds in US government securi-
ties, earning 3 to 4 percent risk-free. If interest rates rise, then Circle
stands to reap greater profits. Will banks like JPMorgan Chase and
HSBC issue their own stablecoins? Not likely, said Allaire. Banks
have a different ideology about money: they lend out five, ten, and
sometimes fifteen times the capital they have on reserve. Allaire said,
"There's a new physics of money: money at the speed and utility and
cost efficiency of data on the Internet."[44] As we saw with Terra LUNA
and later with legacy lender Silicon Valley Bank, these new physics
make for flash bank runs, and so the bank had better have either full
reserves or plenty of liquidity to meet redemptions, or risk collapse.

On CBDCs, Allaire said that the developed world has no need and no precedent for governments to build national, end-user-facing infrastructure. "The history of electronic money innovation in the West is a history of private sector innovation, whether it's the wire messaging system, checks themselves, automated check-clearing systems, credit cards, debit cards, ATMs, PayPal, Apple Pay, stablecoins," he said.[45]

Central banks have an important role in setting federal prudential standards for dollar digital currency, he said. "We are supportive of federal regulation, and that's the key. The public sector should regulate the safety and soundness parameters, and the private sector should innovate at the technology and distribution layer."[46] Some central bankers agree with Allaire: in a November 2021 speech, former Federal Reserve governor Christopher J. Waller said that the government and private industry have long worked side by side and sometimes in concert in advancing the national and global financial system and promoting competition. "With the right network design, stablecoins might help deliver faster, more efficient retail payments," especially cross-border, and reach more consumers, Waller said.[47] Because they're blockchain based, the greater transparency could make the job of central bankers easier. Until government comes around fully, the Web3 industry can follow Circle's example by focusing on growing relentlessly and responsibly on public blockchain infrastructure.

DeFi Functions

We can extend Satoshi Nakamoto's concept of peer-to-peer electronic cash to eight other financial services. Taken together, these functions of financial services, which I have called the "Golden Nine," are undergoing a profound transition as Web3 tools begin to replace, augment, or enhance what traditional intermediaries do.[48]

1. **Moving value and payments:** We are moving from SWIFT, federal automated clearing house (ACH) services and other legacy systems to stablecoins and perhaps CBDCs.

2. **Authenticating value and identity:** We are moving from bank-verified compliance with know-your-customer (KYC), anti–money laundering (AML), and counter-terrorist financing (CTF) rules to on-chain credit scoring and Web3 reputation systems.

3. **Storing value:** We are moving from relying only on banks and other institutions to multisig wallets, self-custody solutions, and other methods. Banks and other intermediaries will continue to play important roles as trusted third parties, especially for institutions.

4. **Lending and borrowing value:** We are moving from banks as lenders to smart-contract-based lending pools, which connect borrowers and lenders automatically and peer-to-peer.

5. **Funding and investing value:** We are moving from initial public offerings (IPOs), venture capital, and Kickstarter campaigns to initial decentralized exchange offerings (IDOs) and other token-based crowdfunding models where the barrier and cost to launching a new asset or organization converge to zero.

6. **Exchanging value:** We are moving from centralized exchanges with order books maintained by companies or some other trusted intermediary to decentralized exchanges where users transact peer-to-peer and atomically via self-enforcing smart contracts, such as automated market makers (AMMs).

7. **Insuring value and managing risk:** We are moving from centralized insurance providers to prediction markets for investors, businesses, and everyday people who wish to offset risk.

8. **Accounting for and auditing value:** We are moving from traditional accounting and audit firms that prepare financial and audit statements to on-chain automated auditors. Blockchains leave a vast trove of immutable and trustworthy data that innovators can organize and audit via tools and dashboards to help investors and businesses make sense of these new complex systems.

9. **Analyzing value:** We are moving from analyzing financial statements to analyzing blockchain data on-chain.

DeFi can minimize friction and costs in financial services through its own set of primitives. To qualify as a DeFi dapp, an app must be difficult to shut down, run on a blockchain, and be trustless. Rune Christensen, founder of MakerDAO, said, "The main advantage and characteristic of DeFi is very similar to open-source software in that it's really about unlocking network effects and the value of people working together seamlessly and in a permissionless manner without intermediaries."[49] Venture capitalist Matt Huang, cofounder of Paradigm, added that some of these primitives "will transfer over from traditional finance (e.g., MakerDAO is a margin loan with automatic liquidation). Others will be wholly new (e.g., Uniswap opened up a broad design space around AMMs)."[50] The benefits are fivefold: lower costs, efficient accounting, total transparency, low switching costs, and broader access. Bankers ought to take notice: decentralized models can disrupt or replace much of the industry. Let's explore.

People in emerging markets often lack access to banking services. DeFi is permissionless—no gatekeepers—and so the main barrier to entry is an Internet connection, access to an Internet-connected device, and a decent helping of financial literacy. Uniswap founder Hayden Adams argued that because data and analytical tools are free and publicly accessible in DeFi, and "the balance sheets supporting lending or trading are transparent, anyone with an Internet connection can track a protocol's assets and liabilities on a per-second basis."[51] He cited this as a reason for venerable firms like JPMorgan Chase, Goldman Sachs, and the European Investment Bank to issue and trade assets on-chain to reduce "the settlement, operational, and liquidity risks vis-à-vis existing issuances."[52]

DeFi has pioneered several innovations, such as AMMs, which are decentralized exchanges like Uniswap, through which users can trade digital assets without a middleman. In their book, *DeFi and the Future of Finance*, Campbell Harvey, Ashwin Ramachandran, and Joey Santoro wrote, "An AMM is a smart contract that holds assets on both sides of a trading pair and continuously quotes a price for buying and selling. . . . From the contract's perspective, the price should be risk-neutral where it is indifferent to buying or selling."[53] In other words, the smart contract performs the same function as a centralized market maker at an exchange.

Consider Bancor, a DeFi trading and staking protocol governed by a DAO and credited with launching the first AMM.[54] Its founder, Galia Benartzi, explained that Bancor didn't develop the AMM as a financial primitive for traders and speculators but as a platform for bootstrapping community currencies for small populations with special needs. "If you're an island, or you want to join the United Nations, you want to become a new nation, you want to issue your own currency, that's great. But if no other country is going to accept your currency, then you're not going to be able to import or export anything, and so you'd better have a full-stack economy at your service."[55] Bancor saw an opportunity "in this new world of blockchain-based currencies." Benartzi said, "You could program liquidity into the currency itself, meaning you could program that exchangeability, that interoperability," so that the token itself would "mathematically 'know' its own exchange rate with any other token at any given moment."[56]

Indeed, AMMs are the dominant model for peer-to-peer trading in digital assets, but we could easily apply the model to most other assets and upend the traditional order books of mainstream finance, maintained by the New York Stock Exchange (NYSE) and other august organizations. For example, with lending protocols, lenders and borrowers can earn yields and access credit, respectively. New derivatives such as *perpetual futures* contracts allow users to speculate on the future value of assets or insure against risk. Unlike traditional futures contracts, they do not have a fixed expiry date. One specific lending innovation that could disrupt finance is the *flash loan*, "an instantaneous loan paid back within the same transaction," according to Harvey, Ramachandran, and Santoro.[57] They likened the flash loan "to an overnight loan in traditional finance but with a crucial difference: repayment is required within the transaction and enforced by the smart contract."[58] As a result, it eliminates both *duration risk* (the sensitivity to interest rates and time) and counterparty risk, but it introduces smart contract risk where hackers can exploit buggy code and drain the assets that the smart contract is holding on behalf of its users.

Because DeFi is open-source, people can easily copy and improve a

DeFi project or platform, in some cases "to poach liquidity or users by offering larger incentives than the platform it is copying."[59] This practice is known in the industry as *vampirism*, which can be good or bad. On one hand, offering a larger up-front share of a user-owned DeFi project can incentivize early adopters and help bootstrap a startup in the space. On the other hand, unscrupulous actors may offer, and indeed have offered, unsustainably high yields that come crashing down, harming everyone.

Another DeFi innovation is the *initial DeFi offering* (IDO) or *initial decentralized exchange* (DEX) offering—where an entrepreneur can launch a token, set a price by making a market against a stablecoin like USDC, and wait for buyers. If the token has utility and offers access to a nascent user-owner network, then it may be more valuable. The offspring of ICOs, IDOs are becoming an increasingly popular method for raising capital in Web3-native startups. Prediction markets are another DeFi-native innovation. To be sure, people have been wagering on the outcome of events like elections and sporting events for centuries. But DeFi makes it fully transparent and peer-to-peer and expands it to other hard-to-predict but easy-to-bet-on events like the weather. American essayist Charles Dudley Warner once quipped, "Everybody complains about the weather, but nobody does anything about it."[60] Prediction markets help us do something. We can use them to hedge against failed crops, if we're farmers. If we're Wall Street traders, we can offset the risk to our portfolio from failed trade deals, peace negotiations, interest rate hikes, or any other event-based risk.

New DeFi innovations like "flash loans" aside, good old-fashioned lending is foundational to financial services. A very smart banker once told me, "We move money. Because we move money, we get to store money. Because we store money, we get to lend money, and lending is pretty much our whole business." His point was that Web3 technologies like stablecoins could cut into the bank's role as payments provider, thus undercutting the foundation of his core business, lending. How is Web3 transforming lending? A DeFi lending pool is a platform for users to lend and borrow cryptocurrency or other digital assets without a TradFi institution.

Consider Compound, a lending market that offers several different assets for lending and borrowing. All the tokens are pooled together so that "every lender earns the same variable rate, and every borrower pays the same variable rate." All loans are overcollateralized. If a user's collateral dips below a certain threshold, the user's holdings are automatically liquidated. Compound has many advantages: lenders do not have counterparty risk that the borrower will default because all loans are overcollateralized. The ability to borrow and lend many different assets creates choice for users. Finally, Compound is composable with other applications: users can borrow money in one place and easily spend somewhere else. However, the platform also has risks and inefficiencies. Creditworthiness, for example, is irrelevant because loans are made anonymously. So someone with a stellar credit rating "in real life" borrows at the same rate as someone with no credit rating.

DeFi has another, more fundamental challenge to overcome: it is still largely a closed-loop system, meaning it does not export much economic value beyond the borrowing, lending, storing, moving, and exchanging of tokens. The reasons for this are threefold: First, to access services, most DeFi applications require users to post collateral, because DeFi today is anonymous. The second is that, by and large, collateral is exclusively cryptoassets rather than securities, cash, real estate, and so forth. In other words, prospective users must first acquire cryptoassets before they can use DeFi. Third, in TradFi, lenders use a person's credit score to evaluate the person's likelihood of paying a regular bill or repaying a periodic loan. In DeFi, reputation systems that gauge a user's ability and willingness to repay a loan are still in development, and so protocols default to overcollateralized loans.

Let's address these challenges head on. People may choose to borrow against their tokens to avoid triggering a capital gain, but that borrowed money could very well go to pay for a new car or a family vacation. That's a means of exporting economic value to the real world. People use home equity lines of credit and margin accounts in much the same way. Some businesses are using centralized stablecoins like USDC to make payroll or compensate contractors such as Korapay. Individuals are using stablecoins to store wealth, pay rent, and buy goods and services, and so we could similarly use a decentralized stablecoin like Maker Foundation's DAI. But so far, people are tinkering at the margin of DeFi today.

Lending pools do offer unsecured loans, but they typically target known institutional borrowers, not retail, that is, individuals. Sidney Powell of Maple, a DeFi lending pool, said, "Maple takes in deposits and aggregates them and then originates loans."[61] It sounds simple enough, but what makes it work are Web3 tools. Said Powell, "What smart contracts gave us was a really, really efficient tool to run a credit fund or that nonbank lending business on-chain. Because it's very easy to aggregate capital and to pass back repayments through to those LPs," meaning limited partners, or depositors in the pool.[62] At first Maple dealt only with crypto-native organizations like market makers and hedge funds. Soon other financial firms started to use it, and many instantly seized on the ease of use. Powell said, "The entirety of the workflow is occurring on-chain and facilitated by smart contracts." He added, "It's like I hit a button and then smart contract goes, 'Okay, now I'm disbursing and creating a loan. So, what's the interest rate on the loan? How frequently is it being repaid? Who's it going to? What term?' All of that's happening on-chain. That would otherwise be a bunch of data fields in a ledger at a bank [that] nobody else can see."[63] Maple had to work through some bad loans as fallout from the FTX collapse but is otherwise proving that businesses can borrow and lend using crypto-native platforms. However, this does not solve the issue of on-chain identity for regular users.

So how do we overcome these challenges? First, we must digitize more assets—not just traditional stocks and bonds, but titles and deeds to houses, property, and more. The push to onboard real-world assets is a focus of DeFi entrepreneurs. Ethereum founder Vitalik Buterin thinks DAO-governed, real-world, asset-backed stablecoins could be the bridge to connect DeFi and TradFi, while minimizing reliance on a single currency issuer like the United States.[64] That may take a while, but we are clearly heading in that direction. For example, MakerDAO has added US treasuries to the collateral for its native stablecoin, DAI. The DeFi project Parcl provides a simple way for Web3 users to buy digital tokens representing investments in real estate in major markets such as Manhattan and San Francisco.[65] This melding of traditional and digital markets will improve liquidity, stability, and functionality of DeFi tools. Second, we extend DeFi into the world of uncollateralized or retail credit, what we might consider *microloans*, and we create a Web3 credit score based on a user's on-chain reputation.

Reputation and Identity

Everyone has a reputation. We wrote about this in *Blockchain Revolution*, long before DeFi entered the vernacular: "Reputation is critical to trust in business and in everyday life. To date, financial intermediaries have not used reputation as the basis for establishing trust," preferring our FICO scores, Social Security numbers, and other identifiers. Credit scoring is a great business—companies voluntarily give customer information to the credit-scoring firms like Equifax, Experian, and TransUnion, and those firms package it with other information and sell it back to the companies that gave it customer data in the first place. Web3 entrepreneurs want to use on-chain reputation as a complement and eventually a substitute to conventional credit scoring.

Consider Sishir Varghese, founder of Spectral, who arrived in crypto from a typically atypical route—online poker. Perhaps his time at the poker table assessing probabilities gave him an innate feeling for risk, as he soon realized that DeFi lacked risk analysis of customers. Rather than bridge over a FICO score on-chain, he wondered whether he could "build permissionless or programmable creditworthiness," that is, an on-chain credit score.[66] Spectral has built the equivalent to a traditional FICO score, called the Multi-Asset Credit Risk Oracle (MACRO) score, for users to check their on-chain scores through its platform.

Unlike in traditional credit scores, the data are all on-chain.

Varghese said, "We want to make credit scoring a publicly accessible network so it's not gatekept by three credit bureaus in the West, and it's not controlled by the Chinese government issuing social credit scores in the East in the extreme dystopian version."[67] Despite aiming to replace the FICO score, Spectral is sticking with FICO's 300–850 score range, in a skeuomorphic nod to its off-chain predecessor.

Right now, Spectral, the company, is a chokepoint, and it is still developing a road map for fully decentralizing. It faces many challenges to building such a system, and surely many would seek to exploit or game it. As fintech writer Alex Johnson pointed out, "One of the benefits of centralization and KYC is that [they allow] lenders to feel confident that they are evaluating applicants' full credit histories." Regarding MACRO, Johnson imagined users opening "a bunch of Web3 wallets for interacting with DeFi protocols" so that, when they wanted to borrow, they could connect only those wallets that contributed positively to their MACRO scores.[68] Moreover, MACRO measures liquidation risk whereas FICO measures an individual's ability and willingness to repay a loan. Those are different metrics, and the former may not represent someone's creditworthiness. Identity is an important primitive of Web3, and an on-chain credit score could help strengthen it to open up a new range of services and products for Web3 users. If successful, DeFi could finally fulfill its potential to build a better financial system for everyone, not just the dedicated few.

In essence, on-chain identity comes with convenience and control. Said Stepan Gershuni of Gyde One, "Any Web3 identity service that I know, I can authenticate with my Ethereum address. If I have MetaMask, which is my single identity, I can even have zero tokens and zero cryptocurrency in it and still authenticate on any website."[69] That's more convenient than having eighty versions of identity on eighty Web2 platforms. As for control, he said, "You have all your data points attached to this identity, and you choose which application gets what. Today, when I sign in with Twitter, applications can request information from Twitter, but only what I have on Twitter." Twitter also gates the flow. "If Twitter decides that it wants to block something from the API, which it did a few times in the past, then nobody can get this information."[70] In a Web3 world, users hold the power, not the services they interact with.

Risks and Opportunities in DeFi

Of course, like many new industries, DeFi is a minefield of unprecedented and unforeseen risks. For example, while transactions in DeFi generate vast tracts of immutable and trustworthy on-chain data, they also rely on information from the real world. Let's say we have a smart contract that pays the holder if the price of Apple goes to X dollars, like a TradFi call option. How does the contract track the price of Apple? Enter *oracles*, data sources external to the blockchain that our smart contract calls on. This bridge to the off-chain world is an area needing greater investment and innovation, according to Harvey, Ramachandran, and Santoro: "Oracles are surely an open design question and challenge for DeFi to achieve utility beyond its own isolated chain."[71]

While DeFi eliminates counterparty risk, it adds to *regulatory risk*: with the exception of the Central Committee of the Chinese Communist Party and a handful of other countries that have banned crypto altogether, regulators are still wrapping their heads around DeFi.[72] The uncertainty weighs on innovation. Moreover, composability between different applications is aspirational, theoretical rather than real, because of interoperability challenges. DeFi also presents *governance risks*. Sure, token holders have a vote, but will they bother to participate?

DeFi innovators are already competing with the very institutions they hope to displace. Ethan Buchman of Cosmos worries that we are "replicating a lot of the existing patterns of behavior from Wall Street, the speculation, the casinos, rich-get-richer schemes, insiders, and so on." He added that if Wall Street co-opts DeFi and extends its high-tech shenanigan games to Web3, "that would be quite unfortunate."[73] The financial industry serves a critical role in the economy, and plenty of good actors work in it, but Buchman is correct that it's not known for restraint. Indeed, Wall Street traders have flocked to the moneymaking opportunities in DeFi as they did subprime mortgage-backed securities and collateralized debt obligations in the oughts. The industry has attracted the "peculiar collection of shrewd businessmen, criminals, adventurers, and smooth-talking hustlers who always seek opportunity in an unexplored land," to quote from novelist and historian Irene Vallejo's work *Papyrus*.[74] Buchman thinks the industry needs to leap forward from degenerate behavior to regenerative behavior, focused on building new, more inclusive, and sustainable models.

Another risk is that this new financial frontier foments the same mercenary zero-sum mentality that characterizes the darker and weirder sides of traditional markets. At the peak of the first wave in 2022, I interviewed Lex Sokolin, chief economist at ConsenSys. He said, "Every fourteen-year-old on TikTok is now a derivatives CDO financial engineer. If you don't like that, then it's too bad because it's too late. It's literally too late to put that back into the Pandora's box. So you've got millions of amateur financial engineers in this extremely complex but unbelievably compelling dopamine world, who are sticking together into tribes organized through trolling, memes, cartoon characters, and populist anarchocapitalism, and it's just wildness, right?"[75] It sounds exciting and sexy but not stable footing for the world's next financial infrastructure.

DeFi also adds *smart contract risk*, the risk that clever hackers will exploit a flaw in the coding or design or the rules of a system. "A key tenet of economic analysis is that enterprises are unable to devise contracts that cover all possible eventualities," according to the Bank for International Settlements. "Centralization allows firms to deal with this 'contract incompleteness.'"[76] In DeFi, the equivalent concept is "algorithm incompleteness," where writing code that addresses all contingencies is impossible.[77] Web3 die-hards will say that, because the code of each contract is totally transparent, a hacker is merely using it as explicitly "written." Caveat emptor.

Matt Levine, a columnist for Bloomberg, pointed out that "[i]n crypto, explicit rules are very popular." Developers often code rules into computer programs and open-source smart contracts that anyone can read. "If you find a clever way to exploit them—to 'hack' the smart contract, or to 'manipulate' the market, to use loaded, traditional terms—then you can do that, quickly and efficiently and at scale."[78] Levine speculated that unwritten "norms" of behavior might regulate this kind of behavior and even make it useful. Describing this new norm, Levine said, "If you hack a decentralized finance protocol and run off with a bunch of money, you can keep some of it as a reward for your cleverness, but you have to return most of it because keeping it all would be mean and perhaps a crime." This effectively turns a malicious attack into an ex post facto "bug bounty," of the kind paid to beta testers who point out flaws in code before software is released. Levine added, "If you find a flaw in a protocol's security, they should pay you a reward for pointing it out, but you should not get to take all their money."[79] As in most social groups, norms will develop. But is putting our trust into the hands of a criminal or malicious actor in keeping with Web3? Is it a reliable and replicable approach on a large scale? Does it matter whether the exploiter is a teenager honing his skills in his parents' basement, a state-sponsored cyber terrorist, or a malicious hacker from one of the world's largest criminal syndicates?

Instead, we need technological solutions to strengthen and foolproof these systems, when possible. "Some programming languages are better than others for building secure systems because they provide safeguards, checks that show how the program will work," said Ali Yahya of Andreessen Horowitz. "There's a broad spectrum of tools that you could use, like [Facebook's] Move programming language." Based on Rust and developed in conjunction with Facebook's Libra cryptocurrency initiative, Move has native support for what Facebook calls "resource types," that is, data types that represent money or assets in the language.[80] "The compiler and the execution environment protect against [possibilities] that you wouldn't ever want to happen to an asset, like duplication. You can go all the way to what's known as 'formal verification,'" Yahya said.[81] He summarized his thoughts: "The combination of better human practices with better technology will get us there. It's not an intractable problem, and these apply not just to smart contract risk but also to bridging."[82]

Another old-fashioned solution to smart contracting risk is to hire a company to audit the code before it ships. The better their reputation, the more weight their "Good Housekeeping Seal of Approval" will carry. Zeppelin, a favorite of companies like Coinbase as well as the Ethereum Foundation, Compound, Aave, and others, tries to solve for three related problems: (1) security, namely exposure to hacking or attack, (2) the developer experience, namely lack of proper development and testing tools, which can create errors, and (3) operations, specifically managing and fixing problems in dapps once deployed, which can be tricky. A security audit verifies that the system works as intended. Sometimes it's okay to put some trust in the experts.

How Should We Value Web3 Assets?

The first-ever stock market popped up spontaneously in Amsterdam in 1602, as a venue to trade shares in the newly incorporated Dutch East India Company, one of the first of a novel breed of organization known as the joint-stock company, discussed earlier. Since then, publicly traded companies have become increasingly dominant forces in business and the economy.

Despite the long and illustrious history of the public company, *securities analysis*—how we determine the worth of shares in a company or some other asset—is relatively modern. Benjamin Graham and David Dodd wrote what has become the sacred text of value investing, *Security Analysis*, in 1934.[83]

If most capital formation occurs at the protocol and distributed application level in Web3, then we need to develop a methodology and framework for valuing digital assets, just as Graham and Dodd developed a method for the analog assets of their time. As with traditional corporations, we can look at the people involved, the business model, product offering, and market position, and come up with a value. To these traditional metrics we can add community: How engaged are participants? What is the size of the blockchain economy they're building? How quickly does money circulate through it? We can analyze the tokenomic model, the governance model, and the technology's performance. We can look at the token distribution model, the fee structure, and the token float, roughly akin to the share count of a company. Just as the number of shares can increase and shrink, so too can the number of tokens outstanding. Whatever valuation we ascribe to a digital asset depends on this all-important number, because it is the denominator in many of our quantitative metrics.

Network participants need incentives to contribute their time, energy, and computers to processing transactions and securing the network. User-owned networks offer rewards to early participants, adding new tokens to the ones outstanding, thus increasing the float. Right now, bitcoin miners receive newly minted bitcoin in exchange for their efforts. PoS networks like Cosmos and Cardano have token floats that grow steadily. Applications built on top of these kinds of networks like Uniswap (a decentralized exchange) or Compound (a decentralized lending product) also issue tokens that, over time, increase the float of tokens outstanding. Users can take tokens out of circulation by "burning" them, that is, by sending them to a wallet address to which no one has the keys (that is, no one can retrieve them). In TradFi markets, we call this "retiring stock." In a company, if the share count increases without earnings increasing by an equivalent amount, then the additional shares are dilutive. Similarly, if the token float increases more than the underlying protocol revenue, it dilutes token-holder value.

Web3 investors are reimagining elements such as earnings per share and stock buybacks as "protocol revenue per token" and "token burns." Consider Ethereum. Its recent upgrades, known as "the Merge" and Ethereum Improvement Proposal-1559, were watersheds for Web3 because they reduced the carbon footprint of Ethereum by more than 99 percent and cut the inflation rate of ETH by 90 percent—and they did so by implementing proof of stake and changing Ethereum's market mechanism, so that it burns a portion of the ETH used to pay for transaction fees, increasing the scarcity of ETH.[84] Stakers still receive new ETH, but as network demand has steadied, the amount burned has begun to match (and even exceed) the amount issued.

Tim Beiko, a core contributor to Ethereum and one of the lead architects of the Ethereum Merge, broke down the process: "If you give validators issuance and part of transaction fees, but burn the rest of transaction fees, when the burn offsets issuance, you get both rewards and deflation, along with a sustainable security budget."[85] The key driver of this process is the sustained growing interest in using the Ethereum network. If nobody wants to transact on the network, then no fees will offset the issuance of new tokens. This unsustainable dilution spiral has weighed on many would-be competitors to Ethereum. At the time of this writing, Ethereum has a steady to declining float and flat or growing earnings. In traditional financial parlance, this system is *accretive* to token holders. Like Apple, which uses a portion of its profits to buy its own stock, thereby reducing the float and increasing earnings per share, Ethereum's burn mechanism drives value long-term to token holders.

Charting the Financial Frontier of Web3

Just as cell phones allowed billions to leapfrog landlines, DeFi might allow people to leapfrog traditional banks and other intermediaries, particularly in the Global South. Uniswap has had many days where its volumes exceeded those on Coinbase, an NYSE-listed company. The automated investment aggregator YFI (pronounced "Wi-fi"), through which investors pool capital into a smart contract that makes investments on their behalf, hit a total value locked of $7 billion within its first year. By contrast, Wealthsimple took more than six years to reach the same level. The stablecoin DAI does around $500 million a day in volume, which is more than Venmo, a popular payment app in the United States.[86] The stablecoin USDC, while not strictly a DeFi asset because it holds its collateral in centralized financial institutions, facilitated $4.5 trillion worth of transactions on the Ethereum blockchain in 2022 alone, or more than $12 billion per day.[87]

The experience with cell phones taught us that building out infrastructure is costly, whether it's 5G or satellite. Does DeFi have the same problem? On one hand, DeFi is permissionless and available to anyone with an Internet connection. On the other hand, you need to own cryptoassets and have access to an Internet-enabled device and decent Internet. So, there are still huge barriers. The history of telecommunications in emerging markets may provide a road map for those looking to deliver DeFi at scale. Cell phone providers gave away handsets when rolling out mobile service. DeFi protocols give something else away—ownership of the platform itself—but that may not entice most people better than a free phone. Moreover, DeFi protocols are nowhere near as well capitalized as telecommunications companies and cannot subsidize growth to the same extent.

An enlightened government could build its own user interface for a DeFi protocol to broaden access to financial services in a given region where banks are currently failing, as in remittances. According to the World Bank, despite the benefits of traditional fintech (not DeFi, but the same logic applies), the burden of compliance with AML and CTF regulations continues to restrict access of new service providers to correspondent banks in developing countries. These regulations also affect migrants' access to digital remittance services. To sum up, DeFi innovators face challenges to widespread adoption, including regulatory uncertainty, security risks, and lack of accessibility. Despite all of these, the potential benefits of DeFi are too great to ignore. Today's financial giants should take note.

Conclusion and Takeaways

Web2 has several shortcomings: it funneled Internet users into walled gardens and mined them for insights as advertising became the Web2's business model. Financial intermediaries enriched themselves with little innovation. Centralized platforms created monopolies, stifling innovation. These limits created opportunities for new solutions in various industries:

1. Financial services have an opportunity to reimagine everything the industry does: identity, moving and storing money, providing credit, raising growth capital, insuring against risk, market making in financial products, and much more. This is not digital wallpaper but a new architecture for the world's most important industry.

2. DeFi is the vanguard in building a truly Internet-native financial industry. DeFi benefits from greater composability, liquidity, and programmability. It does not require formal verification and thus is easier to access for the unbanked.

3. DeFi has various shortcomings, including regulatory uncertainty, smart contract risk, oracle risk, and fraud. These are implementation challenges that can be overcome with time.

4. Stablecoins are driving deeper connections and integrations between TradFi and DeFi. Stablecoins are a hybrid model (Web2.5) that will become the norm as banks and other enterprises adopt the Web3 toolkit.

CHAPTER 7

Gaming

In Web2, gamers may pay for digital goods, but they do not own them. Players are, at best, renting them for a period. The industry's business model has evolved to a so-called "freemium" model where players can purchase in-game assets. As mentioned, this does not deter Internet users from supporting the market for these digital rentals: we spend $100 billion a year on digital goods that we don't truly own. Roblox, for example, makes almost all its $1.9 billion in annual revenue from selling an in-game currency called "Robux."[1] With 50 million daily users, Robux is one of the most widely used "virtual currencies" in the world. However, it is not a digital bearer asset in a true sense. While users can trade Roblox for money, it still exists at the whim of the company. Users have no property rights.

This lack of rights has not stopped people from building markets in virtual assets. Since those early days, a market for virtual assets has thrived, however illicit. Said Yat Siu of Animoca Brands, "The black market of selling virtual items existed for decades, first in a small, and eventually in a larger way, but always black market. Even today, if you go on eBay, you can see people selling accounts, which is a proxy for selling digital assets."[2]

Some entrepreneurs have tried to build legitimate businesses trading in virtual assets, only for gaming companies to shut them down because the businesses were against the gaming terms of service. "You actually don't own your stuff," said Siu. "So, this struggle existed in our industry before blockchain. When blockchain came about, with this distributed, independent, decentralized way of storing assets outside centralized control, that's where it clicked for us, and we said, 'Okay, building on top of that, we think, will change everything.'"[3]

Web3 videogames will augment the freemium model by allowing players to own rather than rent their virtual goods. For our purposes, Web3 gaming refers to games that offer true digital asset ownership and may include monetary rewards as part of gameplay. Web3 will also challenge the rent-seeking model of the leading operating systems of Android and Apple by enabling players to buy and sell assets to each other directly, thus disintermediating these companies from in-app purchases. Token-gated communities could replace traditional social networks while community-owned content will empower fans and challenge the traditional studio production model for all kinds of content, including games.

From Free-to-Play to Play-to-Earn

Mobile free-to-play games first became popular shortly after the invention of the iPhone. Offering users a fun and simplistic form of gameplay, these downloadable apps appealed to commuters with a few minutes to shoot down some *Angry Birds* with a slingshot, for example. Users could download and even play the game for free, but to unlock certain features they needed to pay. These early games were inferior to the traditional gaming model in most ways that mattered to the core market. Most people were not paying to play because they were not serious gamers. For an executive at Sony or Microsoft, this kind of customer was not valuable compared to a core console gamer, who would spend $500 for a PlayStation or Xbox, and hundreds more on games (discs played like DVDs in consoles) and hardware accessories. Consequently, the big companies in the core market ignored the free-to-play market initially. They focused on their core customers at the time, not on some small, low-revenue segment that was unproven and even a bit gimmicky. That's good business, right? That's the innovator's dilemma, whether to develop new products that your best customers don't care about. Even when corporate executives do embrace them, often they get the timing wrong, spend too little (and occasionally too much), or fail to grasp what makes the new market or technology so disruptive.

An iPhone in 2009 did not pack the same punch as an Xbox. But an iPhone in 2022 does. Free-to-play games we downloaded to our phones were initially gimmicky and simplistic. Today, mobile gaming accounts for 57 percent of all gaming revenue, half of which are free to play. The sideshow market became the market.[4] The growth of free-to-play was not a zero-sum outcome for traditional platforms. Its success, along with mobile gaming, significantly grew the total size of the market for gamers as it lowered the barriers significantly for people to play, effectively acting as an on-ramp and leading to growth in so-called "premium console games" such as *Call of Duty* as well.

Yat Siu credited the mobile gaming revolution and free-to-play games for rescuing the gaming business from a deep slump. "Most people may not remember that, between 2009 and 2010, the gaming industry stagnated. . . . A lot of people became very bearish on Sony" because sales of the PlayStation were stagnating.[5] Game studios and technology companies were targeting "the one customer who was going to buy twenty games a month. And the customer would go to Target, or GameStop, or wherever to buy these games, and everything centered around that. Eventually, it hit a limit."[6]

The big breakthrough? Free-to-play gaming amateurized gameplay just as Instagram amateurized photography, according to Siu. "Everyone, from my grandma to my mom, became an expert gamer, starting with *Angry Birds* and *Candy Crush*. A subset of those ended up going, 'Oh, actually, I love gaming. I didn't know it was that much fun.'"[7] The try-it-for-free business model helped gaming expand beyond a "niche" market of 400 million players to the more than 3 billion gamers today. Mobile free-to-play games became a gateway for many who ended up becoming more serious, buying consoles. "Suddenly, sales of console games went up and the entire industry increased because . . . the mobile industry brought them billions of users," said Siu.[8]

"Before NFT gaming, the revolution was the free-to-play market. In the past, the bigger companies had difficulty transitioning from the traditional way of doing gaming into mobile free-to-play," said Ria Lu of Web3 gaming startup Laguna Games. She added, "It was not because they lacked resources or anything. Usually, it's the indie game companies who are into the new thing . . . because they enjoy playing around with it. Versus large companies who usually get in on it because the market is going that way, and therefore it's a business decision."[9] Lu pointed out how initially "smaller and more independent developers made free-to-play games like *Angry Birds*" and that "only much later did we have large companies getting into mobiles because that's where the market was going to be."[10]

We may see these dynamics play out with NFT games, too. Today many NFT games may seem inferior, but a small segment of the market thinks ownership of digital goods and economic consequences are incredibly important. Token-gated communities create a sense of shared ownership that has gained traction. Plus, some people like making money inside the economies of NFT-based games. If we combine all these factors, we have a recipe for continuous improvement as it encourages Web3 developers to continue building out new titles. Aleksander Larsen, cofounder and chief operating officer of game publisher Sky Mavis, believes that when Web3 games reach "feature parity" with Web2 games, meaning the gameplay is the same quality and immersiveness, the Web3 game will win "10 out of 10 times."[11] Larsen may be correct that Web3 gaming will come to dominate the industry, "winning out" over other models. But it is also possible that it merely grows the whole pie, bringing in new people to gaming who previously were not drawn to it, just as free-to-play gaming grew the overall market.

Earning and Owning Should Enhance Gameplay, Not Replace It

Lu said that ownership was one of several features of Web3 applications, but utility and fun should come first. She likened the digital goods in her game *Crypto Unicorns* to jewelry.[12] People buy emeralds because they like to wear them. Perhaps they will sell the gems someday but selling and realizing a profit was not what drew them to buy emeralds in the first place. "Do I buy the jewelry because I can sell it? Not necessarily. I buy it because I enjoy wearing it, because I enjoy having it, and I want people to see NFT gaming as like that," she said. "You buy NFTs for the game because you want to play the game. It just so happens that it has value. That's my dream for the industry if it's going to move forward."[13] She said that "when NFT games started really blowing up, people never really went into NFT gaming because they liked the game. They came in because they could make money. But it's a game. You have to like the game, you have to like the experience, right?"[14]

Siu used a similar analogy: games that have a strong community and culture are likely to succeed because people have an emotional attachment to cultural artifacts beyond their intrinsic worth. He gave the example of wedding rings. "Wedding rings are very fungible. They all cost the same, and they're all made of the same material. But the moment that you buy a wedding ring, it becomes very meaningful. It becomes priceless. You can't sell it, if you treasure your relationship."[15]

In Lu's view, since players own assets of the NFT game, they have more ownership in the game. "You are more invested in it. You feel that the game is partly yours." Contrast that with free-to-play games, said Lu, where gamers spend money on "virtual coins" like Robux, but "[i]f you're tired of the game, it's like, okay, I'm done, I'm going to stop playing. Whatever you put in, it's lost. It's gone, because it's virtual and it isn't going to be important anywhere else."[16] If the main character is your NFT, like a unicorn in Lu's game *Crypto Unicorns*, then you can resell it when you no longer want to play the game. "So, it's not like a total loss." In that sense, Lu said, the Web3 gaming experience is a little different from the Web2 game, "because I don't have to lose everything that I put in."[17] On the player side, owning tokens creates a Web3 community and may lead to more collaboration and connections among players.

Another member of the Laguna Games team is product director Katrina Wolfe. An avid gamer herself, she knew she wanted to make a career of her passion and work with diverse people with varied skill sets. She joined Laguna Games in 2022 after a seven-year stint at another independent studio, Kongregate. Wolfe thinks ownership can enrich existing gameplay. She told me she's the kind of person who spends hours developing avatars for different games, so even pfp NFT projects appealed to her. The idea of owning that avatar appeals to gamers like herself. Aleksander Larsen of Sky Mavis had something similar to say: "Looking back at my history as a competitive gamer, when I was winning these massively important matches, I had no way to prove that it really happened, because it's legacy Internet. You might google my name, find me or my nickname mentioned somewhere in the dregs of Internet history. But if I had an NFT issued by the creator of that game, as a representation as an achievement, that could be mine, a part of my digital identity."[18]

Wolfe said that user-generated content also enriches games. "I played so many *Skyrim* mods and different mods from other games, and there are so many people with amazing ideas all over the world," she said. "I think this ability to have ownership and revenue—and having systems that support very creative people to generate content all over the world—is unlocking the potential of games."[19]

Sascha Mojtahedi proposed a different spin on the play-to-earn game when developing *Parallel*, an NFT card game: "We thought about it more as 'win to earn.' We didn't reward people for playing. Just because you don't reward people in a videogame if you lose. You reward them only if they win."[20] But, like others, Mojtahedi sees the social aspect of gameplay as foundational to any success with Web3 gaming. The experience must be fun to overcome gamers' initial apprehension about Web3 games, which he chalks up to fears about overmonetization. What gets gamers coming back? "One, they're super fun to play. Two, they're social. People want to play these games to interact socially with each other," said Mojtahedi. "We play *Warzone* because we get to chat on voice headset. It's like taking a phone call with your friends where you're running around and shooting stuff."[21]

Benjamin Lee of Blowfish Studios has been developing games since 1998. With his partner Aaron Grove, he has created some popular titles like *Siegecraft*, which topped the gaming charts in the Apple App Store for a period. Lee always has his eye on what's next: first, it was PCs, then mobile and VR, and now Web3. Like Ria Lu, Lee saw flaws in the early Web3 model: most players were "getting in and cashing out straightaway," as if they were "doing a job." Second, "the gameplay layer was very shallow. It was more just clickers . . . which didn't suit Blowfish because we're a traditional game developer. For the last twelve years, we've been focusing on premium games."[22] At the same time, ownership as a user experience resonated with Lee: "Transferring money around the world instantly without going through banks was quite powerful."[23] Lee wanted to apply it to gaming.

Lee described his vision for players of Blowfish's first Web3 game, *Phantom Galaxies*: "You're playing because you're just having fun. You're engaged with the world and building up your character, your ships, and the assets that you own. . . . Even *World of Warcraft* is about your items, and so people are playing that for fun. They're not playing it for monetary gain."[24] He said, "We were confident *Phantom Galaxies* was going to be a fun game to play because we had pitched it initially to some partners just as a traditional game, and they were very positive on it. We were going to have a retail distribution. Taking it to the blockchain meant we didn't have to go with the traditional route or traditional partners, which let us be a lot more experimental, more innovative with the way we're handling it."[25] As someone who likes to work on the bleeding edge of the gaming industry, Lee found Web3 liberating.

Lu of Laguna Games had this advice for developers who are newcomers to Web3 games: "Treat it as a normal game. Have the elements that a normal game would have—interesting gameplay, interesting characters, interesting art." Regarding her game *Crypto Unicorns*, her studio wanted it to feel like a great game. Her team consists of "traditional game people—people who've been in the game industry for quite some time." She made it clear: "We didn't form Laguna Games to make NFT games. We're a game company. We're game people. We have pride in our work." She also said, "Be thoughtful. We really thought out how to design these unicorns, how we name them, how we breed them, which classes we're going to release, and what fun stuff they can do. Can they farm? Can they do this, can they do that?"

Defining the Role of Digital Goods in Web3 Games

Digital goods play as many roles in Web3 games as they do in other Web3 applications. They can be collectibles, prizes, or useful assets like a sword or shield. They can be virtual land or some other productive asset that exists only in the game. They can be status symbols for a player's digital identity, like a profile picture or building blocks for the player's in-game reputation. They can be credentials to unlock in-game experiences. Though nascent, these games could begin to mirror economies in the real world. For example, games are using digital goods as rewards for players' time and energy. This incentive has the potential to enhance gameplay and drive new users. Or it could sour people on a game before it even has a chance to get off the ground. *Axie Infinity* is a play-to-earn game that users in the Philippines flocked to, to earn in-game rewards. "In the Global South, there is the incentive to learn, and that incentive is high enough for them to bother doing that. But in the West, the incentive relative to what they might earn or the time they might spend to learn it and the risk they take is not equivalent to the labor they have to put in," according to Aleksander Larsen of Sky Mavis.[26] The only catch is, users need to buy their characters to play it.

For a period, players were earning $800 a month just from playing the videogame, so the cost of the player was not a big deal. In one stretch of thirty days in 2021, 2.5 million were playing the game.[27] "*Axie Infinity* is a game where you can earn tokenized resources. These may or may not have value; it's an open market as created and defined by the players themselves. There's a speculative nature to the game," Larsen said. "I have seen how the crypto narrative oftentimes gets very perverted and driven by those who might be purely profit oriented. To me, that's very scary because we tried to create a game that should be fun."[28] To Larsen, it was about the shared journey, not the destination. As with so many Web3 inventions, a creator releases something into the world, and a community forms around it and builds on it in unexpected ways.

For example, to cover the cost of joining—as much as $1,500—some players seek sponsorship from managers or "guilds" that fund the new players' entry into the game, in exchange for a cut of these players' in-game earnings. According to journalist Vittoria Elliott, "Guilds can sprawl hundreds of members managing various accounts, honing *Axie* characters and churning the value of the *Axie*'s Infinity Shard token ever higher."[29] Whether in guilds or as individuals, *Axie* players have made enough money that the Philippine government wanted to subject *Axie* awards to income taxes.[30] Alas, within a year, that reward had plummeted to ten dollars. Some people were out of pocket and unable to earn it back. Many soured on the game.

Other problems beset *Axie*, such as the March 2022 hack of a bridge to *Axie*, which players were using to move assets into the game environment.[31] The North Korean hackers diverted more than $600 million, $30 million of which law enforcement was able to recover.[32] Despite these setbacks, this pioneer of Web3 gaming is working to regain its momentum.[33] For Beryl Li, whose company Yield Guild Games helped organize many *Axie* guilds, it has "proven that people demand games to have rewards. It was the first game and has inspired several developers and game designers to create games designed after *Axie*, or slightly improved from what they've learned from *Axie*."[34] Of course, earning money playing videogames is not an entirely new concept: in games like *World of Warcraft*, players could earn the in-game asset "gold." However, in play-to-earn games, individuals can earn far more fungible assets that they own and can manage outside the game itself.

One lesson is, speculators and mercenaries will play games, take advantage of token rewards, flip their in-game assets, and move on. Once again, the raison d'être of the game cannot be merely to earn tokens. The lesson seems to be that, while the assets themselves can be an important part of the gameplay, they should probably not be the sole reason for a game existing.

How Should Incumbents React?

Will game studios and other industry leaders realize this late, as they did with F2P games? As of December 2022, there were 1,873 Web3 games, an increase of 34 percent in less than a year.[35]

So far, the reaction to NFT games from these circles has been mixed. Tim Sweeney, founder of Epic Games, has been positive on the underlying technology, saying that we will soon "come to the realization that the blockchain is really a general mechanism for running programs, storing data, and verifiably carrying out transactions. It's a superset of everything that exists in computing." He said, "We'll eventually come to look at it as a computer that's distributed and runs a billion times faster than the computers we have on our desktops, because it's the combination of everyone's computer."[36] Epic has allowed others to sell NFT games on the Epic Games store. When asked about Microsoft's decision to block NFTs in *Minecraft*, Sweeney said, "Developers should be free to decide how to build their games, and you are free to decide whether to play them. I believe stores and operating system makers shouldn't interfere by forcing their views onto others. We definitely won't."[37]

Sweeney's Epic Games has recently stumbled in a way we normally associate with Web2 companies. In December 2022, the company reached a settlement with the FTC and agreed to pay $520 million in fines and rebates to users. The FTC said *Fortnite*'s "counterintuitive, inconsistent, and confusing button configuration led players to incur unwanted charges based on the press of a single button." The FTC added that design tactics like dark patterns "led to hundreds of millions of dollars in unauthorized charges for consumers." *Fortnite*, Epic's most popular title, counts kids as players, and the regulatory action reflected that. In an interview with Canada's CBC, independent technology analyst Carmi Levy said, "I think this sends a hugely important and historic message to the rest of the industry that, when you're dealing with kids online, you have an additional standard of care that you have to adhere to."[38]

The FTC also said the game developer violated privacy laws and "required parents who requested that their children's personal information be deleted to jump through unreasonable hoops, and sometimes failed to honor such requests."[39] In response to the settlement, Epic said, "We accepted this agreement because we want Epic to be at the forefront of consumer protection and provide the best experience for our players. Over the past few years, we've been making changes to ensure our ecosystem meets the expectations of our players and regulators, which we hope will be a helpful guide for others in our industry."[40] Epic makes great games. Despite what appears to be an obvious oversight on its part, it has been a pioneer in a new model for gaming and unlocked real innovation.

Of course, a Web3 game developer could just as easily build a front-end user interface to its online world or a game with dark patterns that confuses people into buying digital goods. But a user typically needs to sign any transaction in the user's wallet of choice, like signing a bill at the end of the meal, and that added friction could deter such "accidental charges." Also, in the Web3 hypothetical, the fooled party at least truly owns the digital asset and can resell it, but that would be cold comfort to someone who felt deceived or duped. More likely, Web3 game users would have better protection of their personal data from the outset, as they can play games pseudo-anonymously via their wallets.

As an innovative game publisher, Epic could benefit from the growth of the digital goods market, as a great game could have a thriving economy with assets whose value could accrue to their creators. There is a bigger play here: digital assets like NFTs existentially threaten the platform monopoly on in-game purchases. "Allowing *Call of Duty: Mobile* to connect a cryptocurrency wallet would be akin to a user connecting the game directly to their bank account, rather than paying through the app store," Matthew Ball wrote.[41] He wondered how such a platform could continue justifying its 30 percent take of all sales and resales of NFTs: "if such commissions did apply, the entirety of the NFT's value would be devoured if it traded hands enough times."[42]

Traditional gaming developers and the platforms themselves face other risks under the current model. For example, they can't block the sale of assets bought in a game. "They're not even actively informed of it (though the transaction is recorded on a public ledger)," Ball wrote. In his analysis, developers couldn't "'lock' blockchain-based assets into a virtual world. If Game A sells an NFT, Games B, C, D, and so on can incorporate it if the owner so chooses," meaning that some games might be very popular but not profitable because people are importing digital goods bought elsewhere.[43] Indeed, how would Game B "know" the utility of the asset designed for Game A?

Sascha Mojtahedi of *Parallel* said this composability is one of Web3 gaming's biggest breakthroughs, freeing digital goods from closed worlds. But he also acknowledged that this will be difficult to implement: "What happens when you have a shield from some medieval NFT, and it's 3D. I have a laser rifle from *Parallel*, and it's 3D. What happens when I shoot your shield with my laser rifle? You need a framework for this to work," Mojtahedi said, adding, "We can create all these objects, but then we have no idea how they interact."[44]

NFT games not only challenge the videogames studio model but the entire Web2 model of centralized control by platforms like Apple and Google. Gaming is the starting point for many when trying out Web3, and so it can be an important building block to someone's on-chain identity. Earlier we spoke about a DeFi credit score, but someone could just as easily build a solid reputation by how they behave in games. For some projects, that goal is explicit. Beryl Li of Yield Guild Games said that YGG is focused on building reputation-based identities for its users. Li said its reputation system uses soulbound tokens, "where individuals or participants are members of the DAO and can enhance their identities to access future applications—such as uncollateralized loans, insurance, and other dapps within the entire Web3 network."[45] YGG's fastest-growing markets are not what one might expect. "We started in the Philippines, so that has always been our biggest market. Then it widely spread to Indonesia, Vietnam. We were really surprised to see visitors from Latin America, like Venezuela. Yes, Venezuela, Colombia, and then Peru. Suddenly we see players from Brazil and India as well."[46]

Overcoming the Apple and Google duopoly will be key to Web3 gaming's success, especially in the Global South. "There are more mobile phones in the Philippines than there are people in the Philippines. Most of the country has access to the mobile phone, to the smartphone. If the company aims to reach the Philippine market, it has to be on mobile," distributed via mobile, said Ria Lu of Laguna Games.[47] The trouble is, Google and Apple app stores tend to exclude Web3 gaming apps. "That's what we need to figure out—how we can distribute our games. If we want to be in the hands of the majority of the population of the Philippines, we need to be on mobile. Because not everybody has a computer or laptop in the Philippines."[48]

Look past Web3 gaming's growing pains and you'll uncover a fundamental truth: if people are willing to spend money on in-game assets, they might as well own them outright. If they own them outright, they're going to care more about the economy of the game. If they care more about the economy of the game, they may choose to play longer, so long as the gameplay is as fun as any other game. As in-game economies grow more complex, they push the design frontier for Web3 developers and widen the market for potential players.

Incumbents should pay heed. Indeed, Web3 has been poaching Web2 managerial talent. In December 2022, Yuga Labs announced that it had hired away Daniel Alegre, chief operating officer of Activision Blizzard, to serve as Yuga's CEO and steward its efforts in gaming and the metaverse.[49] Alegre's departure said a lot about how rapidly Web3 gaming is maturing. After all, Activision is an industry juggernaut and publishes the *Call of Duty*, *Tony Hawk's Pro Skater*, and *Crash Bandicoot* franchises. It's also the target of a takeover bid by Microsoft, which the US government is fiercely contesting on antitrust grounds. Yuga, by contrast, publishes the Bored Ape Yacht Club.[50] But Alegre will oversee the development of *Otherside*, the virtual world funded by an ongoing NFT sale of virtual goods called Otherdeeds.[51]

Traditional game publishers have clearly taken notice, but can they disrupt themselves smartly so that they position themselves for the next era of gaming, whatever it may be? "It's almost like the innovator's dilemma with the big gaming studios," said Messari's Ryan Selkis. "Maybe it's an opportunity for one of the laggards to refocus their efforts on Web3-native games and lean in there for a long-term play and how they could outflank some of their rivals."[52] Industry leaders who are as "resolutely opposed to all innovation," as media philosopher Marshall McLuhan was, would be wise to do what McLuhan did: "I am determined to understand what's happening. I don't choose to just sit back and let the juggernaut roll over me."[53]

Gamification Beyond Videogames

The success of Web3 games with their play-to-earn economics has motivated other entrepreneurs to try out other creative ways to induce users to sign up. One category, the so-called "move-to-earn" applications, targets people who want to exercise and like earning a bit on the side for doing it. In the wake of the success of move-to-earn apps, developers have experimented with other X-to-earn concepts, including "learn-to-earn," such as RabbitHole and Hooked. RabbitHole is an ingenious concept—it pays users in rewards for learning about Web3, thus inviting new Web3 users to "build an on-chain résumé," an immutable record of their accomplishments that they could use to prove to an employer they are well trained.[54] This could be the model for credentialing in many professions.

Research firm The Block recently reported, "StepN's success hinges on the gamification of its fitness app and the incorporation of in-game rewards via the move-to-earn mechanism. As the market leader in move-to-earn, it attracted more than three million monthly active users at its peak in April, resulting in a high trading volume of its Sneaker NFTs, which generated $149.3 million of revenue in H1 2022," adding that, "despite the impressive revenue, StepN's tokenomics has proven unsustainable as [its] token supply has continued to become net inflationary in the absence of sufficient user demand."[55] As with play-to-earn games, many X-to-earn concepts still need to work out some growing pains with their tokenomics.

Done correctly, move-to-earn dapps could have a big and unexpected impact, not only on gaming but on healthcare, finance, and government budgets. "Nature doesn't want us to be active," said Oleg Fomenko, founder of Sweatcoin, because "burning calories is actually detrimental to your survival action." Fomenko noticed his own health deteriorating after a lifetime climbing mountains for fun. "I could barely run a 5K," he said. He needed an incentive, an inducement—

some form of instant gratification. That was the inspiration for Sweat-coin, "a currency backed by the value of physical activity," founded in 2017.[56] Fast-forward to today and Sweatcoin is arguably the most pop-ular Web3 application out there. According to its website, Sweatcoin has 120 million users in more than 60 different countries. The dapp is simple: users earn Sweatcoins for provably moving.

Rather than Bitcoin's proof of work, Sweatcoin relies on proof of physical activity as its consensus mechanism. At $50 million market capitalization, the GDP of the so-called "movement economy" is very small indeed, though Sweatcoin's current value plus the value of all future rewards is closer to $1 billion.[57] But Fomenko believes the eco-nomic upside is significant, and the market needs time to reflect this upside in the asset value. Obesity, for example, creates incalculable billions in external costs for healthcare providers and individuals in the form of higher insurance premiums. During the pandemic, Fo-menko saw from the dapp's data that "Spain lost eighty-five percent of all physical activity overnight. That loss of physical activity has ripple effects. You can recalculate it into calories. You can recalculate it into extra weight gained. You can recalculate it in extra healthcare costs."[58] This data is enormously valuable to the government, private healthcare providers, and insurers, to name a few. Apparently, incentives work: a study in the *British Journal of Sports Medicine* showed Sweatcoin users increased their physical activity by 20 percent. Fomenko thinks we are at day zero of the movement economy. Is he right?

Perhaps the movement economy will be worth billions someday. Today the rewards are small. A dedicated user might earn $25 to $50 a year at the current price, which is hardly a life changer. Also, Sweat-coin owns users' data: it's a Web2.5 company that hasn't fully trans-formed into Web3. Fomenko acknowledged that his team is tinkering with the Web3 toolkit and wants users to own their data, but feels that blockchains are not performant enough to support that kind of functionality. For now, Sweatcoin is collecting user data in compliance with the EU General Data Protection Regulation.[59] Despite these implementation challenges, the opportunity is significant. If Sweat-coin can reach a place where users earn tokens and own their health data, they get all the value. They can volunteer their anonymized data to clinical trials, earn rewards from brands, and get rebates from insurers while maintaining sovereignty over their data, without sharing it with anyone else.

Conclusion and Takeaways

Every industry will be impacted in some way by Web3. In this chapter we discussed three areas where Web3 entrepreneurs are reimagining business models based on ownership and user control. Here are the key takeaways for this chapter:

1. In gaming, we are on the brink of an upheaval to business models that will empower gamers, already accustomed to buying stuff, with the power to own stuff.
2. Ownership will introduce new gameplay and features that will probably grow the industry, just as free-to-play unlocked new gamers and revenue sources.
3. NFT gaming creates new ways for cash-strapped studios in the developing world to fund development. At the same time, Web3 games need to get their token models right.
4. It turns out on the last point that we may require all the computing power we can get our hands on if we want to fulfil the promise of the metaverse, not to mention the opportunities in AI and beyond.

The next chapter looks at the metaverse and the physical infrastructure supporting industry innovation.

CHAPTER 8

The Metaverse

A Utopia, a Panopticon, or the New Global Village?

Promise and Peril

The metaverse is one of the hottest topics in business, but for something with so much excitement and anticipation around it, the idea has a dubious past in literature. Neal Stephenson coined the term *metaverse* in his 1992 novel *Snow Crash*, set in a near future where governments have ceded control to large corporations and other private organizations. In Ernest Cline's 2011 novel, *Ready Player One*, the main character, Wade Watts, enters OASIS, an immersive virtual world, to escape the drudgery of daily life in a polluted and overcrowded earth. In the film *The Matrix*, human beings are hooked into a simulation mimicking life at the end of the twentieth century while robots harvest their bioelectricity. This tethering people to a global collective or central nervous system takes a less dark turn in William Gibson's novel *Neuromancer* (1984), where cyberspace is "a consensual hallucination experienced daily by billions of legitimate operators, in every nation . . . a graphic representation of data abstracted from the bank of every computer in the human system."[1] We might view these as commentary on the perceived isolating effects of videogames and technology at the end of the twentieth century.

But long before modern computers came along, authors have been wrestling with the idea of how humankind uses technology to transcend the normal boundaries of existence. In *Brave New World* (1932), novelist Aldous Huxley has engineered human beings to live in harmony with one another and access virtual reality–like experiences. In the novel, a character called the Assistant Predestinator asks the protagonist Henry whether he is "going to the feelies." The Assistant Predestinator adds, "I hear the new one at the Alhambra is first-rate. There's a love scene on a bearskin rug; they say it's marvelous. Every hair of the bear reproduced. The most amazing tactual effects."[2] In the book, those in power breed and separate people at birth into "pre-destined" paths. Fortunately, Henry is at the top rung of the social ladder: his peer group spends much of its time taking drugs, having sex, and going to the feelies—anything to escape reality or actual emotions. Despite having all his basic desires fulfilled, he is hollow and miserable. In each of these tellings, the virtual world is at best an escape from the drudgery of daily life (*Ready Player One*) and at worst a prison of the mind where humans are born, live, and die without ever truly living (*The Matrix*). Furthermore, often a sovereign, enemy, or all-powerful corporation compels the characters to plug in to these systems.

Plato's cave is a thought experiment in Plato's work *The Republic*. In this experiment, Plato imagines a group of people who have lived their entire lives in a cave, chained in such a way that they can see only the shadows of passing objects on the cave wall in front of them. These shadows are the prisoners' only reality, the true nature of the world.

In a way, we can view Plato's cave as a metaphor for the metaverse. If we spend time hooked up to a shared virtual reality controlled by companies with a profit motive and governments with a political agenda, then we may experience only what they want us to experience in our headsets, and we may take this "experience" for reality. Think of Orson Welles's live radio broadcast of H. G. Wells's *The War of the Worlds* in 1938; Welles adapted the novel into a series of "fake news bulletins describing a Martian invasion of New Jersey."[3] Radio listeners panicked. Now imagine the metaverse as a kind of panopticon, a world where a central authority constantly surveils users, tracks their movements, collects their data (including biometrics), and feeds the data into artificial intelligence, training it to develop ever-finer methods for shaping each user's behavior. I'd prefer the Martians.

The metaverse could also extend what media theorist Marshall McLuhan called the "global village" to virtual reality without changing much. In McLuhan's mind, the global village reduced the world to a virtual small town of busybodies. No one had privacy. "It doesn't necessarily mean harmony and peace and quiet, but it does mean huge involvement in everybody else's affairs," McLuhan said.[4] Social media erode the sovereign private self, which the metaverse could exacerbate, along with surveillance by companies and governments.

Through our hopeful lens, we can view Plato's cave as a metaphor for how people experience the world through their senses and their biases. Community-governed DAOs could inform the metaverse experience and invite people to transcend the boundaries of their physical world and immerse themselves in worlds beyond, learning more about themselves and perhaps gaining a deeper understanding of others in the process.

Matthew Ball described the metaverse as "a massively scaled and interoperable network of real time rendered 3D virtual worlds" that an infinite number of users can experience "synchronously, persistently, and effectively . . . with an individual sense of presence, and with continuity of data, such as identity, history, entitlements, objects, communication, and payments."[5] Where the fundamental backbone of the Internet was a public good, Ball said the mainstay of the metaverse is a private one, engineered for "commerce, data collection, advertising, and the sale of virtual products."[6] Tim Sweeney of Epic Games said, "This metaverse is going to be far more pervasive and powerful than anything else. If one central company gains control of this, it will become more powerful than any government and be god on earth."[7]

Yat Siu of Animoca Brands has a simpler definition: "The metaverse is the construction of new shared realities as opposed to virtual reality, and these shared realities come about because we have shared common concepts of values that we believe in, which is how societies are constructed."[8]

The metaverse is just another human fabrication—a shared delusion we all agree to participate in. As human beings, Siu said, "We coalesce in communal states around shared realities and shared beliefs, whether this is capitalism, whether this is socialism, whether this is a political belief, whether you have a perspective on property rights, for instance, that becomes the center of that." Human beings have a unique ability to "create these fictional realities and make them real to us. Money is fictional, right? Societies are fictional, political systems are fictional. These are stories we tell ourselves that become a shared reality."[9]

When it comes to the metaverse, "if we don't have digital property rights, none of it matters." What does Siu think of Meta and other corporate virtual worlds? He sees them more like theme parks than real economies or societies. "Disneyland is fun, it's an experience, but you don't have ownership in this. There's no stake in it. Therefore, it's meaningless, except for those who own it." Referring to Meta, he added, "It means something for the people at Facebook. It means something for shareholders of Facebook. But it doesn't mean anything to users. They're just consuming it," while it extracts their data.[10]

The economics of the metaverse must be shared, meaning everyone participates in them. Digital property rights come first. "Things like VR or AR or any of the toolsets, or even the screen, are just mechanisms in which we can experience our digital ownership, the shared reality we have within games." VR and AR are simply the tools we use to access the metaverse. Perhaps they become necessary as we move to immersive digital spaces, but they alone are insufficient, in the same way PCs were necessary to access the Web in the 1990s but owning a PC alone did not mean that we were online.

How do we ensure that the metaverse becomes the individual's tool for greater empathy, autonomy, and self-actualization in relationship to each other, rather than the institution's tool for digitally enslaving the masses, each of us in our custom-made cell? The answer— what's missing from Ball's lists—is individual property rights. For now, corporations are exploiting the confusion around the metaverse to advance their own vision. If you're Epic Games, the metaverse is a powerful tool to create a more immersive gaming experience. If you're Microsoft CEO Satya Nadella, the metaverse is a new interface for customers to engage with Microsoft's software suite—think virtual PowerPoint presentations. If you're Meta's Mark Zuckerberg, the metaverse adds a third dimension to your walled garden, for harvesting user data and running ads in Sensurround, perpetuating your ad-based model, so that you can scale well beyond three billion users and half a trillion in market cap.

Huxley's book is so farsighted that, with a few minor tweaks, we can imagine a 2030 version of it. In our updated version, global warming has ravaged the earth. Many citizens turn to now-legalized psychedelics to escape reality, while the government uses a CBDC to monitor and control people. A handful of giant companies ply us with a new kind of immersive virtual escapism that distances us farther from reality. The social media echo chambers have now become virtual worlds where we feed on a steady stream of misinformation that reinforces our prejudices as social fabric comes apart at the seams.

The vision of a Web3 metaverse is far more hopeful and ambitious, and it could revolutionize how we interact with each other and the world around us. A Web3 metaverse is a decentralized, open, and interconnected fabric of virtual spaces, sometimes—but not necessarily—accessible via virtual reality or augmented reality, and powered by blockchain technologies and other open-source protocols. The metaverse is not just some new plane of digital human experience that will interconnect with our physical world and where we will spend more of our time. In the Web3 version, users will also have full control over their data and identities and property rights to their virtual goods, with the ability to interact with each other and build applications on top of the platform freely. The Web3 vision for the metaverse is about freedom on a new plane of human existence that mimics the same autonomy and rights we have in our physical world. This new realm offers an unprecedented opportunity to exercise those rights and transform how we experience the world, conduct business, learn, find companionship, and entertain ourselves and each other.

To be clear, we can have Web3 without the metaverse, but we don't want the metaverse without Web3. Web3 applications in DeFi, art, gaming, and countless other fields require no immersive VR experience. We can create immersive experiences without Web3. But we need Web3 to secure our rights and privileges against centralizing forces in the metaverse. Otherwise, it's just VR Facebook at best, and

VR North Korea at worst. Ball wrote, "In the metaverse, everything costs 30 percent," controlled by conglomerates who "forcibly bundle" services and stifle competition.[11] This is the Web2 model for a virtual reality experience, not a new plane of human existence.

Why the Metaverse Must Be Built with Web3 Tools

For a period, Second Life was the closest innovation we've had to a metaverse-type of experience. The pioneering virtual world launched in 2003 and quickly gained a large user base. It delivered a collective virtual shared space where users could interact with each other and with virtual objects and experiences. Second Life offered several features—such as its native digital currency, Linden dollars—for creating and owning virtual property, conducting business transactions, and participating in a wide range of activities and communities.

As Second Life gained in popularity a robust little economy developed. It had a million regular users, as well as a presence from real-world organizations and companies like the BBC, Wells Fargo, and others. Harvard University offered courses in Second Life. Linden Labs, the company that started it, was not an intermediary but a facilitator. It acted more like a limited government than a game maker in the traditional sense. Second Life at its peak had a half-billion-dollar GDP and stock exchange where users cashed out $55 million Linden dollars into real-world currency.[12]

The presence of Wells Fargo in Second Life sounds ripped from today's headlines. In February 2022, J.P.Morgan announced it was opening a "branch" in the Web3 metaverse project Decentraland.[13] The metaverse hype cycle has drawn more big brands to this space like bees to blossoms. Some see it as more than a PR stunt. They see themselves as first movers in virtual commerce and entertainment.

Despite its initial success, Second Life has not had staying power. I'd argue that a lack of Web3 technologies such as digital property rights, sovereign identity, and true peer-to-peer transactions prevented it from scaling. Not long after Second Life launched, Zuckerberg introduced Facebook. Compared to Second Life, Facebook was not particularly innovative; it was the latest in a string of social media sites like Myspace and Friendster with similar offers. But it succeeded where Second Life failed—in driving user adoption. Unlike Second Life's Linden Labs, which governed with a light touch, Facebook was more controlling, choosing not to seek input from its users on matters relevant to the community. In Web2, Facebook's approach was the winning one—for Facebook.

Today, Facebook is betting big on the metaverse, with a vision that is at odds with the promise of a free and open Web3. For example, Facebook recently announced that transactions involving digital goods inside its metaverse environment would be subject to a *50 percent tax* and that all assets would live on an internally controlled system, not on a public blockchain. In other words, Facebook is using the metaverse as a pretense to build its own app store, a walled garden where all subjects pay tribute to the company. This model worked in Web2 for Apple, but so far investors are not convinced. Since Facebook announced its name change to Meta, its stock has plunged, though it has recouped some of those losses. By comparison, investors put a record $25 billion in Web3 companies and digital assets in 2021. According to Web3 research firm The Block, NFTs and gaming also drove investment into 2022: "The vertical raised $8.3 billion in 2022, a 51 percent year-on-year increase. Half of these investments were in VR/metaverse, blockchain-based gaming, and game studio subcategories. Most of the deals reflected seed and pre-series A stages."[14]

Perhaps investors are now realizing that the open frontier of Web3 could be more lucrative than the walled gardens of Web2. Business leaders pay attention to what savvy investors value as a signal of where they should invest their money, and so this will be a trend to watch.

Web3's unique capabilities, such as digital property rights, sovereign identity, and peer-to-peer transactions, are critical for enabling a fair, prosperous, sustainable, and inclusive metaverse. They provide users with the ability to truly own and control their digital goods and identities, and facilitate secure, private, and efficient transactions within the metaverse—secure because they clear and settle on-chain, private because they are peer-to-peer, and efficient because they avoid toll-taking Web2 platforms.

With digital property rights, users can have full ownership and control over their virtual assets, allowing them to build wealth in the metaverse and take it with them. This can also help to create a more sustainable metaverse, as users can invest in and maintain their digital assets for all time, rather than over the lifetime of a game release or a software update from a big company.

A Web3 metaverse also enables users to have control over their own personal data and online identity (or identities, if they like). They can decide who gets to see what, when, and where in the metaverse. They can use digital assets to enter token-gated communities without revealing personal information or their credit card number or their global location. It is time to give the metaverse a second life—and we can do that with Web3 tools.

Web2 companies are flexing their muscle to control the metaverse, contain Web3 innovation, and influence related industries. Apple has prohibited mining apps on its phone, because they "rapidly drain battery, generate excessive heat, or put unnecessary strain on device resources." As Ball pointed out, shouldn't users get to decide that? The maker of your refrigerator does not prohibit you from storing processed cheese and ice cream even though they may be bad for your health.[15] Platforms have already refused to allow Web3 games because they "simply do not work" with their business model.[16]

Brett Winton of Ark Investment Management sees ways to work around the app stores to make the business model even more lucrative for game developers building in the metaverse. "Think of the consumer experience of playing a game as distilling into a cost per hour decision," he suggested.[17] "Having digital ownership of items within that game actually means that you'd be willing to pay a higher price per hour for that experience."[18] Publishers could offer "incentives for game developers to allow digital ownership systems to plug into their games," ranging from "an economic overlay . . . to a more completely embedded experience, like, if you have digital Nike shoes, then you can move quicker" in the game.[19] Creative people will come up with new ways to integrate digital goods into game and metaverse applications.

In so many ways, a true metaverse is incompatible with Web2 business models. Web3 enshrines digital property rights, which include possession and the unrestricted right of resale—that is, you can do with your property what you like as long as it is lawful. "When a user buys an NFT from a given game, the trustless and permissionless nature of a blockchain means that the game's makers cannot block the sale of that NFT at any point," according to Ball.[20] Not surprisingly, many Web2 companies and other technology giants are the largest builders in virtual worlds, what we might call the "anti-Web3 metaverse," because they are actively hostile toward Web3 innovations such as peer-to-peer transactions in and between decentralized applications that sidestep Web2 transaction fees. In blockchain games, tech giants limit users to collecting rather than transacting in assets and keep them to more rudimentary gameplay.

The data back this up. According to The Block, the majority of Web3 games (64 percent) "choose web browsers to host their games, followed by Android (37%) and Windows (33%)"; we presume this number adds up to more than 100 because publishers can host games in multiple locations. "Web browser as the preferred platform is likely because it is easier for players to connect their crypto wallets and self-custody their game assets while engaging with the game's RMT services (e.g., trading, minting, and staking)," researchers at The Block wrote.[21] Apple is missing entirely from this list because it has effectively banned in-app purchase and sale of NFTs.

Digital Twins

"A digital twin is a digital representation of a real-world entity or system," according to consultancy Gartner. "The implementation of a digital twin is an encapsulated software object or model that mirrors a unique physical object, process, organization, person, or other abstraction." Gartner expects innovators to aggregate "data from multiple digital twins . . . for a composite view across a number of real-world entities, such as a power plant or a city, and their related processes."[22]

However, implementation is next to impossible without Web3 tools. Consider the most obvious use case: you. To be sure, there is a "real you" in the physical world and a "virtual you" in the digital. But in a Web2 world, the virtual you is not a unique version of you: it is a fragmented image of many versions of you spread across a growing number of apps and platforms, like when you stand between two mirrors, creating an infinity mirror with an infinite number of you. Some versions of the virtual you are incomplete or distorted: not the reflected but the funhouse version. None of these is a true digital twin. What's more, none of these belongs to you; they belong to the apps and platforms.

Web3 changes this paradigm by allowing for self-sovereign and completely unique digital twins for places, assets, and our identities. As a metaverse user, you will need a digital twin that you own and control, not one managed for you by several big companies.

But there are various implementation challenges to fully realizing a virtual you in the metaverse. In an ideal world, the virtual Alex is as robust and rich and unique as the real Alex, and I own me in the truest sense. I can walk or fly or swim my virtual self, with my wallet of assets, my history of experience, and my reputation, wherever I want in an open and permissionless metaverse. I can take myself and play games or watch movies or socialize or whatever else the metaverse supports. These experiences are all uniquely mine. Once we reach a standard for importing and exporting digital assets, as if we are leaving one country and entering another, then I can take whatever I need with me to the next environment. Cofounder of Parallel Studios Sascha Mojtahedi said, "That world becomes the social consensus mechanism where people decide what to do, and how to contribute as a community."[23] Clearly, we have a long way to go, which leads us to our next section, on challenges.

Implementation Challenges for the Metaverse and Web3

Right now, the metaverse lacks standards for moving assets and identities from one virtual world to another. Let's revisit gaming. Can you move the Formula One car you bought in one game to a game set in ancient Rome and race it against the chariots? The standards for digital goods like NFTs allow us to view and trade these assets in compatible blockchain environments. Not so in the metaverse and across different gaming titles. A Formula One car may handle beautifully in one environment, but who knows how it will look, feel, and perform in ancient Rome? Not only do we lack asset composability between chains; we face innumerable challenges in migrating assets and other digital goods between virtual environments.

Another huge implementation challenge is the underlying hardware. Most people think of virtual reality or augmented reality as the hardware interface for the metaverse. "I think VR and AR are still quite a ways away, in just fidelity, from truly being awesome. I can't tell if it's iPhone 1 stage or Palm Pilot stage. That means it's probably closer to the Palm Pilot stage, right?" Anatoly Yakovenko, cofounder of Solana, told me in 2022.[24] But he still thinks there's a need for a dedicated hardware interface for Web3 and that a dedicated phone is the answer for now, for three reasons.

The first is user experience and functionality. Cryptoassets are digital bearer assets, so if you're going to be taking them on the move, you should have a safe and convenient way of holding them. Solana has announced its own phone with secure private key management that allows it to be a hardware wallet and have the Solana application ecosystem built right in. "This is not a competitor with Ledger for cold storage. For things that are secure, you should still use a very dedicated device, but this is a daily driver," said Yakovenko.[25] Having a Web3-native integration on your phone opens up some fun possibilities. The phone frees up developers to deliver higher-level applications as "the OS handles the nitty-gritty hard part of actually securing the assets. Those translate into UX improvements."

The second is the experience. "When the devs are constantly telling me we can't do the things that we want to do in mobile, that we have to build these weird Web view integrations that link through wallets and stuff, I start pacing around the room and trying to figure out how do I help them."[26] Having a dedicated platform makes the developers' job easier.

The third relates to the first and second, that it leapfrogs Apple's and Google's app stores and unleashes innovation. The Solana phone "doesn't have restrictions on NFTs bought and sold, is not charging twenty, thirty percent on every NFT sale, which doesn't make any sense with user-generated content, but with true digital ownership that business model just totally doesn't make sense."[27] Yakovenko is making a big bet that even with fifty thousand dedicated Web3 users this phone is viable—and so small that, in the grand scheme of things, it won't raise alarms at Apple and Google.

Another challenge is the current limitations of blockchains themselves. After more than a decade, this industry is scaling rapidly, but questions remain. Perhaps digital property rights, decentralization, and token incentives will be powerful tools that help bring about a more open metaverse, but are blockchain solutions really ready for prime time, to run other aspects of the metaverse like real-time rendering and computation, as some skeptics assert?

Rendering a truly disruptive metaverse is impossible on a centralized cloud like AWS, and may not be possible on a decentralized cloud for a long while. In general, I tend to put these critiques into "implementation challenges" that we can overcome. Web3 tools like digital assets and sovereign identity will be foundational to building an open metaverse, and we will need decentralized networks for storing data and running computations, with token incentives driving adoption. For Web3 to fulfill its potential in the long run, it cannot rely on centralized clouds. The metaverse should be free from these shackles, too. For now, many Web3 applications run on AWS. Metadata for NFTs sit on centralized servers at OpenSea. But innovators can overcome this challenge, and Web3 itself provides the toolset and economic incentives to do it. Critics allege that decentralized clouds will not be as performant as their centralized counterparts. Since AWS and Azure are a long way from rendering real-life persistent virtual worlds, a Web3 version could never support the metaverse. Render Network should compel naysayers to rethink these assumptions.

Rendering the Metaverse with Web3 Tools: Render Network Case Study

For Jules Urbach, CEO of cloud graphics company OTOY, Web3 is an idea whose time has finally come. Urbach told me that, twenty years ago, his thesis was "at some point, you're going to have a lot of latent compute power."[28] Urbach knows a thing or two about compute power: his company, OTOY, is a pioneer in cloud graphics. Its flagship product, OctaneRender, is what's known as an "unbiased, spatially correct GPU render engine," which is the industry's way of describing powerful software that can render more lifelike images and video than what came before. Urbach said it's "like Adobe Photoshop, you rent it for twenty bucks a month."[29] Marvel Studios used Octane-Render in the opening of *Ant-Man and the Wasp*, and TV shows on HBO, Amazon, and Netflix have experimented with the technology, according to Urbach.

More importantly, OTOY democratized rendering, so that you can now render in a couple of minutes what used to take hours. How? By harnessing dozens and sometimes hundreds of graphics processing units (GPUs) at a time to break down projects into smaller parts. "We showed that you can take one hundred GPUs, you can render the *Transformers* movie from hours to seconds. The proof was that with GPUs, unlike CPUs, it's really easy to take one hundred of them together for a single frame and get back a render that's a hundred times faster." Urbach's customers include Hollywood studios and upstart artists, and he counts former Google CEO Eric Schmidt and Hollywood power broker Ari Emanuel (the inspiration for *Entourage*'s Ari Gold) as investors and advisors. The popularity of cloud rendering was pushing them to the limit. One reason was cost: "When you're buying data-center-render GPUs, it's an insane amount of money. The weird part is, it doesn't render any faster than a local GPU that is one-tenth the price." Data centers may update their GPUs every few years or so, whereas hard-core gamers and other users of GPUs, namely Ethereum miners, have up-to-the-minute tech. So the graphics card a hard-core gamer buys at Best Buy is more powerful than the cards in data centers. The average Joe has more power than Amazon . . . at least, when pooled with thousands of other average Joes. What if we could harness the latest and greatest GPUs all over the world?

Until very recently, Ethereum's PoW consensus algorithm ran on state-of-the-art NVIDIA graphics cards. Urbach said, "I was thinking the following, which was that if it costs $1 to run this on Amazon, but the cost of electricity for somebody's Ethereum mining rig is $0.10, what if I were to pay these Ethereum miners $0.25 or $0.50?" He reasoned that, if he offered a better deal to GPU owners, then they would pool their assets. Thus, the Render Network was born. Users pool their GPUs and get paid for their time and energy in the native RNDR token. Since launching in 2017, Render Network users have rendered more than 16 million frames and almost half a million scenes on the network.[30] Artists using the network have created crypto art and NFTs with combined sales of half a billion dollars in primary and secondary markets, according to the company.[31] Many of the leading 3D crypto artists, like Pak and FVCKRENDER, use Render. Urbach told me that the artist Blake Kathryn used Render to create the visuals for musician Lil Nas X's Montero Tour and that Render was also used for the 2021 UEFA Champions League in a halftime show.[32]

Urbach expects a purely Web3-based decentralized cloud of GPUs to perform better than anything a single company can produce. It may hold the key to powering a decentralized metaverse. Urbach called the metaverse a spatially aware browser. Online, we use uniform resource locators, better known as URLs, to hop from website to website. Building something new for the Internet's next era requires more than real-time rendering. It requires a new public architecture for the metaverse, specifically standards for 3D, equivalent to what we have for HTML or JPEGs. Urbach has worked on this process for years and is a founding member of the Metaverse Standards Forum group, with two thousand members and counting.[33] We also need to figure out provenance, said Urbach. He sees a Web3 solution: anything rendered in the Render Network creates a hash on a blockchain, for the verifiable provenance essential to transporting digital goods from world to world and managing creators' IP rights.

In our conversation, Urbach told me that his childhood friend wanted to preserve the legacy of his father, Gene Roddenberry. OTOY's LightStage technology could create a hyperrealistic digital twin of the *Star Trek* creator, but everyone's expectations would be astronomical.[34] OTOY had to figure out how to do it at warp speed.

Using Render, Urbach hired a team to rebuild all of *Star Trek*'s history visually, starting with a digital twin of the USS *Enterprise* with provenance back to the original IP. "That's how the starship *Enterprise* in the metaverse is going to work. It's not an experience, it's not a videogame, it's not a world—it's the whole thing."[35] So far, OTOY's team has used Render to scan a million documents between Roddenberry's archive, "the equivalent to the Smithsonian's storage of the eleven-foot physical model from the show," said Urbach.[36] The final frontier will be rendering the *Enterprise* in real time, eliminating the impossible, however improbable.

Decentralized Physical Infrastructure

Decentralized models for problem solving are appearing in a range of areas, such as decentralized physical infrastructure (DePIN), where networks use tokens as incentives to pool and coordinate the physical resources of many individuals, turning them into decentralized and resilient systems.

Web3 researcher Sami Kassab of Messari breaks down DePIN into four categories: cloud networks, wireless networks, sensor networks, and energy networks. He estimated that DePIN's total addressable market is more than $2.2 trillion, growing to $3.5 trillion by 2028.[37] Consider decentralized storage and computing, where startups like Filecoin, Storj, Sia, Skynet, Arweave, and Akash Network are competing alongside giants like Amazon's cloud service, better known as AWS. Or the decentralized wireless network Helium, which already has hot spots in 182 countries.

In two weeks, ChatGPT exceeded 200 million users, straining the company's limited computing resources and funds and throwing into stark relief how much AI will drive compute demand, along with the metaverse and the Internet of Things (IoT), putting pressure on centralized cloud computing resources. Enterprise users may need new solutions. Decentralized networks can bridge the supply-demand gap, tapping the vast pool of underutilized computing hardware. "Think about all those gaming computers with powerful GPUs that go unused for most of the day," said Kassab. With decentralized compute networks, "people can monetize their GPUs and CPUs when not in use, making a significant impact on the total available compute capacity on cloud networks."[38]

Like DeFi, DePIN will likely have the greatest impact in developing countries for many of the same reasons: the physical infrastructure for banking, communications, and electricity is often unreliable, underdeveloped, and underserving vulnerable people, especially those in remote locations. By pooling their resources, the millions of individuals who use this infrastructure can own it, too. "This bottom-up approach has the potential to drive greater decentralization and empower local communities to meet their own infrastructure needs," said Kassab.[39] We expand upon this opportunity in the next chapter.

Distributed Storage and Computation

Filecoin is a protocol with incentives to participate in a decentralized cloud storage marketplace, designed to "store humanity's most important information."[40] Consider the potential benefits of this model. First of all, protocols like Filecoin reward users for pooling their storage and compute power and doing "proof of physical work," that is, proving they are dedicating the resources to support the network. These built-in incentives, such as data storage and retrieval fees paid to stakeholders, have garnered Filecoin an ever-growing community of 1,100 unique providers and nearly 18,000 storage deals at the time of this writing.[41]

Second, in a decentralized system, data and computing power are distributed across multiple devices, so that if one device fails or goes offline, the system can still function and access the data. In contrast, traditional storage solutions can break down if the central server or cloud goes down.

Third, because data and computing power are distributed, attackers cannot easily access or manipulate the data, or shut the hardware down, compared to centralized honeypots controlled by single entities. No dictator can switch off Web3 because he doesn't like what people are saying and saving online.

Fourth, making use of unused resources reduces the need for expensive, specialized hardware. Historically, large corporations undertook the capital-intensive job of building physical infrastructure like wireless networks or cloud facilities. But pooling a bunch of individuals or even small businesses together with a coordination and incentive mechanism is cheaper than building everything alone, and the peers can decide whether to pass those savings through to end users.[42]

Finally, decentralized storage may last longer than centralized clouds. What happens to our data if a cloud provider goes bankrupt, gets acquired, or is seized by a government? In contrast, decentralized cloud service providers have an economic incentive to continue running their hardware forever, as they receive compensation for their contributions to network computing power. As a species, we need ways to keep our shared memory alive in perpetuity. Consider the work of the USC Shoah Foundation and Stanford University, which have partnered with Filecoin to ensure the digital preservation and eternal storage of the testimony of Holocaust survivors.

These benefits are finding product/market fit with different kinds of entrepreneurs and builders. Greg Osuri, founder of Akash Network, said there are three categories of users on Akash: "One, I would put in a bucket of innovators—DeFi projects, NFT projects, games. Osmosis is a big one. Several media projects like Omniflex are running on Akash, and several games like *Strange Clan*."[43] He also pointed out that Akash works for DAOs, too, because it removes the "key person risk" in deployment. "Anyone with a key can control the deployment, and that key can be multisig. If you want a multisig-based cloud infrastructure, then Akash is the only solution."[44] Second are so-called "arbitrageurs" looking for a price mismatch between centralized clouds and Akash. "Right now, Akash offers a price point that is one-third to one-fifth lower than Amazon. When you see that arbitrage opportunity, the best way to realize it is to mine" the native token of the network, which is required to use the service, rather than purchase it in the market. The third group are what Osuri called "ecosystem builders," with names like Akashlytics and ArGo.

Will companies with cloud needs like Walmart or Goldman Sachs use Akash over AWS? Yes, but not right away, said Osuri. "You don't want a Goldman Sachs or a Walmart user who is so used to clicking, clicking, clicking, and complaining a million times, and expecting support. You don't want that user. You want a user who, when there's an issue, will dig into it themselves, find a solution, and come up with an idea. That's how you scale," presumably in exchange for the benefits Akash offers. When early iterations of new technologies fail to meet the most lucrative customers' needs, the biggest vendors tend to dismiss the technology as a toy. Osuri said that's fine, for now: "By focusing on composability and not usability, we made a conscious choice that we can attract high-end developers. We're doing that right now. In five to six years' time, you're going to see some of these enterprises adopt."[45]

Another example of Web3 and physical infrastructure is Helium, a decentralized Internet provider that uses incentives to bootstrap networking infrastructure for low-power, wireless devices such as IoT devices. The network uses a so-called "proof-of-coverage" consensus mechanism: to earn the native HNT token, a participating node on the network must prove that it is providing coverage to other devices by solving a cryptographic puzzle. The difficulty of the puzzle is adjusted based on the number of nodes (called HotSpots) in a given geographic area, so that the network maintains a desired level of coverage. T-Mobile thought Helium was interesting enough to partner with Nova Labs, a company founded by the founding team of Helium, on a distributed wireless deal. Helium gets to fall back on T-Mobile's network as it scales. If it succeeds, then Helium's network would help T-Mobile reach remote customers.[46] Helium faces many of the same challenges from bots as other Web3-enabled applications do, such as in the Web3 gaming space where players can earn token rewards for participating. In Helium's case, users "simulate" wireless nodes without any true wireless coverage, and so honest nodes constantly battle to shut down fake nodes that are cheating to earn rewards. Today, proof of coverage is still too hard to prove.

Another challenge is just the sheer supply of resources that must be pooled in order to compete with or exceed a traditional network. Filecoin's storage capacity stands at approximately 13.8 exbibytes, enough to store the entire Internet Archive more than 200 times.[47] Helium's IoT network has 980,000 hot spots in more than 182 countries, according to Kassab's research. They will need to grow much larger to begin making a meaningful impact.

DePIN and Mapping Data

Could DePIN upset the Web2 applecart in other areas, beyond cloud computing? Ariel Seidman, founder of Hivemapper, thinks so. He is going after Google's monopoly in mapping and map data. "I'm more of a mapping guy than I am into crypto," said Seidman, who was a senior executive at Yahoo Maps at a time when Yahoo was the dominant search engine and Google was a scrappy upstart that was gaining market share. Yahoo and other map providers at the time were licensing data from third parties. Google, at enormous cost, decided to create the data themselves, mapping every road in the world. When Seidman's boss rejected his plan to do the same thing, he quit.[48]

Today, Google Maps is the dominant mapping application, but more importantly, it provides access to its application programming interface (API) for a price to hundreds of companies and even governments. Uber, Lyft, and Airbnb use Google Maps. There's a good chance your local statehouse and insurance company do as well. Since ancient times, maps have been a source of power. "A map is a weapon," said a World War I soldier who understood that precise, detailed, and up-to-date information could be used against the enemy.[49] In the mapping business, Google wields a howitzer against competitors with slings and arrows.

Waze, a popular mapping application, competed with Google for a while, by harnessing the wisdom of crowds. For one, the app turned users into prosumers, gamifying the application (drop a pin when you see a stalled car and earn a sticker). But more importantly, it tapped into a vast community of thousands of map lovers, or cartophiles, who would voluntarily spend thirty to forty hours a week fixing maps and teaching other editors.[50]

"Those twenty thousand to thirty thousand people literally would go into a desktop application and tediously edit a map. Quite frankly, they made the map. Without them, there is no Waze, period." Then Google bought the company in 2013 for $1.2 billion. Said Seidman, "The investors made out, as they should, the employees made out, as they should, but all these twenty-five thousand or thirty thousand editors got zero. That's bullshit." The value proposition for a Web3 solution is obvious to Seidman: "You help build a map with us, and you collect this data, we're going to be very open and very transparent about, here's the data you're collecting and here's how much you're going to be earning" in its native HONEY token.[51] How? Hivemapper sells dashcams preloaded with state-of-the-art AI and mapping software that anyone can install in their car in minutes. The device captures reams of data that are later uploaded to the cloud via a smartphone app. Like Sweatcoin, Hivemapper wants users to earn some income for what they were already going to do—drive to work, run errands, and so on. Drivers in big cities or with longer commutes might earn more. Uber drivers or FedEx delivery people are extra valuable.

This leads to an obvious opportunity: a fleet owner like UPS or FedEx could partner with Hivemapper. No matter how many cars Google deploys to snap pics, Uber and Lyft will likely have more drivers. FedEx, Uber, and others might like to reduce their need for Google's mapping data, and so this feels like a win-win. Carmakers also use Google's API. If cars are computers on wheels, then they do not own their operating system or other data. They are dumb hardware. Hivemapper technology could turn them into stakeholders in a mapping network where they could access data without relying on Google or someone else.

Anyone who spends five hundred dollars on a Hivemapper dashcam probably expects a return on that investment at some point. The token model is clever: Hivemappers earn the native token equitably for the data they create. When businesses want to license the data, they buy and burn tokens, just as enterprises burn money on Google Maps' APIs. If the number of tokens burned is greater than the number of tokens issued, then more value accrues to existing holders. Like the cartophiles who helped to build Waze, Seidman wants to attract community members to this project for more than financial reasons. Seidman seems indifferent to the token, at least for now. "What matters in the early days is, Are you building something useful to other human beings and other businesses? If not—if you don't pass that hurdle—then it's like, 'Who cares?'" On a grand adventure, we want missionaries, not mercenaries, as fellow travelers.

The Trivergence

The convergence of smartphones and wireless networks led to the rise of mobile apps, location-based services, and mobile-centric business models, transforming human behavior. Innovators combined advances in metallurgy and manufacturing processes to create the steam engine, which revolutionized transportation, agriculture, and production; and they strung telegraph lines along railways, conveying freight and information in tandem.

As these examples show, more often the combination or convergence of several technologies leads to the greatest economic, social, and cultural impact.

Today, we stand on the brink of a new era where the technologies of Web3 are converging with AI and IoT. Call it the *trivergence*.

First, a primer. IoT denotes the growing connectivity of everyday objects and our physical environments to the Internet. Today's IoT applications range from the mundane—such as your fridge ordering milk from Amazon or a dashcam recording traffic data—to the miraculous, such as remote health monitoring of those with Parkinson's disease. Physicians could observe their patients' symptoms remotely, collect and analyze data that might help to adjust their medications and improve their lives, and contribute to advances in treatments and earlier detection of the disease.[52] AI describes the ability for computers to perform tasks that once required human intelligence, from writing computer code, investment memos, and poetry to generating art and music. Of course, blockchains have unleashed Web3. With Web3, we can store, manage, and exchange our own things of value—like anonymized medical data—in a secure, private, and peer-to-peer manner.

Sam Altman is perhaps best known as the CEO of Open AI, creator of Chat GPT, but he also focuses on the trivergence of these technologies through another project, Worldcoin, founded in 2019. Altman's understanding of the impact of AI on human work, how massive gains in productivity could dislocate and displace workers, informs his vision for Worldcoin as a global public financial utility. Through Worldcoin, all of humanity could share in global prosperity in the form of a universal basic income (UBI), regardless of who they were or where they lived.[53]

To access Worldcoin, users must first verify their "humanness" via an eye scanning device that looks like the love child of HAL 9000 and a basketball. From there, they receive a wallet with access to a free token with future utility and governance rights as a reward. This project has continued to gain momentum with over 1.7 million sign-ups.[54]

Worldcoin shows the trivergence in action. The retinal scanning orb is an example of cheap, durable, and useful IoT technology, while the Worldcoin token and wallet promise to deliver Web3 to billions. Worldcoin uses zero-knowledge proofs so individuals can "prove" their hummanness without revealing any information about themselves. And Worldcoin's ID system could be useful to the billions who lack an easy way to verify themselves digitally. As the AI enabled wealth piles up, more token holders stand to benefit.

OpenAI has courted controversy, with some critics alleging that those retinal scans undermine privacy because ownership of the biometric data is unclear. But Worldcoin's bold plan is worth understanding better and worth watching closely as a trivergence experiment.

Conclusion and Takeaways

The potential of a Web3 metaverse is immense, and we will feel its implications in all aspects of our lives, from how individuals and businesses interact, to how governments and other stakeholders in society organize. Here are the key takeaways for this chapter:

1. The opportunity of the metaverse is immense. We have an opportunity to build a new shared reality online, which could bring us closer together as a species and create untold opportunities for businesses, creators, and Internet users.
2. We cannot ignore the technical, social, and economic challenges that will arise as we create and inhabit this type of technology.
3. The biggest risk is that we simply perpetuate the same Web2 model where users lack rights or ownership of their data or digital selves. This is not an "open metaverse" but a closed virtual world. It's Disney World. It can be fun, but it is not a "second life."
4. The metaverse must be open and where possible built with Web3 tools: the biggest investments today in core technology like AR and VR and in content is happening by the traditional platforms of Web2. If desktops were how we interacted with Web1, and smartphones were how we interacted with Web2, then VR and AR and, by extension, "the metaverse" may be how we experience Web3. That means we need open worlds, common standards, and user rights.
5. Web3 tools, specifically decentralized computing and graphics rendering, may provide us with the toolset we need to actually make the metaverse possible, while ensuring the back-end technology itself is not owned or controlled by a single company.
6. Web3 provides a road map on how to harness excess capacity in the economy—whether computers in your home or drivers on the

road—into coordinated systems that can begin to complement and strengthen (and perhaps one day replace) existing infrastructure. DePIN is already seeing early success in graphics rendering, distributed storage, and mapping. Web3 is converging with other revolutionary technologies, namely AI and IoT. This trivergence will create new business opportunities and challenges for society.

The metaverse may bring people around the world closer together, something that we are seeing in Web3 today. As we will see in chapter nine, the world is getting flatter and Web3 is paving the way.

CHAPTER 9

Civilization

The World of Web3 Is Getting Flatter

We are living in a time of the greatest global prosperity ever but also a time of great uncertainty about the future. There is a creeping feeling that our system creates tremendous wealth but at the expense of our planet. "It was the best of times, it was the worst of times, it was the age of wisdom, it was the age of foolishness, it was the epoch of belief, it was the epoch of incredulity, it was the season of Light, it was the season of Darkness," wrote Charles Dickens. On the one hand, we have made enormous progress in our health and material well-being thanks in large part to the global spread of goods, capital, technical know-how, and technology. Humans have added twenty years to the average life expectancy from just sixty years ago. In the developing world, the situation is even more dramatic. In Africa, people live 60 percent longer than they did in 1960.[1] Infant mortality has declined in the same period by more than 80 percent.[2] But not all is well and there are many problems in the world. For starters, people have not shared the prosperity of our global economy equally. Thomas Friedman once wrote *The World Is Flat*; in reality, most of the world's people still face a daunting ascent. According to the World Bank, 1.4 billion adults were unbanked in 2022.[3] In *The Sovereign Individual*, written in 1997, authors James Dale Davidson and William Rees-Mogg describe how the rise of the information age will dissolve borders, allowing individuals to "transcend locality." The book was farsighted in describing today's digital nomads, typically young and affluent knowledge workers who have a passport and a laptop and can work from anywhere. But for most of the world's population this is not a realistic option.[4] Web3 or any other tool alone will not close the economic gap between the developing and developed world because these folks need an Internet connection and other financial tools and knowledge, but only 5.16 billion people are connected today—that's 64.4 percent of the world's population.[5]

Creators and entrepreneurs in the developing world have lacked the toolset to reach beyond their local markets and economies to fund business projects or creative ventures. The Internet has undeniably made the world "flatter," and Web3 will make it even more so. Consider the following three stories.

Case Study 1: Creators Can Monetize Their Global Fan Base

April Agregado lives in the Philippines with her husband and four children. She works as the office manager at a financial advisory firm, and he's an executive recruiter. They are typical of the emerging Filipino professional class. Like so many families, their youngest son, Sevi, was born with autism. As in so many countries, they received no government assistance in helping their son to be all they believed he could be.

April and her husband enrolled Sevi at an early age in programs like art therapy, gymnastics, and football. For five hours a day, he learned how to handle social interactions and perform tasks involving skill. The Agregados dug into their savings to give Sevi every chance at life. Eventually the cost became too great, and the family needed to drop all but one of the programs. They asked eight-year-old Sevi to decide. He chose art.

April told me how important art is to Sevi, how his paintings speak for him when words don't come easily. His work often surprises her. It gives her a window into his mind and his growth as a person. He paints a wide range of subjects, but favors animals, landscapes, and portraits of April and other family members. He works with an instructor-therapist who helps him express himself in bright colors.

Ever the proud parent, April started posting pictures of his pieces to Facebook, where they caught the eyes of friends and family. A few people asked to buy them. April was reluctant—Sevi prefers to give his art to his three sisters. She considered selling a few pieces to close family, but there was no way for Sevi's small fan base to buy his art without taking possession of the paintings. Then, in March 2021, a friend told April about NFTs. The Philippines was emerging as a hotbed of crypto innovation.

Unlike prior eras of the Web, the world's emerging economies are driving Web3 adoption and experimentation, partly due to the wider distribution of digital tools like smartphones and Internet and partly due to decades of offshoring and outsourcing that have made Southeast Asia a thriving technology ecosystem. For example, the Philippines is known for its videogame studios, which develop their own games and work on big American titles like *Gears of War*, *Red Dead Redemption*, and *The Last of Us*.

But unlike previous eras of the Web, Web3 is a medium not just for creating but for claiming ownership of assets. People are finding new ways to monetize their time and creative energy on Web3. In many emerging economies, working multiple jobs and gigging for extra cash are essential; through these Web3 tools, locals can connect to global markets and capture more value from their work. This new capability resonates with people in emerging economies perhaps more than it does in the West, which is why Vietnam, the Philippines, and other Southeast Asian countries outrank all Western European countries in Web3 adoption.[6]

With the help of her friend, April learned to mint an NFT (that is, to create a unique digital version) of each of Sevi's pieces. She listed a few of them on the NFT marketplace OpenSea, along with some information about Sevi. Sevi's story struck a chord with people in the burgeoning Web3 scene, and he recorded his first few sales. Soon after, the leading NFT art fair NFT.NYC started following Sevi on Facebook and Instagram.[7] April's friends encouraged her to apply to the fair in the hopes that its hosts would select Sevi as a featured artist. April said, "At first, we were very hesitant to share his story and his work because it's a space with a lot of amazing established artists, and here's this eight-year-old kid with autism, and we're sharing his work from therapy."[8] But, seeing no downside, they decided to give it a go.

Sevi's first foray into the global art scene came at a fortuitous time. Not only had NFTs emerged as a medium for creative expression online, but collectors were paying attention to the category of "child art" itself. Ten-year-old New Yorker Andres Valencia, dubbed "little Picasso," made headlines for selling his paintings (not NFTs) for more than $100,000 apiece.[9] By the summer of 2021, NFT.NYC was showcasing the work of Sevi and other young artists on hundred-foot billboards in Times Square. Sevi's art was a hit at the fair, and he started recording multiple sales. Today he has about four thousand followers on Twitter, and CNN recently featured him. Since April started selling Sevi's art as NFTs, the family has earned about eight ETH, worth around $16,000 as of April 17, 2023, more than the average Filipino makes in a year. These life-changing funds were but a drop in the bucket of the NFT market, with $23 billion in transactions in 2021.[10]

April explained how Sevi's art "became a way for us to safeguard and support Sevi's future." She added, "It's very likely that he will continue to need therapy for a very long time. To sell his work through NFTs provides a future for him that we're building now, today."[11] Sevi's family is middle-class, but like so many families striving for a better life, they always carry the risk of slipping backward. "We're okay for now, but you never know. Things can turn on a dime," April said.[12] Sevi's NFT nest egg helps.

Sevi's story would not have been possible in Web2. To be sure, Sevi benefited from Web2 tools. Through Facebook and Twitter, April published copies of his work and built his fan base. But NFT and Web3 platforms like OpenSea gave him ownership online so that she could monetize his creativity on his behalf. Through Web3, an autistic kid from a normal Filipino family tapped into a global market of art collectors. April said, "His art was featured in NFT galleries in Singapore and in Chicago. It's getting to places, to people, and into countries that we didn't think would happen until he was much older."[13] All the while, Sevi retains the physical copies of his work, which he and his family cherish so much and are instrumental to his therapy. Finally, with his NFTs, Sevi earns his fair share when collectors resell his art, an option most visual artists never had. On average, more than half of all NFT sales in the art and collectibles category are resales, and asset creators can program their NFTs to pay them a royalty in perpetuity, to their original wallet address. Of course, not every kid who paints can go on to the same success as Sevi. His story as an artist is not necessarily replicable, but the technology tools that make it possible are, because they empower individuals with ownership over their digital goods, in this case a talented autistic boy's art. According to April, Sevi's earnings help secure his future.

For now, Sevi is happy and thriving. April told us, "He has improved so much that we haven't needed to add therapy," though he continues with his art because he enjoys it so much, and it helps him focus. Of course, Sevi is a kid; he may not love painting forever. "We're hoping that he will continue to enjoy it, but he's only ten, and his interests can still change." April would be happy for Sevi to pick up football or gymnastics again. Thanks to his NFTs, they can now afford to give him all the help he needs.

Case Study 2: Entrepreneurs Can Connect to Global Markets

Sevi's story illuminates the ways in which the Internet as communication tool combined with a digital medium for value (in this case NFTs) allows creators in far-flung parts of the world to connect into a global market, reach buyers, and earn a living. Without these innovations there is no way that a young autistic artist in Manila could ever connect with a buyer, let alone sell their creation. Sevi's story is unique but there are plenty of others in the Philippines who see Web3's potential to create a better life for themselves. Web3 innovation extends globalization to the plane of digital experiences and digital assets. Like previous waves of globalization, it comes with risks and opportunities. The experience of others is not always exclusively positive. Web3 can help create new economic opportunities and exacerbate inequality. Nowhere is this more true than in the Web3 gaming space.

Earlier in our analysis on how Web3 is transforming the gaming industry, we described how so-called "play-to-earn" games had captured imaginations in developing countries, especially the Philippines, where young people had flocked to *Axie Infinity* and other titles. Many Web3 games require players to first acquire the playable character, which is in effect a digital asset. Young people in the Philippines were keen to make money but many were starting from scratch. But there was also a genuine feeling that NFT-based games had unlocked a secret, that they were radically *different*. Katrina Wolfe, who works at Laguna in the United States as a product director, said that early on when she first joined, she was startled by "the sheer optimism pouring out of the communities" (of players in different geographies). People were thinking "we'll fundamentally change the entire world. Well, maybe. Technology doesn't always do that. There's still a lot of culture and policy and all these other things that need to happen, too."[14] Still, she said, it was fun to be in a space where every playbook was getting thrown out the door.[15]

In response, some entrepreneurs created a new industry for so-called "Web3 gaming guilds." These are different from the "guilds" of massive multiplayer open online games like *World of Warcraft*, where a group of players band together to go on adventures and quests. They are certainly different from medieval guilds, which were in effect professional associations that set standards for the quality of goods produced by their members and negotiated with feudal lords for favorable treatment and rights, also providing a means for artisans to pool their resources and knowledge, helping to train new members. If anything, the closest comparison to feudal times is not to medieval guilds but to the relationship between landlord and tenant farmer. Players who sign up for Web3 gaming guilds become "scholars" who get to play the game with borrowed assets they otherwise could not afford, paying back a share of their earnings to the guild organizer. Sometimes they borrow money to buy in, with the promise of making a living playing a game. For a young, unemployed person who loves gaming, what could be a better vocation?

As with all things, there are risks and unintended consequences to this innovation. During the pandemic, *Axie Infinity* became a popular game in the Philippines as many people found themselves out of work and more than a bit bored. "The whole concept of scholarships got popular in the Philippines. During the pandemic when everybody was home, or lost their jobs, *Axie Infinity* NFT gaming became really popular in the Philippines," said Ria Lu, country manager for the Philippines for Laguna Games, a US-based Web3 gaming project.[16] "At the end of the day a big part of Southeast Asia is still considered developing. And so money is a big thing. People are always figuring out ways of making money. Getting into blockchain, crypto, NFTs is really primarily a way to make money for most people in Southeast Asia." And for a while, there was money to be made playing the game for rewards that could be easily converted to cash. But she adds, "players really need to understand that treating it as a normal money-making job is not sustainable. Because NFTs go up, they go down. You can't treat that as your main source of income."

Lu thinks that NFT-based gaming is not a real vocation, "especially for Filipinos who are still in poverty who don't have a lot of savings. If they rely on one source of income, and it suddenly stops or drops, it's not good for them. That's why I don't really think that [earning money] is a good motivation for NFT gaming. In the Philippines, people would borrow money to buy NFTs for *Axie*, treating it as a business investment. Which I really don't think people should treat it that way. It should be thought of differently."[17]

Ultimately, people will play how they want, but for Lu it is "kind of sad that you're playing the game not for the experience. Because that's the whole point of a game. The whole point of a game is an experience. That happens a lot in the Philippines. Where you have guilds, whose jobs are really to go into all these NFT games, have their scholars play, and then make money, and then they split the profit after that."[18]

Lu has been in the gaming industry in the Philippines for fifteen years. During that time, she has seen how global forces have transformed the business. The Filipino-born executive's career has blossomed along with her home country's gaming industry, which has become a major player in the industry. Globalization led a wave of outsourcing and offshoring, and game development was no exception, said Lu. "We were under contract to not say that we were making parts of the games for these companies." They had to fight for recognition: "Of course over the years we fought back. It's like, 'Dude, this is intellectual property. We designed this for you, we made this for you, at least acknowledge us in your credits.' Eventually, they started putting us in the credits. You would see Philippine game companies in the credits now."[19]

What began as an offshore game development factory has blossomed into a thriving industry with a few, but not many, independent studios: "I feel that we don't have enough of the independent games. When I say independent games, I'm referring to these studios that make their own games." Independents struggle because developing a game is expensive. Said Lu, "Not a lot of studios have that kind of runway."[20]

To get over that, a lot of companies do both nowadays. That is, "They have a side of the company that does the outsourcing, and then there's a side that's doing their own game as well." Most investors are still from outside the country. Web3 helps to level the playing field for developers in these countries. Already, the Philippines is getting recognized for its role in driving Web3 adoption. Yield Guild Games has raised more than $20 million from Andreessen Horowitz and other top VCs.

More interestingly, these projects can bootstrap by sharing ownership with their community, so long as the game is fun. The early backing from users can help the game become more valuable, and everyone benefits. "Games take a while to make. There are a lot of game companies who run out of funds midway, before they even finish the game that they're making. With NFT gaming, since people buy NFTs right from the start, even before the game is launched, there's funds for the company to run. There's a better chance of finishing the game than a traditional game company," said Lu. "If you're developing a game, nothing's coming in. Because you haven't launched yet. That's the risk for small games to do so in the Philippines. In terms of business, it might be more sustainable for smaller game businesses to do NFT gaming." Play-to-earn gaming may never work at scale as a vocation, but for cash-strapped but creative studios across the developing world, the Web3 model could help them fulfill their potential where the old model failed. That is reason enough to want it to succeed.

Case Study 3: Dollarization, Destabilization, and Survival

"It's faster to drive money from Nigeria to Ghana than it is to send a wire transfer because, with a wire, the money must first go to New York and then to London before coming back to Africa," said Dickson Nsofor, CEO of Korapay. He was describing how the global financial system fails African countries, businesses, and individuals. Nsofor set out to serve these parties four years ago when he launched Korapay, a Pan-African payment infrastructure company.

"I've never believed in bitcoin as a speculative asset, never believed in bitcoin as a store of value. But I've always believed in cryptocurrency and blockchain as a medium of exchange," said Nsofor, who likens the technology to electricity—powering financial solutions the way electricity powers your toaster or fridge.[21]

Korapay employs more than one hundred people in Canada, Nigeria, and elsewhere in Africa. It has become the largest cross-border business-to-business remitter in Nigeria. Since launching, it has processed billions in cross-border payments, using cryptoassets like bitcoin and USDC as the underlying payment tool, but settling transactions to traditional fiat currencies. Nsofor told me in an interview that many of the world's largest companies doing business in Nigeria use Korapay to exchange Nigerian naira (NGN) to US dollars, often completely under the hood. In other words, many brand-name companies are using crypto for payments and don't even know it.

Nsofor said, "We are bridging the gap by using global financial tools like blockchain to connect Africa to the world." He is integrating

Web3 tools into traditional business processes, and Korapay is a model for the transition from TradFi to DeFi. For Nsofor, bitcoin and other cryptoassets are media of exchange through a peer-to-peer technology. But he also acknowledged these tools empower people, especially if they're underbanked, in countries where the local currency is hyperinflationary and the government corrupt.

Alex Gladstein told us that he has met people in the Global South who are skeptical, even hostile, toward Europe and America because of the history of colonialism and, more recently, neocolonialism. "There's a growing number of people in the Global South who don't want to be controlled by their dictator or by their own local government. They also don't want to be controlled by Washington or by Brussels."[22] Places like Africa "thirst for something else, for something different, when it comes to money and payments. I think you see bitcoin and stablecoins filling that gap big-time." The data back this up. More Nigerians own cryptoassets than in any other country, at 22 million people, or 10 percent of the population, according to research firm Triple-A.[23] Nigeria is the number one country in the world by Google keyword searches for "Bitcoin" and "Crypto."[24]

In 2023, I visited South Africa as a guest of Standard Bank to better understand how Web3 was taking shape there and across the continent. This is a continent with a young, digitally native population, where technology tools are widely available, but existing financial infrastructure is out of reach to most and many people are underemployed. Strangely, these weaknesses may prove to be strengths in adapting to and adopting Web3, as Africa has the potential to leapfrog legacy *financial* infrastructure and tap into Web3—the ownership web—seizing the digital property rights and payment tools that they otherwise lack in the physical world. "Africans innovate out of necessity," said Ian Putter, an executive at Standard Bank. Indeed, more than once, a South African used the word *survive* to describe their livelihood, as in "I drive an Uber, but I also help my brother with his business to *survive*." The hustler mentality of underemployed people in places like Africa, borne of necessity, has driven them to experiment with Web3. In the long run, this may be their great advantage.

In the early days, many crypto believers had high hopes that this asset class could help onboard the unbanked and shelter them from currency debasement. In 2013, Arianna Simpson of Andreessen Horowitz traveled across southern Africa. In Zimbabwe, she witnessed the effects of really bad hyperinflation and heard heartbreaking stories of loss. One family lost a child because hospitals had no penicillin. Others lost their jobs and suffered financially. When she returned to the States, her friend—a cofounder of Blockstack—explained how bitcoin was deflationary and could provide an alternative system to Zimbabwe's. She thought, "It's not certain that bitcoin is going to work. But if it does work, then it feels really transformational."[25]

Alas, it was an idea whose time had not yet come. But Simpson was undaunted and today Andreessen Horowitz (also known as a16z) is actively funding projects in emerging markets: "We're seeing Web3 start to permeate the rest of the world, and it's taken some time. There's a long-standing narrative around financial inclusion, bringing other parts of the world into our financial system through Web3. I think it's starting to work now. Some of these projects have boots on the ground and are really affecting people in emerging markets."[26]

Simpson supports Web3 applications aimed at consumers: "They're positive for both the creators and builders who are actually launching Web3 products and services." She thinks that the infrastructure has improved significantly, supporting the creation of "more approachable consumer interfaces and experiences."[27] In Korapay's case, Nsofor has gone one step further and concealed cryptoassets entirely from the product.

In February 2022, I joined a panel with economist and noted Web3 skeptic Nouriel Roubini and Reza Baqir, then governor of the State Bank of Pakistan, the country's central bank. A few days before the session, the State Bank recommended that the country ban all cryptocurrencies, something that bank officials were still debating.[28] Of course, such a law would have the unintended consequence of outlawing all digital goods, including NFTs, securities tokens, and stablecoins, to name a few. This kind of ban would be bad for Pakistan's fledgling innovation economy. Baqir had his reasons: an influx of digital assets could further destabilize the already weak economy and currency, thanks to dollarization, the process by which people swap out a local currency for USD or some other asset.

Nigerians, Nsofor said, have a similar view. "Go to every young person in Lagos, Nigeria, or across Africa and ask them, 'Would you rather get paid in USDC or naira?' And they'll say, 'USDC.' There's so much pressure on African countries to dollarize." He added, "You see businesses changing their invoices to dollars, freelancers changing their bills to dollars. You even find local Nigerian talent all shipping out to take foreign jobs because they want to get paid in a currency that's not the local currency."[29]

Of Nsofor's more than one hundred employees, most are Gen-Z Nigerians who are, in Nsofor's words, "crypto-native," meaning they prefer to do all their finances in crypto rather than fiat. "I think every one of my employees would prefer to get paid in USDC or bitcoin rather than naira, because it's easier to use and it doesn't get inflated away." Government rules prevent him from doing that. Indeed, the Central Bank of Nigeria has advocated for a similar ban to the one proposed in Pakistan. Are these central banks waging a hopeless battle? Forty percent of Africans are under fifteen years old.[30] In Nigeria, mobile Internet penetration is at 34 percent and will hit 50 percent in five years based on current projections. Will freelancers working for American companies or (increasingly) DAOs and Internet-native organizations "opt out" of their local currency now that a US dollar stablecoin is available? If local merchants begin accepting USDC or equivalent, then the last true demand for local currency is tax collection. The government manufactures demand for a currency by requiring you to pay your taxes in it. But in Nigeria, 57 percent of the economy is considered "informal" and so most people are bypassing taxes anyway.[31]

Whether the dollarization of these economies would be a net positive to the world is unclear. On the one hand, locals have a way to move and store value that is relatively stable. They can use these financial rails to work for foreign or Internet-native organizations and build wealth for themselves. This flattens the world and could drive more prosperity. The counterpoint is that already fragile governments in volatile regions could collapse under the weight of a collapsing currency, which historically has been very bad. Initially, the Central Bank of Nigeria was hostile toward cryptoassets, even proposing an outright ban. In January 2023, it released a research report that hinted at a change (or at least a softening) of tone, saying the time had come to create a regulatory framework for stablecoins and other tokens. Whether such a move will slow rather than hasten the dollarization of the Nigerian economy is unclear at this point.[32]

In another sign that digital assets are coming to substitute for more conventional forms of money, in December 2022 the United Nations High Commissioner for Refugees announced its use of the Stellar blockchain network to distribute digital cash to "internally displaced persons (IDPs) and other war-affected people in Ukraine."[33] Users can download the Vibrant wallet app to their smartphones, and the UNHCR confirms their eligibility and distributes Circle's stablecoin (USDC) directly to recipients' digital wallets. "For displaced people around the world, carrying cash is risky because it can be lost or stolen," the UNHCR stated.[34] These displaced persons can receive funds at a MoneyGram location in local currencies, euros, or dollars. Money-Gram has 4,500 agent locations in Ukraine. Digital assets have now found broad appeal for diverse groups such as the underbanked, those living in war zones, groups fighting oppression, or those just fighting the corrosive effect of inflation.

Conclusion and Takeaways

Web3 promises to fulfill the untapped potential of globalization without creating new externalities in the form of a polluted, hotter, and more unstable planet. The protocols and native assets, and not the rail or container ship, will forge the new trade routes of Web3's economic frontier. Here are the other key takeaways for this chapter:

1. With Web2, artists and other professional creators could reach a global audience, as the Web's second era democratized access

to publishing. This was a huge breakthrough, but it did not go far enough. Web3 takes it one step further by giving creators tools for capturing their own returns on assets. This means that even if you are an aspiring child artist, you have a chance of making a decent living.

2. For the first time in human history, all knowledge workers, creators, entrepreneurs, and everyday people can vie for the same capital to start a business, renumeration for work, or compensation for creative output. If we do this right, it should not matter who you are, where you're from, or even what your name is as long as you create value. This kind of concept promises to upend traditional concepts of work and place and "flatten" the earth more.

3. Entrepreneurs and other business builders who have historically been severed from capital pools in Silicon Valley and elsewhere have a new way to reach global investors. They can also "pre-fund'" projects by partitioning key IP and other assets in the form of NFTs and other tokens that represent a claim on their ideas under construction.

4. Stablecoins will displace legacy payment networks and the US dollar will be a big winner. One of the ironies of Web3 is that one of the first killer apps of tokens is to export the US dollar.

5. Dollarization turbocharged by stablecoins will destabilize governments in the Global South because it will reduce the power of central bankers to control the main lever in the economy. Unlike in developed countries where governments can create demand for the local currency by compelling you to pay your taxes, in countries with weak enforcement and where most economic activity happens in the gray market, this will not be effective.

It might seem that Web3 is an unstoppable force, but in fact there are many reasons Web3 may not reach its potential, as well as implementation challenges, a focus of the next chapter. Also, while the risks of destabilization caused by the powerful force of this technology might lead one to believe that governments will have a smaller role to play in our world, in actuality we need government more than ever, to set the conditions for Web3 to succeed.

PART III
LEADERSHIP

CHAPTER 10

Web3's Implementation Challenges

The rise of Web3 is not without doubters, who are quick to point out that, while promising, these capabilities are nascent, and many questions remain unanswered. Will we have solutions to deal with the potential fallout from disintermediation, dollarization via digital assets, and the potential loss of white-collar jobs to automation, smart contracts, and more? Will Web3 create a new powerful caste of elites who own the foundational protocols of the new Internet, trading one oligopoly for another? Do Web3 tools just make it that much easier to conjure up a Ponzi scheme or other illicit con to dupe the gullible and innocent out of their savings? Web3's progress will depend on being able to answer these questions and confront the status quo. In *Blockchain Revolution*, we called these factors "showstoppers," and I have revisited and updated the list of eight issues that we must carefully consider and address.

The Eight Challenges

1. Web3 will get co-opted by those it seeks to disrupt

One huge open question: Will Web2 giants try to co-opt Web3 innovation, and will TradFi middlemen fight disintermediation and the digitization of financial services? Some incumbents of the old paradigm have adopted cryptoassets and are looking seriously at Web3 and other applications. Some may be trying to blunt innovation from startups, as is Facebook, which is making a fulsome push into NFTs and the metaverse. But it's more likely that incumbents will need to accommodate innovation. Consider stablecoins, a tiny sliver of this whole pie: stablecoins are integrating more into the financial system. AngelList, a leading platform for VC investment, now accepts stablecoins for eligible investments.[1] Mastercard announced plans to integrate stablecoins into its network. It also plans to integrate with CBDCs when they come into existence.[2] Visa now supports transaction settlement with the USDC stablecoin.[3] PayPal, a longtime cryptoasset innovator, has explored its own stablecoin.[4] Payment giants want a firm foothold in the world of programmable fiat. Whether they will be able to adapt in time is up for debate. In 2021, Visa announced it was taking another leap forward into stablecoins: it would launch its own Layer 2 "universal payments channel" where customers could use different stablecoins and CBDCs for payments globally.[5]

Banks should fear central bank digital currencies more than Web3 and DeFi. At least in DeFi, there could be a role for the bank as custodian or market participant. The market will decide. CBDCs, by contrast, could disintermediate banks by government fiat. As the *Economist* noted in its cover story on CBDCs, if everyone started banking directly with the government, and "retail banks were sucked dry of funding, someone else would have to do the lending that fuels business creation. This raises the queasy prospect of bureaucrats influencing credit allocation. In a crisis, a digital stampede of savers to the central bank could cause bank runs."[6]

The bigger risk to Web3 has been the creeping growth of outsize centralized crypto companies, notably exchanges like Binance and FTX, the latter of which sent shock waves through the industry when it collapsed in 2022 under the weight of its own mismanagement and, in all likelihood, fraud. On-ramps like Binance and FTX need not dominate the industry. After all, what makes Web3 so compelling is that it allows for trustless and permissionless transactions between parties. It removes intermediaries rather than reintermediates new ones. As Hester Peirce of the SEC said in the wake of FTX's collapse, "At its core, crypto is about solving a trust problem: how can you interact and transact safely with people you do not know. Traditionally, people have looked to centralized intermediaries or government to solve this problem, but technology like cryptography, blockchain, and zero-knowledge proofs offer new solutions."[7] From this simple premise and core primitives flows what Peirce called a "multitude of other uses, including smart contracts, payments, provenance, identity, recordkeeping, data storage, prediction markets, tokenization of assets, and borderless human collaboration."[8] Bitcoin was the first to make this possible, and Ethereum and DeFi applications have turbocharged it. FTX's sleek user interface and functionality drove users like moths to flames before burning them. Companies like FTX served and may continue to serve as important on-ramps to this asset class and the wider world of Web3. However, the on-ramps to an industry must not define the industry. Right now, Binance accounts for more than half of all cryptoasset volumes. Concentration like this should worry everyone.

2. The technology is not ready for prime time

Is the technology ready for prime time, easy enough for people to use? Web3 is a frontier, and like the American frontier in the old Wild West, there is land to be staked and fortunes to be made. But there are also pitfalls and dangers, and some familiarity with the terrain helps. Accessing Web3 requires an Internet connection and a level of computer literacy that not everyone possesses. This is an implementation challenge that Web3 leaders must overcome.

When we first raised this concern in 2016, the Bitcoin network was worth a few billion dollars and Ethereum had yet to launch. Smart contracts, NFTs, DeFi, and DAOs had not yet been realized. Internet enthusiasts who used bitcoin were battling over its future—remember the Bitcoin block-size wars, over how many transactions a single block should record?[9] Corporations held few digital assets, and governments barely noticed the industry. We saw great potential but questioned whether the technology could cross the chasm to mainstream adoption.

At the same time, enterprises are accustomed to centralization and will typically prefer it, meaning they are likely to embrace so-called "Web3 toolkits" that allow them to build new products and services without requiring a full Web3 stack. Kain Warwick, founder of Synthetix, told us, "There are centralized actors right now, representative of our early state, not the end state. As tools get better, decentralized solutions will be able to outcompete centralized solutions. Eventually, most Internet services will be decentralized. But today, at least, some centralization is a necessary stopgap."[10]

We still need a better user interface for many Web3 basics like wallets. In the early days, shipping a "good enough" minimum viable product was the best means of gathering feedback on the user experience. For example, the first Internet browser, Mosaic, shipped as text readable, not just binary readable. In the short term, it worsened the user experience because it made already slow modems slower. In the long term, it sparked an explosion of innovation. Also, privacy and ownership alone may not matter to most users, so we need to build more functionality that stands alone. Do most members of developed economies care about privacy and use of personal data? Most people don't read terms of use and terms of service; many parents don't know how to prepare their children for using social media or are oblivious to how their children use it. People continually forget their passwords; some simply let some accounts lapse and start new ones.

In part, that's because governments really don't like it. "When [European Central Bank president] Christine Lagarde said that bitcoin was not going to work, she didn't say it because she believed it. She said it because she's worried that it might work," said Albert Wenger of Union Square Ventures.[11] When technology has big regulatory headwinds but suffers from scammers and hackers, innovators have a lot to overcome for broad market adoption. The value proposition must be strong.

Plus, immutability and permanence may be a liability as well as an asset—blockchains will become inflexible. Decentralization does not mean disorganization, but the history of computer science suggests centralized entities can scale quicker. Despite the promise of a more decentralized, open, and resilient Web, we are nowhere near reaching the end of the journey. Some critics use the acronym DINO—decentralized in name only—to describe Web3. Moxie Marlinspike, founder of the popular messaging app Signal, wrote an influential blog post in 2022, titled "My First Impressions of Web3." In this post, he challenged Web3's premise and then dissected how it actually worked, revealing the large gap between the reality of Web3 and its promise. "If something is truly decentralized," he wrote, "it becomes very difficult to change, and often remains stuck in time. That is a problem for technology, because the rest of the ecosystem is moving very quickly, and if you don't keep up you will fail."[12] He pointed out that email, an open protocol, has not been encrypted after thirty years while WhatsApp, owned by Facebook, was able to do it in a year.

In trying out numerous Web3 tools like Ethereum, he concluded that Web3 has many centralized chokepoints and, in some instances, is *less* private than Web2 (and certainly more primitive).[13] Marlinspike is correct that Web3 is not completely trustless: Oracles are trusted entities that feed real-world data to smart contracts. Validators help verify transactions on blockchains like Ethereum. Even in Bitcoin, miners help secure the blockchain by verifying transactions and creating new blocks. Marlinspike poses as a newcomer to this space, but his critique was well reasoned, sobering, and required reading for even the most fervent Web3 adherents.

Charles Hoskinson, creator of Cardano, one of the ten largest Web3 protocols by market capitalization, thinks that Marlinspike is correct in many respects. Rather than conclude that Web3 is not worth pursuing, he believes Marlinspike's concerns are implementation challenges that innovators can overcome. Cardano launched in 2017 but introduced smart contracts in 2021. This caution now looks like prudence in light of some of Web3's growing pains. Hoskinson believes many technologists jumped the gun before solving for some of Web3's basic building blocks. "You need identity, you need metadata, you need standards and certification, you need governance, and you need regulation—and you need to do those five things without compromising censorship resistance, decentralization, and accessibility," he said. Some projects tried to walk before they could run and cut corners. "Every project has to be decentralized, if it's to be Web3," he said.[14]

Full decentralization has been hard to achieve. If we look at it through a traditional business lens, we see that it has some drawbacks. If you are not relying on a central party to execute a transaction, you also cannot rely on them to mediate a dispute or reverse a fraudulent transaction. You cannot seek damages because no central party is at fault. Do we need to build more mechanisms for dispute resolution? Indeed, a group of technologists thought this was such a significant concern, they penned a letter to members of Congress stating, "Financial technologies that serve the public must always have mechanisms for fraud mitigation and allow a human-in-the-loop to reverse transactions; blockchain permits neither."[15]

Some argue that blockchains are costlier and slower to use than traditional payment networks. Transaction fees on Ethereum are higher than those on payment networks like Visa, which adds friction to economic activity in Web3, though these fees are dropping precipitously with new scaling solutions and other purpose-built networks, just as the cost of launching a website dropped from tens of thousands of dollars in the 1990s to nearly free today with new software tools.

Should we all hit the pause button until these technologies are fully scaled up and decentralized? In the past, I have advocated for a more pragmatic approach. Though most founders bring a missionary zeal to their companies, some are more pragmatic than others. In an October 2022 opinion piece for *Fortune*, I wrote about how the Jesuit missionaries in North America were rigidly doctrinaire, but also flexible when it suited them, adapting their teachings to existing native customs, languages, and narratives. The Jesuits translated the Bible and Lord's Prayer into Wendat, the local language. Web3 missionaries should consider translating the dogma of decentralization to fit the circumstances.

Finally, we should acknowledge that, while self-custody is a feature for some, it is a significant impediment to Web3 adoption for others. That means users still need trusted service providers in this space. The tools of Web3 are not intuitive to everyone, and many users have a justified apprehension when it comes to holding their own assets. Roneil Rumburg, founder of Web3 music platform Audius, told me that the FTX issue should "lead to more time and resources spent toward improving the usability of fully self-sovereign, decentralized tooling for managing digital assets," though he acknowledged that while "it's possible to be a self-sovereign crypto user today, the usability bar for doing so is still so high that it's out of reach for many mainstream users."[16] Kain Warwick has a different perspective. He hopes that, "over time, infrastructure will become more decentralized, even if there are centralized components, and those centralized components will be more about usability, user experience, or whatever, and less about custody and control."[17] To be sure, Web3 innovators are making more accessible tools, but individuals and businesses particularly will still need trusted agents and partners, if nothing else, to prevent what Tyler Winklevoss called the "five-dollar pipe wrench attack" of getting mugged for what's in your wallet.[18]

3. The energy use is unsustainable

The future of Web3 and distributed applications will be built on proof-of-stake systems like Ethereum, Cosmos, Cardano, and Solana, which are far less energy intensive than Bitcoin. Because Bitcoin uses a lot of energy, opponents call it wasteful, but something "wastes" energy if that energy serves no useful function, whereas the Bitcoin network secures hundreds of billions of dollars and serves millions of people, including many without access to traditional payment tools.

Bitcoin can even help subsidize renewable power projects by providing a rough-and-ready buyer of electricity right at the source; in other words, no need to build expensive power lines to justify a project. ExxonMobil is mining bitcoin in North Dakota to help curb its emissions. The pilot project has been enough of a success that the company plans to roll it out on a much wider basis. ConocoPhillips is reportedly working on a similar project. Here's how it works: A typical Bakken well produces oil but also natural gas, which is burned off or flared into the atmosphere. This is a significant source of carbon entering the atmosphere. Due to natural gas flaring, the Bakken Shale resembles a large city when photographed from outer space. Instead of flaring the gas, ExxonMobil has partnered with Denver-based Crusoe Energy to capture gas and divert it to generators where it mines bitcoin. According to Crusoe, bitcoin mining reduces the footprint by as much as 63 percent.[19]

Still, Bitcoin should work toward a net-zero target like any other industry. The Crypto Climate Accord (CCA), launched with more than forty supporters, including the World Economic Forum, Energy Web Foundation, Rocky Mountain Institute, and ConsenSys, has the goal of making the world's blockchains 100 percent renewable by 2025. This is a laudable goal, so long as it does not force Bitcoin to be something it's not. To wit, some have suggested changing Bitcoin's underlying code so that it uses the less energy-intensive proof-of-stake consensus mechanism. This would be a mistake. Proof of work is a feature that gives the network resiliency and strength, not a bug. As with all things Web3, the answer to simple questions is often "It's complicated." We must acknowledge the progress of problem solvers in addressing its shortcomings while planning for the long term.

DAOs like Flowcarbon, Regen Network, and others are trying to coordinate mass action to address global issues like climate change. The idea that we can use DAOs, a core Web3 primitive, to address climate change seems at odds with the popular image of the Bitcoin blockchain, and by association all Web3, as a polluter. But often the media narrative does not tell the whole story, and sometimes it opposes the truth.

4. Criminals will use it

Understanding this topic requires some nuance. First, criminals use cash more often than crypto. Why? Because paper cash is difficult to track, whereas blockchains leave a tamper-resistant digital trail that any half-decent Federal Bureau of Investigation agent can use to bust a would-be criminal. Chainalysis estimated that 1 percent of bitcoin transactions are linked to illicit activity, and it has built an estimated $3 billion business using blockchains to bust criminals and keep institutions safe.[20]

Anyone who has seen the headlines knows this answer alone is unsatisfactory. After all, the biggest financial scammer since Bernie

Madoff may prove to be Sam Bankman-Fried, former CEO of failed crypto exchange FTX, who has been charged with several crimes. The collapse of FTX eroded public trust. With FTX, we got exactly what Bitcoin's creator, Satoshi Nakamoto, sought to route around: a "too big to fail" organization where the handful of actors in power took excessive risks behind closed doors, leading to FTX's insolvency and ruin.

In periods of economic dislocation or technological innovation throughout history, bad actors have exploited unwitting investors. Niall Ferguson broke this process into four stages. First comes displacement, when a "change in economic circumstances creates new and profitable opportunities." Next comes euphoria or overtrading, a feedback loop where rising expectations drive higher asset prices. Third comes the mania or bubble phase, when first-time investors pile into a now-crowded trade, and swindlers try to rip them off. After the bubble comes distress, when insiders with private information begin to dump their holdings. Finally comes revulsion or discredit, as remaining investors "stampede for the exits."[21]

Ferguson noted that prominent Web3 critics would have been delivering the "last rights to shares" in the aftermath of the South Sea Bubble. Of course, public equities and equity financing became foundational capitalist primitives. Web3 tools offer an off-ramp from the overreliance of intermediaries like FTX. As we have described in this book, creative people around the world have redoubled their efforts to build useful, robust, safe, simple, decentralized tools on open protocols.

We asked a few of them whether the collapse of FTX changed their view of Web3. No, said Ria Lu of Laguna Games. "You need to be aware of what Web3 is, if you want to play in the space, and that includes all its good and bad points."[22] She reflected on the difference between Web2 and Web3 actors: "I've been in the game industry for fifteen years, but I've never encountered as many people trying to exploit our game maliciously as when I started working at Laguna Games and doing NFT games." She said that "fraud, greed, and the lack of accountability" were easily finding their way into Web3 along with the positives of "decentralization, ownership, community, and distributed decision making." In her view, the FTX collapse is "sad and infuriating" but not surprising: "Web3 is a Pandora's box." It strengthened her resolve to advocate for "more decent players in the Web3 space." That there are so many "indecent players" in the space has been a historically big problem that so far nobody has been able to solve for.[23]

So we must hold bad actors accountable while preserving what makes the technology so great. Fortunately, many in government see beyond the crimes of an individual to the value inherent in the industry. At congressional hearings on FTX hosted on December 12, 2022, the day after Bahamian police arrested Bankman-Fried, Congressman Patrick McHenry (R-NC) said this: "Bankman-Fried's play is nothing new; we've seen it before. In the late 1800s when Union Pacific purposefully inflated the price of railroad construction to line its executive's pockets. Or in the 1900s when the con man George C. Parker was arrested for illegally 'selling' the Brooklyn Bridge, Madison Square Garden, and the Statue of Liberty. In the 2000s . . . Enron engaged in a massive corporate fraud and corruption sending shock waves throughout the business world." McHenry said that he could draw many comparisons between these pretenders and Bankman-Fried—in essence, "old-school fraud," new technology.[24] He added, "We still use railroads, we still buy and sell real estate, and we still rely on businesses to provide services." He advised his colleagues "to separate out the bad actions of an individual from the good created by an industry and innovation" because he believes "in the promise of digital assets and those around the world building on blockchain technologies."[25]

Representative Tom Emmer (R-MN) urged his colleagues to "understand Sam Bankman-Fried's fraud for what it is: a failure of centralization, a failure of business ethics, and a crime. It is not a failure of technology." He said that since he assumed office in 2019, he has worked across the aisle so that "the future of crypto reflects American values, the same way the Internet does today. For the most engaged members of Congress on crypto policy, the FTX collapse reminds us why we care so deeply about this technology. Decentralization is the point."[26]

These politicians' remarks remind us that one of Web3's attributes is its peer-to-peer utility: anyone, anywhere, can use it to move assets without intermediation. Ironically, many of Web3's bad actors have been the managers and owners of centralized businesses rather than the users of the technology.

5. Governments will stymie or even crush it

Web3 innovators are still concerned that government officials, politicians, and special interest groups that fund their campaigns will try to kill it, protecting their own interests or fearing what they do not understand. For example, Senator Elizabeth Warren (D-MA) has been a vocal critic of crypto. In her view, only bad actors use crypto, an allegation that has no basis in fact.[27] I hoped that, as a self-styled progressive, Warren would be more open-minded about cryptoassets, because they could undercut the economic power of big banks. On the last point, Warren has tried to rebuff criticisms that she's a socialist by claiming to be a "capitalist to the bones." Her biggest beef has been with powerful vested interests like Wall Street banks that use their proximity to political power to seek gain concessions.

But, in an analysis of Warren's "Digital Asset Anti–Money Laundering Act," Coin Center, a leading nonprofit focused on policy issues facing cryptoassets, called the bill "the most direct attack on the personal freedom and privacy of cryptocurrency users and developers we've yet seen," because it would "force anyone who helps maintain public blockchain infrastructure, either through software development or validating transactions on the network, to register as a financial institution."[28] As financial institutions, these individual volunteers would be legally obligated to "[1] identify and record the personal information of every person who uses their software or sends transactions over their Internet-connected computers, [2] develop risk-calibrated AML programs that block persons from using their software or network throughput if they suspect those people are moving funds related to crime, and [3] file reports about their users without a warrant, government request, or probable cause as the trigger."[29]

Furthermore, privacy technologies like Tornado Cash, Zcash, and Monero have come under scrutiny. In August 2022, "the US Treasury unilaterally and extralegally made it a crime for Americans to use Tornado Cash," a popular privacy tool and "mixer," for conducting private and anonymous crypto transactions.[30] It is a piece of software, some open-source code that nobody owns. Yet the Treasury Department added the website and associated wallets to the Office of Foreign Assets Control (OFAC) sanctioned list, typically reserved for "persons involved in terrorism, enemy states, or other state-sanctioned activities and ensure that these individuals cannot get the benefit of the US financial system."[31] The US government alleged that money launderers had washed $7 billion through it. Elliptic, a blockchain analytics firm, put the figure closer to $1.5 billion.[32] In a 2023 report, Chainalysis concluded it was closer to 34 percent of all the platform's volume.

But are these sanctions even effective? As Chainalysis pointed out, "Tornado Cash runs on smart contracts that can't be taken offline the way a centralized service can, so there's nothing except the legal consequences of sanctions violations stopping anyone from using it."[33] But the closure of Tornado's Cash's "front end," which is sanctionable, has had a big impact: as of December 2022, Tornado Cash had about $111 million in total value on the platform, a 78 percent decrease within a year.[34]

In today's digital economy, large digital platforms and financial intermediaries and their shareholders capture wealth asymmetrically, resulting in growing social inequality. The structural power imbalance between platforms and users has eroded traditional concepts of privacy and autonomy. We must help Senator Warren and others to understand that Web3 can help us solve the problems that governments are not solving. But Web3 cannot fulfill its promise without government participation and regulation. Sheila Warren of the Crypto Council for Innovation sees regulation as a useful tool in driving adoption. Ignoring it is as bad as poorly regulating it: "You can't ostrich your way out of regulation, as much as some in crypto would like to try. The early advocates who thought, 'If we pretend regulation doesn't exist and regulators don't exist, they'll ignore us,' were wrong."[35] In her previous role at the World Economic Forum, she regularly convened stakeholders and gently nudged them until they could work out solutions.

That said, our regulatory and policy infrastructures are inadequate for the digital age. Web3 rewires the Internet for privacy, inclusion, and participation, where individuals who create value in networks—be it social, financial, or other—reap that value. Bad bills like Senator Warren's won't kill Web3 because the technology is globally decentralized and widely used all around the world, but they will drive people, capital, and other resources to offshore jurisdictions.

This is a pivotal moment in this trajectory of digital assets, Web3, and blockchain. Governments understand traditional custodial financial intermediaries, but Web3 is noncustodial. Regulators understand overseeing companies and individuals, not clever code and math. Labeling every digital asset a security is also problematic. Representative Emmer, a member of the growing blockchain caucus in Congress, raised concerns with SEC chair Gary Gensler's approach: "If Gensler deems a coin with a $1 billion market cap and tens of thousands of investors a security, what happens to those investors? The value of the token will plummet, and retail investors won't be able to trade it."[36] At this point, it seems government cannot stop the industry but their approach to regulation will shape its future.

We need clear rules of the road to bring safe and sustainable innovation to this sector. Many new technologies have bumpy starts where incumbents question their utility. The Internet was a victim of this bias but so too was the automobile. Early automobiles were slow, unreliable, and dangerous for driver and pedestrian alike. We created new rules for automakers, built out roads and erected street signs and traffic lights, and made licensing a requirement for drivers, which helped to smooth the transition away from the horse. The same should be true here. Governments share the onus with individual users, companies who operate in this space, and venture capital investors who bankroll entrepreneurs and policymakers to get this right.

6. The incentives are inadequate for adoption:
the bootstrapping problem

Our concerns here when raising this issue in *Blockchain Revolution* were misplaced. In many circumstances, the opposite is true: tokens serve as an immensely powerful incentive for mass collaboration and adoption by turning early adopters and users into economic participants in the network. Chris Dixon said, "In the Web2 era, overcoming the bootstrapping problem meant heroic entrepreneurial efforts, plus in many cases spending lots of money on sales and marketing."[37] This difficult and costly process led to only a few networks reaching global scale. Once firmly entrenched, new networks targeting similar users struggled to compete against Web2 giants like Facebook. Dixon continued: "Web3 introduces a powerful new tool for bootstrapping networks: token incentives. . . . The basic idea is: early on during the bootstrapping phase when network effects haven't kicked in, provide users with financial utility via token rewards to make up for the lack of native utility."[38]

However, there is another dark side to tokenomics that we have explored in this book: that the economic motive to earn money will supersede all other functionality of a Web3 application. Speculators and arbitrageurs will invade Web3 apps to extract as much value as possible before moving on to the next thing, having never actually *used* the application as intended. To overcome this, we need to make applications useful and fun as stand-alone entities. "Incentives are very important," said Arianna Simpson of Andreessen Horowitz, adding, "if you can couple an incentive mechanism with a product or service or network that people want to use, then that's a really powerful combination. You can't have a token, for example, without a product or service that is compelling and interesting to people. But if you have something that already drives a lot of interest and that people are excited to contribute to, then layering in a blockchain element and a token incentive can be a really useful way of powering that ecosystem. Bringing people into the fold, rewarding them for their contributions, and building a more sustainable mechanism."[39] Ownership and the profit motive must be one of many reasons people interact with one of these applications.

7. Blockchain is a job killer

In *Blockchain Revolution*, we questioned whether blockchain would disintermediate many white-collar jobs such as accounting, legal work, and even management. Yes, Web3 is changing the nature of the labor market, but it appears to be creating more work than it is destroying. We're seeing new kinds of jobs such as digital artists, professional videogame players, liquidity miners, and NFT dealers. Software developers are working for DAOs.[40]

In the Web2 era, a bright young person might set her sights on a career in Silicon Valley or Wall Street. But the large intermediaries considered graduates only from top schools, placing formal accreditations at the top of the list. They would require a person to show up to an office, undergo intensive training, and report to a boss in a chain of command to the top.

Web3, with such innovations as DAOs, have minimal formal hierarchy, management teams, home offices, and so forth. Yes, Facebook and Goldman Sachs still attract top talent, but their monopoly is weakening, evidenced by the flight of quality engineers to startups in Web3, AI, IoT, and other areas.

Yield Guild Games (YGG) is one such community that is pioneering in this field of attracting people to moneymaking opportunities in Web3. "We want YGG to be the platform that people turn to when they'd like to go into a Web3 dapp and earn something, like Fiverr, where creators look for gigs to earn income, but within the metaverse," said Beryl Li, cofounder of YGG. "We're also looking at X-to-earn, which could be learn-to-earn, move-to-earn—like Metacrafters, where you complete certain modules, such as coding, whether it's on learning Ethereum and smart contracts, or Solana and smart contracts. Every time you complete modules, you earn rewards, and then you get hired. The chances for getting hired are greater."[41] Li is referring to the growing popularity of "X-to-earn" Web3 applications such as StepN, Sweatcoin, and *Genopets*.

This could potentially open up new moneymaking opportunities for enterprising Web3 users in the Global South. Katrina Wolfe of Laguna Games also thinks DAOs could be the evolution of the gig economy. "Maybe I have a share in fifteen different DAOs and I see what this team is really doing—I actually have time for that, that looks super fun, let me sign up for it and work on it."[42] You could take your pick of fun and financially rewarding opportunities, assuming you have the requisite skill set, but earn equity or governance tokens or some other financial reward that lets you participate in the upside of the project. Also, Web3 itself is creating new jobs. According to The Block, the employment in the "digital asset" industry has jumped 351 percent since 2019, and 421 firms employ 82,248 people within the industry, compared to 158 companies with only 18,200 employees in 2019.[43]

This expanded economic opportunity set will drive adoption, which in turn will help many early users bootstrap the equivalent of a US dollar bank account. After all, if you're getting paid in the native token of some application to complete a useful task, then converting it to USDC, a popular stablecoin, requires only one more step. Suddenly populations of people with no access to US dollars or in some cases no bank account have a new tool to move, store, and perhaps even invest US dollars. In this sense, guilds can serve as an on-ramp to greater economic prosperity.

8. Governance is like herding cats

Blockchain and DAO governance are evolving in real time. Despite the promise of DAOs, the reality is they suffer from many of the same limitations as traditional governance structures, such as voter apathy.[44] Token holders often ignore governance approvals that require their assent, leaving decision making to a few large, tuned-in stakeholders.[45] That's like most proxy votes for corporations under traditional governance. Moreover, radical decentralization may work for certain industries, but vertical integration and a traditional organizational structure may suit situations such as pharmaceutical manufacturing.

These governance challenges are familiar to any shareholder of a public company or citizen of a democracy. When we wrote *Blockchain Revolution*, we questioned not only the ability of PoS networks to push software updates but also the actual viability of proof of stake as a system for organizing and securing a blockchain. So, in comparison, today's problems stem from prior governance successes, such as the launch of dozens of working Layer 1 smart-contracting platforms. Thus DAOs still need to overcome this challenge.

Conclusion and Takeaways

Technology innovation is not some deterministic process whereby the result is a foregone conclusion. Random events and external shocks can change the outcome. As we see in the conclusion in plenty of examples, early failures or use cases set a technology back—just ask the boosters of nuclear power generation. When we look at Web3, we see a lot that needs improvement and more than a few things that could go wrong. But we must ask ourselves whether these are reasons not to pursue and support it, or if they are implementation challenges to be overcome. Here are the takeaways:

1. Do not judge a technology by the first instantiations of it. Web3 is not just about cryptocurrencies, meaning money and payment applications. It is a general-purpose technology. The technology is rapidly maturing to accommodate the needs that users will soon place on it.

2. The criticism that Web3 wastes energy is not credible, as most innovation is now happening on proof-of-stake systems like Ethereum. Bitcoin, despite its carbon footprint, uses less energy than washing machines globally, and draws nearly half its power from renewable sources, making it, as an industry, a global leader.[46] Also, there is no shortage of Western elitism in the view that poor people the world over who use it as a lifeline should somehow feel guilty about it.

3. Powerful forces of the old paradigm can fight or embrace these tools, but they are unlikely to co-opt them. The pull from Web3's native communities is too powerful, and already we are seeing hearty and healthy adoption by many enterprises.

4. Web3 is no job killer. It is an enabler of people the world over to earn money in new and novel ways. However, if we accept the thesis that Web3 makes it possible for a developer in India to vie for the same

work and "stock-based compensation" in the form of token rewards as a developer in Austin, Texas, then the Texan had better bring something bigger and better to the table. Hey, assets are always bigger in Texas, right?

5. Governments can derail the path of Web3. They can also enable it.

On this last point, we need a sensible framework and regulations that protect users and still promote innovation. The status quo of regulation by enforcement must end. "Innovators can't build on quicksand," said Sheila Warren. "They can't move if they don't know what regulators are going to do in response."[47] In the conclusion, we try to resolve this last question and provide recommendations for our readers on how to move forward.

CONCLUSION

The Web3 S-Curve: A Projection More than a Prophecy

"There are decades where nothing happens, and there are weeks where decades happen," said Vladimir Ilyich Ulyanov of the Bolshevik Revolution.[1] He also went by the name Lenin. Such is the tug of pseudonyms in the instigation of change. Digital technology compounds at an exponential rate. Moore's law posits that computing power doubles roughly every eighteen months. For decades it has proven prophetic, though many think that growth rate will slow until innovators commercialize quantum computing. Still, the world today is virtually unrecognizable from the one the late Gordon Moore lived in when he was developing semiconductor technology. The coronavirus pandemic of 2020 accelerated our digital lives and smashed critical links in global supply chains as countries closed borders to protect the health of their citizens and restart local manufacturing. Remote work became the new normal.

The fundamental building blocks of Web3—blockchains—have existed since Bitcoin launched in 2009. Yet, fourteen years later, Web3 feels early. This follows past technologies. "In the early stages of a technology, the rate of progress in performance is relatively slow," Clayton Christensen observed. As it gains adoption and public understanding, it improves and scales at an accelerated rate. Eventually, however, the technology hits a saturation point and the growth in the technology slows. At this stage, "ever greater periods of time or inputs of engineering effort will be required to achieve improvements."[2] This process—slow at the start, accelerating and fast in the middle, decelerating and flattening toward the end—is commonly called the "S-curve."

Charles Hoskinson thinks Web3 has not reached the inflection point of the S-curve, what he calls its "ChatGPT moment" in reference to the AI chatbot from OpenAI, which launched in 2022. "ChatGPT is one of those technologies that, now that it's out, people all acknowledge disruption. Because of that, it's getting mass adoption—five days to a million users." He added, "Everybody's scared shitless about it." That's what blockchain needs, "that ChatGPT moment, where it's obvious that this is the direction that the market is going." In his view, Solana, Binance, Cardano, and Bitcoin each has its own flavor, but nobody's looking at any of them and saying, "This is the model that's going to get a billion users, and all we have to do is add water."[3]

Speaking of just adding water, let's remember that the agricultural revolution occurred over tens of thousands of years of trial and error before most people gave up a nomadic life of hunting and gathering for a settled life of agriculture and animal husbandry. The industrial revolution was seeded in the fifteenth and sixteenth centuries, long before the invention of the steam engine, with advances in chemical weapons and firearms, which made conquest possible; the printing press, which introduced mass communication; the collapse of feudalism, which changed the power balance between capital (lords) and labor (peasants); and the rise of global trade, which accelerated the exchange of goods, ideas, and pathogens. But actual *industrialization* didn't begin until centuries later. The steam engine was a novelty for many decades before Thomas Newcomen applied his version to coal mining in England in the 1710s.[4] Well into the twentieth century, many rural Europeans were living like their peasant forefathers of centuries ago.[5] After World War II, "rural life in Belgium could have been depicted by Millet: the hay gathered with wooden rakes, the straw beaten with flails, fruits and vegetables handpicked and transported by horse-drawn carts."[6]

The information revolution began with advances in the science of computing in the 1930s and the invention of the transistor in 1949, but computers took nearly half a century to became household appliances. Leonard Kleinrock and his graduate students at the University of California, Los Angeles sent the first Internet message in 1969 but the US government took nearly twenty-five more years to release the Web for commercial use and another thirty years for businesses and NGOs to put it into the hands of 5.18 billion people.[7] What took hundreds of years for industrialization and decades for computation has taken Web3 roughly a decade, that is, to hit the inflection point of the S-curve before parabolic growth.

Will individuals and enterprise adopt Web3 on a faster timeline than the first or second era of the Web or other technology innovation like personal computers? Don't be so sure. When Albert Wenger first used the Internet, he was in the computer lab at the Massachusetts Institute of Technology. He discovered Mosaic on his machine and wound up spending the next four hours surfing the Web instead of doing his stats homework. "I was like, 'Oh my God, newspapers are dead tomorrow!' But it took twenty years."[8] With Web3, particularly because of the current incompatibility of the asset class with existing laws, disruption might take longer. "The Internet was far simpler technology," he said. "This technology is way more complicated, plus has headwinds. If that took twenty years, then I think we have to adjust our expectations, that this might take thirty years or forty years."[9] Hoskinson agreed: "There are going to be decades of work long-term, just as there have been decades in the Web. We invented JavaScript, the browser, web certificates, and cookies in the 1990s. . . . Have we achieved the nirvana of the Web?"[10]

Wenger also thinks public perception of a technology can shape its growth and adoption, regardless of the underlying utility. He points to nuclear power. "We've been able to build nuclear power plants since the 1960s and we've just been slow, slow, slow," he said, exasperated. "Even though they make zero-carbon-footprint electric power, and we should have tons of them, people are like, 'Not in my backyard, not in my state, not anywhere near my city.'"[11] Technological adoption and diffusion follow different paths that are not just dependent on the characteristics of the underlying technology. He said they also are impacted by early use cases, complexity, and of course the regulatory environment. Big scandals cannot derail a technology. The South Sea Bubble did not spell the end of joint-stock companies, after all. But they can set it back. The industry must reckon with the collapse of FTX, lest it become our Three Mile Island.

Another Rare Moonshot Moment for Policymakers

Governments have another unique opportunity in human history to lead, and some are answering the call to action. In 2022, the White House released its long-awaited executive order on digital assets and Web3. Winston Churchill is reported to have said, "You can always count on the Americans to do the right thing after they've tried everything else."[12] And, indeed, the report felt at the time as a breakthrough of the logjam that had clogged any progress on the issue. However, in the wake of the FTX collapse, the Biden administration walked back its initial enthusiasm. In the White House's 2023 Economic Report, the administration dedicated an entire chapter to the risks of crypto, rehashing some long-debunked criticisms. Where are we now? Web3 and digital assets are matters of national interest because they are foundational to the next era of economic progress. American entrepreneurs and companies dominated the first twenty-five years of the commercial Internet. Times have changed: access to technology, talent, entrepreneurial verve, and the tools needed to build great businesses and organizations are accessible everywhere. Some countries, such as Singapore and Dubai, have welcomed Web3 businesses with open arms, creating a regulatory arbitrage that is luring some of the industry's top organizations. The United States is not in pole position in this race.

As executive director of the Blockchain Association, Kristin Smith's job is to make the case for why Web3 matters and why those in power should care. She knows a thing or two about getting things done in Washington, DC. A consummate DC insider, she has been around government for twenty years, pushing, nudging, and persuading, effecting real and substantive change in the process. For Smith, Web3 is a rare bipartisan issue. The more lawmakers learn, the more they understand Web3 as a general-purpose technology that can improve the lives of everyone. The FTX collapse has muddied the waters, but Smith is helping lawmakers on both sides of the aisle to look beyond Sam Bankman-Fried and identify how Web3 could benefit their constituents.

For example, financial inclusion gets Democrats' attention. Smith said, "If we look at the demographics of crypto owners, it's an outsize number of African Americans and Hispanics. These individuals find crypto more accessible as a method of investment and more useful to share money, particularly with remittances overseas."[13] Naysayers often mischaracterize tokens as speculative investments or digital playthings for privileged groups. In reality, 37 percent of underbanked individuals own and use digital assets to make payments, store value, invest in emerging technologies, and access an array of other DeFi services to fill the gap in TradFi services.[14] Moreover, 44 percent of digital asset holders in the United States are people of color, according to a survey by the University of Chicago's National Opinion Research Center.[15] By contrast, 10 percent of the fully banked population owns digital assets in the United States.[16]

Outside the United States, the situation is starker. Not only are many people in the Global South unbanked or underbanked, but their local currencies are often hyperinflationary, and they suffer under their governments' draconian capital controls. Consider Nigeria, where nearly 30 percent of residents use bitcoin as an alternative to fiat cash. In El Salvador, people hold more bitcoin wallets than bank accounts.[17] The digital asset wallet MetaMask, through which individuals buy, sell, and store cryptocurrencies and digital art like NFTs, is most popular in the Philippines and Vietnam, where young people earn money in DeFi and play-to-earn videogames such as *Axie Infinity*.[18] During a recent bout of currency volatility in Turkey, digital asset volumes in lira grew to $1.8 billion, more than any of the preceding five quarters, and the lira became "the most traded government-issued currency against Tether" in the fall of 2021.[19] (Tether is a popular US-dollar-based stablecoin, so in effect Turks were looking for an easy way to store value in greenbacks.[20])

Smith said, "The other narrative is Web3, which works for both sides of the aisle, because everybody hates [Web2] companies and wants an alternative, a democratization of web services, whether it's web infrastructure or applications."[21] Many are surprised to discover that "the people who are really passionate about this space aren't all

Libertarian anarchists."[22] In fact, "They're often lifelong Democrats, people who care very much about climate issues, antipoverty issues, people who often align with democratic values," said Smith. Her efforts have worked. Congress has a bipartisan Web3 group including Senators Cynthia Lummis (R-WY) and Kirsten Gillibrand (D-NY), who collaborated on a Web3 bill, and Debbie Stabenow (D-MI) and John Boozman (R-AR), who are also working together. "This bipartisan policymaking leads to the most stable policies, policies that don't fluctuate from one administration or Congress to the next. We hope to keep it in that place," said Smith.[23]

Smith looked back to when the US government opened Internet technologies to the private sector in the 1990s.[24] She recalled that, in 1995, only one office of the Senate's hundred offices had Internet access—Ted Kennedy (D-MA). "Somebody had showed Senator [J. James] Exon (D-NE) the Internet somewhere, and he printed off all this pornography, put it in a little blue binder, and showed his colleagues what the Internet was."[25] Congress's early concerns about the Internet? That it was merely a tool for publishing pornography. Republicans found that particularly offensive.

President Joe Biden's executive order is a first step toward a durable and lasting framework for Web3, a modern-day rethinking of the seminal Telecommunications Act, which was critical to the explosion of innovation in the first era of the Internet.[26] Policymakers and industry leaders can work together today to come up with something roughly akin to the 1996 act. For starters, any new rules must distinguish between the technology and the companies that build services on top of it. Take cues from the Internet—we don't regulate network time or the Hypertext Transfer Protocol (aka the Web) but we do try to regulate platforms like PayPal, Internet service providers like Comcast, and other corporate entities like Amazon that use those protocols. Still, we can try a similar tack here. The problem is not too much decentralization in crypto, but too much centralization in these crypto corporate intermediaries, with their inner machinations and financial health concealed from the public.

"It was the Ron Wydens (D-OR) of the world, the Al Gores

(D-TN), the [Jay] Rockefellers (D-WV)—senators on the Democratic side who saw the Internet as a powerful tool. The 1996 Telecom Act had a lot of activity. The E-Rate Program of Olympia Snowe (R-ME) helped.[27] Conrad Burns (R-MT) did this section 706 in the Telecom Act, talked about tracking Internet usage.[28] It was fairly bipartisan back then, too, with the exception of this antipornography," she said. The Telecommunications Act classified Internet service providers (ISPs) as lightly regulated "information service providers" rather than more heavily regulated "common carriers" like telephone networks, and not liable for the content shared over their infrastructure. That had broadly positive effects on the Internet's explosion in value, and ISPs did have responsibility for taking down or blocking material that broke the law.[29]

What should legislators keep in mind? Smith said, "Policymakers like to talk about the same activity, same risk, same regulation. But the risks are totally different because of this ownership element. We have digital assets because we have digital scarcity for the first time, and we can transact without relying on a third party to manage the transaction for us. That is fundamentally different from how traditional financial services work today."[30] Regulators outsource aspects of the law through, for example, KYC, AML, and CTF checks.

Smith noted that policymakers, institutions, and consumers are all talking about stablecoins. "They want to know that, if it's a dollar-backed stablecoin, then there's a dollar in the bank account. That's not unreasonable. We need a framework for looking at that, because that's very different from fractional reserve banking today. Also, the digital world does custody totally differently from the traditional financial services world. Similarly, everybody wants to know that markets have integrity," that they're not susceptible to manipulation.[31]

"We want somebody keeping an eye on those on behalf of consumers. But there's no commodity spot market regulator. The SEC doesn't have that authority. The CFTC doesn't have that authority. Congress must put forth new regulation. Legislators must look at the different actors in this space and find the right regulation. There's a parallel to the 1996 act in that it treated ISPs differently, not as telecom companies, even though we can do voice over the Internet" through Voice over Internet Protocol (VoIP).[32]

Smith continued: "Similarly, digital assets have different qualities. We need to figure out the actual risks and write a framework to address them. We've had some forward-looking regulators who have put out good guidance, particularly the Financial Crimes Enforcement Network and, to a lesser extent, the Internal Revenue Service."[33]

Smith credited federal agencies for looking at their authority and doing their best to interpret crypto accordingly. But all agencies are now looking to Congress for clarity and new authority to act. She said that Congress could deliver "something in 2023, maybe 2024, because it's a big enough market. We have an educated enough policy-making body. We have champions on both sides of the aisle, and we've had some bad market incidents" that have increased the sense of urgency.[34] "Legislation takes years. It's not something that happens overnight—unless it's attached to a must-pass bill in the middle of the night without anybody's knowing."[35] She underscored this important point: "Without Congress, then we end with regulation by enforcement and that's a really blunt tool because a judge or a jury is limited to the facts of a given case, and 'bad facts make bad laws,'" she said.[36]

Add regulators to the list of stakeholders who want to see big changes in how Web3 is governed and regulated. Hester Peirce of the SEC has said bluntly that "the regulation-by-arbitrary-and-tardy-enforcement-actions approach on which we have relied is the opposite of a rational regulatory framework." In a January 2023 speech, she railed against her own agency, calling its method imprecise, incoherent, inconsistent, arbitrary, random, harmful to innovation, and wasteful of the agency's time and resources.[37] Regulators in other jurisdictions around the world are likewise stumbling without coherence and clarity.

Striking the Right Balance between Public and Individual Rights

Reasonable people can agree that, in the wake of the FTX collapse, policymakers must come up with a framework for Web3 to grow responsibly, as they did with the Telecommunications Act of 1996. But they must do so without trampling other individual rights, foremost of which is privacy. Privacy is foundational to a free society, and members of that society have plenty of good reasons to remain private in transactions. Perhaps you want to donate to a Ukrainian humanitarian group without exposing yourself to Russian recriminations, as Ethereum founder Vitalik Buterin did. He revealed this fact, "doxxing himself" in response to US Department of the Treasury sanctions on Tornado Cash in August 2022.[38]

Increasingly, OFAC has targeted personal cryptoasset wallets addresses. In 2018, there were fewer than 100 addresses on the list; but by 2022, it had grown to 400. In 2021, the office started sanctioning cryptoasset service providers as well.[39] In the eyes of many, this is a textbook example of government overreach. Coin Center's Jerry Brito and Peter Van Valkenburgh wrote: "It appears be the sanctioning of a tool that is neutral in character and that can be put to good or bad uses like any other technology." They argued that the OFAC was not sanctioning a specific bad actor who committed a crime but all Americans who might want to "use this automated tool to protect their own privacy while transacting online."[40] Simply put, the government was curtailing citizens' liberties without due process—and there's nothing more anti-American than that.

Unfortunately, the Treasury Department's action does what Senator Elizabeth Warren's proposed bill would do if enacted: undermine Americans' privacy by extending financial surveillance to an unreasonable and, perhaps, unconstitutional degree. Chris Giancarlo, formerly of the CFTC, thinks that financial surveillance is justified only when (1) there is probable cause of wrongdoing and (2) law enforcement has obtained a warrant. But he thinks that the US legal regime has already gone too far. Governments are now "gathering information *in the event something goes wrong* versus gathering information *with probable cause*," he said in a December 2022 interview (emphasis added).[41] The changes have happened imperceptibly, like the proverbial frog in the pot of water that doesn't realize that the water is near boiling, killing it.

Web3 returns to individuals a degree of autonomy lost to more muscular bank secrecy laws and the ever-invasive big tech companies. When nearly all payments are digital and run through some intermediary, and where the government can gather information on anyone *in the event something goes wrong*, then people lose their privacy. "Citizens in a free society deserve a degree of economic freedom," Giancarlo said. We should be thoughtful and deliberate before implementing new laws or embracing innovations like CBDCs, which China is using as a surveillance tool to "associate and link political conformity with economic choice," he said. "Political nonconformity can lead to a loss of economic livelihood or even poverty."[42]

The collapse of FTX was a failure of corporate control. Lawmakers can advocate for a federal regulatory framework for cryptoasset exchanges that custody user assets to bring them under the purview of federal regulators. Some crypto users might self-custody assets to conduct illegal transactions, just as some gun holders might use weapons to commit crimes. But, as Giancarlo told us, there is no reason to ban "technology that is used for lawful and anonymous transactions." He pointed out that, for centuries, Americans have enjoyed a right to privacy—no unlawful search and seizure.[43] He also acknowledged that most free societies opt to diminish "law enforcement capability in exchange for a degree of personal freedom and presumption of innocence."[44] We must strike a balance. Hester Peirce of the SEC agreed with Giancarlo: "Legitimate law enforcement objectives require the government sometimes to gather information about private activities, but defaulting to government surveillance of all private activities runs counter to fundamental American principles."[45] Empowering individuals to control their own assets and use these assets lawfully and freely should not be controversial.

What is the legal liability of writing code? The uncertainty around the government's response to that question is harming America's lead in Web3, according to Sheila Warren of the Crypto Council for Innovation. "Developers don't want to live here. . . . It's not just about companies offshoring themselves, but people second-guessing where they live. Some, but not all, in government see the potential of Web3 as an area of innovation where America can lead," she said.[46] Kain Warwick of Synthetix is among those who believe that "the state is an inefficient coordination mechanism, at a very fundamental level." He echoed Warren that "to change the system, you need to work from within it. You can't stand on the sidelines and shout slogans at it. When something like [Tornado Cash] happens, and there is an outright clash of the state versus privacy, it brings into stark relief that these two are not compatible."[47]

Peirce, an SEC commissioner, sympathizes with law enforcement and regulators as well as developers, all of whom find themselves dealing with unknowns. She said, "Regulating people who write code is more difficult from a practical and legal perspective . . . because it would impinge on free speech and would raise fairness issues since open-source coders cannot exercise control over how their code is used."[48]

In democratic societies, free speech should not be controversial even if it is expressed in code. Nor should privacy in transactions be controversial, even if conducted through software: privacy is the standard in the "real economy" with banknotes, coins, prepaid cards, and so forth. When you pay for your groceries in cash, the cashier doesn't ask for your driver's license unless you're buying alcohol, and they don't question your motives. Of course, free speech and privacy are not an absolute rights: courts have identified circumstances in which governments can or should limit them, as when they incite violence or undermine national security. But free speech and privacy, including how we spend our money, should generally be protected. The Coin Center blog post spelled it out clearly: "Privacy is normal for a salaried employee, a charitable donor, even a celebrity, but privacy is not normal if you do these things on Ethereum *unless you use Tornado Cash*."[49]

Despite all these valid arguments, one can hardly envy the government's position. Short-term, the decision of many firms to shoot first and ask questions later was probably sensible for them: they wanted to avoid guilt by association. But in the medium to long term, the industry must ensure, to whatever extent possible, that governments recognize software as protected speech and that developers are free to build neutral technology tools.

What Governments Can Do

"Some people in crypto have acted for too long as if Web3 was a given" and will follow the same trajectory of Web1 in the 1990s, said Albert Wenger, partner of Union Square Ventures.[50] But he points out "the Web had real regulatory tailwinds. There was no sales tax on the Internet. There was the safe harbor of the Digital Millennium Copyright Act, the safe harbor of the Communications Decency Act, that famous Section 230. We had all these regulatory tailwinds." Wenger is referring to Section 230 of the Communications Decency Act, which enshrined important legal protections for platforms, enabling them to host and even moderate user-generated content without being held liable for what users said or did. By contrast, "Web3 has regulatory headwinds everywhere in the world and especially in the United States but in many other countries."

Wenger's prescription for scaling Web3 has less to do with technology than regulation. First, we need regulatory clarity: what's a security and what's not. "I think a lot of these tokens are not securities," Wenger said. A growing chorus of academics, economists, and businesspeople agree.[51] In Wenger's telling, the uncertainty around how to classify tokens is pushing innovation offshore. Some regulators agree. Peirce shone a light on the absurd notion that all tokens are securities in a 2023 speech. "Why not set forth a coherent legal framework in a rule?" she mused. "If we continued with our regulation-by-enforcement approach at our current pace, we would approach four hundred years before we got through the tokens that are allegedly securities. By contrast, an SEC rule would have universal— albeit not retroactive—coverage as soon as it took effect."[52]

Peirce suggested that the SEC do away with its old methods and adopt a notice-and-comment process that allows "broad public and internal participation in developing a sound regulatory system." Peirce recommended pitching a big tent, including federal and state regulatory authorities, developers, users, entrepreneurs, consumer protection advocates, and critics. She pointed to creation and governance of the Uniform Commercial Code as an example of effective interstate collaboration. The next era of the Web deserves a policy framework worthy of its tremendous potential, much as the first era of the Internet got its own Telecommunications Act.

Second, the United States should foster US-dollar-based stablecoins as it will strengthen the dollarization that has benefited Americans disproportionately. Wenger said, "If the United States isn't leaning in to having lots of well-regulated USD on-chain, that will hurt rather than help the dollarization."

Finally, regulation of the old Web—such as requiring every platform or system to have an application programming interface—would benefit adoption of the new Web. "If we had mandatory API access for customers, I think Web3 would really take off," said Wenger.[53] Users could interact with multiple social meeting sites through a single program or "client." He might get his wish. In December 2022, Bloomberg reported that Apple was planning to let users install alternative app stores on iOS.[54] Not quite willingly, though: the European Union forced Apple's hand by adopting a new set of standards for regulating Internet gatekeepers, known as the Digital Markets Act of 2022.[55] According to the European Commission, the new regulation will "put an end to unfair practices by companies that act as gatekeepers in the online platform economy."[56] The commission seeks to remove the bottlenecks to innovation and competition.[57] The rules went into effect in January 2023. The commission planned to designate gatekeepers by June 2023, as this book went to press. By the time you read this, Apple and other large tech companies could be changing their tactics to comply with the new law, unblocking avenues for competing Web2 platforms and Web3 builders.

In effect, the European Commission, not exactly the vanguard of economic liberalism, has empowered Web3 entrepreneurs. Web3's impact on governments and other institutions will be immense. For example, with Web3 tools like DAOs and stablecoins, entrepreneurs can employ people anywhere in the world and pay them in a stable digital currency, if the value of the employee's local currency is too volatile. Competition for talent and expertise will get more fierce, and jobs may move elsewhere unless lawmakers and regulators at all levels of government have an open mind.

This notion of competition between governments, of so-called "regulatory arbitrage," has been a hallmark of Silicon Valley's libertarian-leaning intelligentsia for decades. To wit, James Dale Davidson and Lord William Rees-Mogg argued in their 1997 book, *The Sovereign Individual*, "Proliferation of jurisdictions will mean proliferating experimentation in new ways of enforcing contracts and otherwise securing the safety of persons and property. The liberation of a large part of the global economy from political control will oblige whatever remains of government as we have known it to operate on more nearly market terms."[58] While competition among nations for talent and capital is fierce, the notion that governments will wither and bend to the will of the market remains an overstatement. Since that book was released, governments have played a more assertive role in society and in the economy, too, if we factor in the outsize role of central banks since the 2008 global financial crisis. The institutions of government in nation-states are not going anywhere, and they will remain a significant force in society and the economy for years to come. But they must evolve.

The counterpoint is that countries are not companies: treating citizens like customers can be bad for democracy, because companies don't treat customers equally, and large campaign donors already have undue influence over US legislators. Such pay-to-play policymaking erodes the democratic principle that all people are equal under the law and that the country's government reflects all its citizens' values and principles, not just those of the wealthiest. As Davidson and Rees-Mogg observed, digital technology rapidly erodes most current jurisdictional advantages: "New types of advantages will emerge. Falling communication costs have already reduced the need for proximity as a necessary condition of doing business."[59] This is undoubtedly true, especially after the pandemic.

Web3 may help to revitalize democratic institutions, through experimentation with new modes of governance such as DAOs. In *The Wealth of Networks*, Yochai Benkler wrote that Internet users were exercising "their newly expanded practical freedom to act and cooperate with others in ways that [improved] the practiced experience of democracy, justice and development, a critical culture and community." He noted, "Individuals can do more for themselves independently of the permission or cooperation of others."[60] We see that in Web3.

Free enterprise and a market economy are the main drivers of economic prosperity. But time and again, governments have played a critical and sometimes deciding role in guaranteeing such prosperity and creating the conditions for companies to succeed. Governments gave royal charters to early seafarers, guaranteeing them trade and allowing them to raise capital to pursue risky ventures. Governments in the United States backed the early steamship entrepreneurs and later underwrote the growth of railroads. Patent and trademark laws encouraged innovation while property laws helped level the playing field, at least for white, literate, and educated property-owning men. Most people were deprived these rights and, to the shame of those in power, millions of individuals were property themselves.

Environmental regulations ensured that industry could not dump poison in waterways and forced them to clean up after themselves. For decades, NASA bought most of Silicon Valley's microprocessors, helping industry on the southern shores of San Francisco Bay to get its footing. The Internet itself was the by-product of public sector investment and private-public collaboration. So, we need governments to stay with the times so this collaboration between public and private sector can continue.

In *The Wealth of Nations*, Adam Smith put forth the idea of an "invisible hand" of the market, whereby the pursuit of individual self-interest can lead to the greater good of society at the whole. This powerful and enduring metaphor has backstopped laissez-faire and free-market economics since its publication in 1776 and has, broadly speaking, worked. But did Smith really believe the market was always right? No. In fact, in *The Wealth of Nations*, he argued that this pursuit of self-interest could lead to market failures like monopolies, that government intervention was sometimes necessary to prevent or minimize such failures. Just because a market works most of the time, does not mean it will work all of the time. This is as true today as it was in late-eighteenth-century Scotland. Free-market capitalism is the best solution most of the time. Web3 and peer-to-peer technologies are the best solution most of the time. But sometimes we need some centralization, coordination, governance, and regulation to move a technology forward. Decentralized does not mean disorganized.[61] Smith argued that government could intervene for the benefit of the economy and society. Ironically, the rise of Web3 and other innovative technologies like AI necessitates bold, farsighted, and innovative leadership from governments. Let's hope we get it.

Where Will Web3 Get Built? Go East, Young One, and Grow Up with the Industry

This evolution creates opportunities and concerns. Unlike the first era of the Internet, we will have different Silicon Valleys—different Silicon networks that are open and decentralized—where people can thrive and build businesses that create wealth, jobs, and prosperity. The days of American exceptionalism are over, according to Sheila Warren of the Crypto Council for Innovation. "America is not leading the adoption in this industry. *It just isn't*. That's not surprising—it's extremely obvious—and that shouldn't upset anybody. Also, yes, the United States will have an outsize role in the policy, the trajectory of policy."[62] Indeed, many countries, like Dubai, are courting Web3 entrepreneurs.

Yat Siu thinks that Asia will lead the way in Web3. "Every major Korean game company has already openly spoken about a Web3 plan or a Web2.5 plan. They may be faulty in their ideas, they may not be fully embracing decentralization, but they're talking about it openly, and their customers are not rejecting or resisting it." He compared that with the West: "Electronic Arts, Activision, any company uttering the word *NFT* has to dial back aggressively because gamers have been rejecting it."[63]

Why are some American gamers rejecting Web3 games? "It's more of a rejection of capitalism broadly than a rejection of ownership," said Siu.[64] "The rejection is not so much related to 'Should I own this?' It's more a rejection of a digital form of capitalism." The government of Japan has been coordinating global regulations, with Prime Minister Fumio Kishida putting the metaverse and Web3 on Japan's national growth agenda. "I think Japan is maybe the only government in the world that has an NFT white paper," said Siu.[65]

The Road Ahead

The COVID pandemic punctuated modern human history. It forced us as a society to rethink our day-to-day existence. Do I need to commute to an office every day to be productive with colleagues? Do I need to travel so much to cultivate business relationships? The pandemic also forced us to ask bigger questions and rethink concepts like globalization, at least, in terms of moving physical assets around the world. We may have hit the pinnacle of the global supply chain just as the flow of information rises steadily, digital goods begin their ascent, and the industrial age of the twentieth century accelerates its miniaturization and localization with innovations in materials science and additive manufacturing.[66] More and more, we will be containerizing value, not commodities.

Is Web3 defining a new Internet-native counterculture analogous to the counterculture of the 1960s? In the same way Baby Boomers rebelled against the institutions and cultural mores of their parents' generation, today's crypto-native generation is rebelling against a strict and permissioned financial system, the rigid hierarchy of institutions in art and culture, and the closed and stifling systems of Web2. In 1960s, counterculture icon Timothy Leary encouraged his followers to "turn on, tune in, and drop out."[67] Today's youth are applying that mantra to technology—turning their brains on to tokens, tuning in to Web3 and its myriad applications, and dropping out (or at least opting out) of the legacy financial system. Soon they may find themselves existing simultaneously on two planes of human existence, driving an avatar in the metaverse with an identity, assets, lived experience, community, and relationships as rich or richer than those they possess in the physical world. In the process of rethinking how to live online, they will transform every industry.

Web3 is global: its users, developers, builders, and influencers come from all around the world, from Manila to Lagos, Toronto to Bogotá. Web3 is distributed—its Internet-native organizations are not based anywhere and seek contributions from all kinds of people. Web3 is permissionless—you do not need a bank account, ID, permanent residence, or other credential to access it, just an Internet-enabled device. Web3 is commercial—as a medium for value, blockchains promise to upend every industry in the world. The first era of the Internet, which includes Web1 and Web2, upended information industries like news, advertising, music, retail, and ICT services. It democratized access to information for those who had access to reading online and later democratized access to publishing, provided that you played by the rules of the dominant platforms. This new era will make those disruptions—important as they were—look quaint. For example, financial services, foundational to all industry, enterprise, and human economic activity, is undergoing a metamorphosis from a lumbering caterpillar, devouring everything in its path, to a soaring butterfly thanks to Web3 innovations of tokens, smart contracts, and the other core DeFi primitives. But like every new being starting out in the world, our Web3 caterpillar is fragile and may require care, attention, and nurturing for it to soar to new heights. What can you do? It's not just crypto-native Gen Zers who can seize the mantle of Web3. Everyone has a role to play.

For business leaders in all industries, Web3 comes with immense promise and potential peril. On the one hand, these tools can improve transparency, trust, and efficiency and reduce costs. They can help you engage more closely with customers through NFT loyalty programs, token-gated community efforts, and more, or improve the metabolism of global trade by using stablecoins, or lead to new and undiscovered markets both online and in the real world. They may also require significant investments in technology and disrupt traditional business models. Incumbents need to thread Christensen's needle—the innovator's dilemma—to manage the transition. Start by staying informed about Web3 technologies and how your industry can use them. Explore pilot projects or partnerships to test the potential benefits and challenges of Web3 technologies. Engage with regulatory bodies and policymakers to ensure that businesses have clarity on the rules of the road. You can be difference makers.

For entrepreneurs the world over, Web3 is a wide-open frontier for you to make an imprint and build something that will create value and change the world. As we have shown in this book, geography, gender, creed, or color matter less in Web3 than in any period before. We have showcased entrepreneurs who are using these tools on all five continents to flatten the earth, which is to say, level the playing field. What can you do? Start now. Try launching a DAO with a group of like-minded individuals around a common goal and see where it takes you and what you learn. Maybe even learn-to-*earn*. Attend meetups in your area. Web3 is global—these gatherings happen *everywhere*. Think long-term: Web3 may feel like a discrete segment of the Internet today, but in the Web3 toolset are general-purpose technologies that you can wield to change the world in ways similar to and more powerful than the first era of the Web.

For financial services executives, Web3 is shaking the windows and rattling the walls of banks. Rather than put in earplugs to cancel the noise, step outside. As incumbents, you face many risks and opportunities. Don't prop up declining businesses (active inertia) but don't disrupt yourself too quickly. Use your legacy products and services to bankroll experimentation and growth in other areas. Build out a digital asset custody business—most of your customers will want to keep banking with you but only if you innovate. Collaborate with peers in the industry to launch a stablecoin. Consider creating "compliant DeFi" gateways that anyone with credentials can access. Launch your own branded on-chain credential that users can passport to other banks and financial institutions. While you're at it, form an on-chain diagnostic team that can help your clients and industry partners make sense of the technology where more economic activity will occur. Be bold.

For government leaders, you have a tough assignment. Web3 forces you to confront long-outdated laws and concepts and compels you to come up with a framework for the future. We need government leaders to act. What are tokens, and how should we classify them under law? How can we bring DAOs into the legal framework without putting undue burdens on startups? Are "smart contracts" really contracts? If not, how can we reconcile the common law with the law of code? How can we apply IP law to NFT artwork, or in-game assets, or storytelling assets like in Shibuya or MV3? There is no easy answer to every question. Here's what you can do: Be welcoming to entrepreneurs in this industry. Develop a clear and simple message and stick to it. Realize you're competing for talent and capital on a global playing field with fewer obstacles than ever before. Be a model user of technology. Protect citizens from criminals but trust adults to make reasonable judgments with their money. Start now.

Students, you are the luckiest group of all. The future belongs to those who understand new technologies and harness them responsibly for good. Web3 tools like learn-to-earn create new ways to creatively gain new insights and credentials. Consider seeking out mentors or advisors with experience in Web3 to guide you as you navigate this new landscape. Start on Twitter, Discord, and other venues where Web3 builders congregate. If my generation, the Millennials, were the first to be "bathed in bits," then Gen Z and its successors were the first *born* in bits—digital natives in the truest sense of the word. That is your superpower—use it.

Everyday Internet users will see their experience online change in ways that I hope are broadly positive. Web1 and Web2 were immensely powerful forces for good, but they had drawbacks that Web3 can correct, if we will it. The future is not something to be predicted; it is something to be achieved. Whether you are the American CEO of a Fortune 500 company, or a student in India, or an artist in Barcelona, or a kid in the Philippines, you have a chance to make your mark on the world. Web3 can help you do it.

ACKNOWLEDGMENTS

Writing a book while building a business and being a dad to two kids under four always felt like a fanciful, if not impossible, proposition until it was done. If it takes a village to raise a child, it took me a small town to make this book a reality, and so I owe a debt of gratitude to dozens (if not hundreds) of friends, family members, colleagues, clients, teachers, and others who have generously shared their wisdom and insights and shaped my thinking on this subject.

They say if you're the smartest person in the room, find another room. Fortunately, this has never been my problem. Every room I enter floors me with the knowledge, passion, and breadth of understanding of so many of this industry's builders and advocates. During the research process, I spoke with many pioneers, among them Gabriel Abed, Sunny Aggarwal, April and Sevi Agregado, Jeremy Allaire, Tim Beiko, Mark Cheng, Gennaro "Jerry" Cuomo, Chris Dixon, Jelena Djuric, Mike Dudas, Oleg Fomenko, Stepan Gershuni, Christopher Giancarlo, Alex Gladstein, Brett Harrison, Charles Hoskinson, Sami Kassab, Torey Kohara, Gregory Landua, Aleksander Larsen, Beryl Li, Ria Lu, Sarah Grace Manski, Dan Mapes, Charlie Morris, Sascha Darius Mojtahedi, Scott Moore, Jesse Nickson-Lopez, Kevin Owocki, Sidney Powell, pplpleasr, Yorke E. Rhodes III, Roneil Rumburg, Ariel Seidman, Ryan Selkis, Arianna Simpson, Yat Siu, Kristin Smith, Sadie St. Lawrence, Jules Urbach, Sishir Varghese, Jesse Walden, Jimmy Wales, Sheila Warren, Kain Warwick, Albert Wenger, Alex Wilson, Tyler Winklevoss, Brett Winton, Katrina Wolfe, John Wu, and Ali Yahya. On our podcast *DeFi Decoded*, cohost Andrew Young and I have interviewed dozens more, including Sam Andrew, Bill Barhydt, Adrian Brink, Sharon

Byrne-Cotter, Mike Belshe, Galia Benartzi, Ethan Buchman, Luigi DeMeo, Anthony Di Iorio, Jake Hannah, Ben Lee, Jon Lister, Zaki Manian, Scott Melker, Dickson Nsofor, Greg Osuri, Lex Sokolin, Eric Turner, Anatoly Yakovenko, Rodney Yesep and Peng Zhong. My thanks to all these experts for discussing their perspectives and experiences with me.

However, I owe a few folks a great deal of thanks for their outsized role in this project and I want to acknowledge them:

First among them is Kirsten Sandberg, this book's editor, who somehow found time amidst her duties as editor-in-chief of the Blockchain Research Institute, and as a university professor to dedicate the better part of a year to this book project. Kirsten, you are much more than an editor. You helped to shape many of the book's core concepts. Your countless days and nights turning around drafts, taking my calls to hear out my half-baked ideas, conducting background research, preparing interview questions, *interviewing* dozens of people with me, then parsing those transcripts, and adding your own insights was Herculean and critical.

I would also like to thank my long-time agent and friend Wes Neff who pushed me to write this book. Wes, your wise counsel, and unwavering support have helped immeasurably. I also got lucky with my publisher: from the moment Hollis Heimbouch at HarperCollins agreed to take on this book, she has been in my corner as a coach, editor, thoughtful critic, and altogether great partner. James Neidhardt, Amanda Pritzker, Heather Drucker, and others at HarperCollins have played and will continue to play key roles in this process, and I thank you all mightily.

At the Blockchain Research Institute (BRI), Dr. Alisa Acosta, director of research and education, was an invaluable resource. She has taken our research on Web3 and run with it, developing several blockbuster courses on the Coursera platform. Her work has helped extend its influence to more than 100,000 individual learners all over the world. At the BRI, Roya Hussaini and Jody Stevens bring professionalism, energy, and expertise to everything they do, and this book project was no exception. Other BRI team members—Global Director Joan Bigham, Director of Client Experience Andrew Facciolo, Chief Catalyst Douglas Heintzman, and Head of Growth Michael Glavich—contributed in many ways. Thanks also to the BRI's regional directors—Aline Daoud in the Middle East, Carl Amorin in Brazil, Ian Putter in Africa, Inhwan Kim in Korea, and Simon Tribelhorn in Europe—for carrying these ideas to an engaged global audience. My thanks to Juliano Lissoni, managing director of MCI Canada and co-producer of our Web3 & Blockchain World conference; he and his team have been excellent partners. Finally, a shout out to Meagan O'Hara for her superb web design skills.

I also want to acknowledge my colleagues and friends at Ninepoint Partners, specifically Co-CEOs James Fox and John Wilson, and Chief Compliance Officer Kirstin McTaggart. Seemingly every day I learn something new from each of you. You are great partners and long-term strategic thinkers who understand Web3's immense potential and have supported me in everything we have done together, including giving me the flexibility to write this book.

This book would not have been possible without my parents. My mom, Ana Lopes, has always been my staunchest supporter and has been a great help on this book, closely scrutinizing early drafts and providing comments, suggestions, and even some pointed criticisms, but always wrapped lovingly in the praise that only a mom can muster. As for my dad, Don Tapscott, where to begin? Nearly a decade ago, on the side of a mountain in Mont Tremblant, Quebec, over rib eyes and red wine, we chose to collaborate on our first research report. I could not have anticipated then how that one conversation would change my life so profoundly. Dad, you are my mentor, business partner, and friend.

Above all, I want to acknowledge my wife, Amy Welsman, who has been by my side through life's many twists and turns, and who has always pushed me to take risks and go outside my comfort zone. Thank you for encouraging me to write this book and for supporting me unwaveringly through the long and sometimes difficult process.

You have taught me how to be more resilient, nurtured my nascent creativity, and set an example in life that I marvel at daily. I would not be the person I am today without you. You have also given me life's greatest gifts in our two daughters, Eleanor and Josephine, and those girls are so fortunate to have you as a mom and role model. This book is for them and for you.

NOTES

Introduction

1. Margaret O'Mara, *The Code: Silicon Valley and the Remaking of America* (New York: Penguin Books, 2019).
2. Federica Laricchia, "Smartphone Penetration Worldwide as Share of Global Population 2016–2021," Statista, Jan. 17, 2023, https://www.statista.com /statistics/203734/global-smartphone-penetration-per-capita-since-2005/#.
3. https://a16zcrypto.com/posts/announcement/expanding-uk-andreessen-horowitz/.
4. Penny Crosman, "What Does the Future Look Like for Crypto Lenders?" *American Banker*, Jan. 23, 2023, https://www.americanbanker.com/news/what -does-the-future-look-like-for-crypto-lenders.
5. Irene Vallejo, *Papyrus: The Invention of Books in the Ancient World*, trans. Charlotte Whittle (New York: Knopf, 2022).
6. "State of the USDC Economy," *Circle*, Circle Internet Financial Limited, March 10, 2023, https://www.circle.com/hubfs/PDFs/2301StateofUSDCEconomy _Web.pdf, accessed April 12, 2023.

Chapter 1: The Web Is Entering a Third Era

1. "skeuomorph, n.," *Oxford Advanced Learner's Dictionary*, Oxford University Press, accessed Sept. 2022, https://www.oxfordlearnersdictionaries.com/us/definition /english/skeuomorph.
2. Laurence Iliff, "EV Designers Are Seeing Grilles in a Whole New Way," *Automotive News*, July 3, 2021, https://www.autonews.com/design/ev-designers -are-seeing-grilles-whole-new-way.
3. Chris Dixon, interview by Alex Tapscott via Zoom, Sept. 2, 2022.
4. More than anyone else, Tim O'Reilly helped to popularize the term *Web2*. Technologist Gavin Wood was the first to use the term *Web3* when describing the evolution of blockchain and cryptoassets into a new web. See Tim O'Reilly, "What Is Web 2.0: Design Patterns and Business Models for the Next Generation of Software," O'Reilly Media, Sept. 30, 2005, https://www.oreilly .com/pub/a/web2/archive/what-is-web-20.html; and Gavin Wood, "Why We Need Web 3.0," *Gav of York Blog*, Medium, Sept. 12, 2018, https://gavofyork .medium.com/why-we-need-web-3-0-5da4f2bf95ab.
5. Jimmy Wales and Larry Sanger of Wikipedia; Julian Assange of WikiLeaks.
6. "The Ownership Economy 2022," Variant Fund, April 28, 2022, https://variant .fund/articles/the-ownership-economy-2022/.
7. Chris Dixon, "Five Mental Models for the Web," interviewed by Ryan Sean Adams and David Hoffman, *Bankless Podcast*, ep. 90, Nov. 1, 2021, https://www .youtube.com/watch?v=jezH_7qEk50.

8. "Tim Berners-Lee on 30 Years of the Web," *Guardian*, March 12, 2019, https://www.theguardian.com/technology/2019/mar/12/tim-berners-lee-on-30-years-of-the-web-if-we-dream-a-little-we-can-get-the-web-we-want.

9. According to Wall Street Zen, institutional shareholders hold 71.80 percent of Uber, and Uber insiders hold 30.20 percent, with zero percent retail investors. "Uber Technologies Inc. Stock Ownership: Who Owns Uber?" *WallStreetZen* (Hong Kong), as of Nov. 25, 2022, https://www.wallstreetzen.com/stocks/us/nyse/uber/ownership.

10. "Tim Berners-Lee Wants Us to Ignore Web3," CNBC.com, Nov. 4, 2022, https://www.cnbc.com/2022/11/04/web-inventor-tim-berners-lee-wants-us-to-ignore-web3.html.

11. Tim Berners-Lee, James Hendler, and Ora Lassila, "The Semantic Web," *Scientific American*, May 1, 2001, https://www.scientificamerican.com/article/the-semantic-web/.

12. Max Fisher, *The Chaos Machine: The Inside Story of How Social Media Rewired Our Minds and Our World* (New York: Little, Brown, 2022), 332–33, https://www.news.com.au/technology/online/social/shock-casualties-of-facebooks-news-block-bom-betoota-advocate-wa-fire-australian-government-pages-wiped/news-story/.

13. Fisher, *The Chaos Machine*, 8–9.

14. Fisher, 9–10.

15. "World's Biggest Data Breaches," Information Is Beautiful, as of April 14, 2022, https://informationisbeautiful.net/visualizations/worlds-biggest-data-breaches-hacks/.

16. Steve Lohr, "Calls Mount to Ease Big Tech's Grip on Our Data," *New York Times,* July 25, 2019, https://www.nytimes.com/2019/07/25/business/calls-mount-to-ease-big-techs-grip-on-your-data.html.

17. Carly Hallman, "Everything Facebook Owns: Mergers and Acquisitions from the Past 15 Years," TitleMax, Sept. 2019, https://www.titlemax.com/discovery-center/lifestyle/everything-facebook-owns-mergers-and-acquisitions-from-the-past-15-years/.

18. Satoshi Nakamoto, "Bitcoin: A Peer-to-Peer Electronic Cash System," Bitcoin, Oct. 31, 2008, https://bitcoin.org/bitcoin.pdf.

19. Arianna Simpson, interview by Alex Tapscott via Zoom, Sept. 13, 2022.

20. Matthew L. Ball, *The Metaverse: And How It Will Revolutionize Everything* (New York: Liveright, 2022), 59.

21. Kevin Owocki, interview by Alex Tapscott via Google Meet, Aug. 17, 2022.

22. Beryl Li, interview by Alex Tapscott via Zoom, Oct. 3, 2022.

23. Owocki interview by Alex Tapscott.

24. Tim Beiko, interview by Alex Tapscott via Zoom, Aug. 9, 2022.

25. Paraphrasing a quote from Tracy Kidder, *The Soul of a New Machine* (New York: Avon, 1981), 33.

26. Thomas Hobbes, *Leviathan or the Matter, Forme, and Power of a Common-Wealth*

Ecclesiastical and Civill (printed for Andrew Crooke, at the Green Dragon in St. Paul's Churchyard, 1651), https://www.gutenberg.org/cache/epub/3207/pg3207 -images.html.

27. John Locke, *Two Treatises of Government and A Letter Concerning Toleration*, 1690, https://www.gutenberg.org/files/7370/old/trgov10h.htm.

28. Don Tapscott and Alex Tapscott, *Blockchain Revolution: How the Technology Behind Bitcoin and Other Cryptocurrencies Is Changing the World* (New York: Penguin Portfolio, 2016).

29. Adrian Shahbaz, "Rise of Digital Authoritarianism," Freedom House, 2018, https://freedomhouse.org/report/freedom-net/2018/rise-digital -authoritarianism.

30. Sunny Aggarwal, interview by Alex Tapscott via Zoom, Aug. 8, 2022.

31. James Dale Davidson and Lord William Rees-Mogg, *The Sovereign Individual: Mastering the Transition to the Information Age* (New York: Simon & Schuster, 1997), 189.

32. "token, n.," *Oxford Advanced Learner's Dictionary*, Oxford University Press, accessed Jan. 15, 2023, https://www.oxfordlearnersdictionaries.com/us /definition/english/token_1.

33. Chris Dixon (@cdixon), Twitter posts, Sept. 20, 2021 (2:56 p.m.), https://twitter .com/cdixon/status/1440026974903230464 and https://twitter.com/cdixon /status/1440026978048958467, accessed Oct. 16, 2021.

34. Brett Winton, interview by Alex Tapscott via Zoom, Aug. 25, 2022.

35. This quote first appeared in Thomas Draxe, *Bibliotecha Scholastica Instructissima: A Treasury of Ancient Adages and Sententious Proverbs* (London: John Billius, 1616).

36. Andrew L. Russell, "'Rough Consensus and Running Code' and the Internet-OSI Standards War," *IEEE Annals of the History of Computing* 28, no. 3 (July–Sept. 2006): 48–61, https://ieeexplore.ieee.org/document/1677461.

37. "The History of Email: Major Milestones from 50 Years," email on Acid LLC, Jan. 28, 2021, https://www.emailonacid.com/blog/article/email-marketing /history-of-email/; and Sean Michael Kerner and John Burke, "What Is FTP (File Transfer Protocol)?" TechTarget, n.d., https://www.techtarget.com /searchnetworking/definition/File-Transfer-Protocol-FTP#, accessed April 23, 2023.

38. Matto Mildenberger, "The Tragedy of the Tragedy of the Commons," *Scientific American*, April 23, 2019, https://blogs.scientificamerican.com/voices/the -tragedy-of-the-tragedy-of-the-commons/.

39. Michael J. Casey, "The Token Economy, When Money Becomes Programmable," Blockchain Research Institute, 6–7.

40. Peter Cihon, "Open Source Creates Value, But How Do You Measure It?" *GitHub Blog*, Jan. 20, 2022, https://github.blog/2022-01-20-open-source -creates-value-but-how-do-you-measure-it/#footnote2.

41. Owocki interview by Alex Tapscott.

42. Michael J. Casey, "The Token Economy: When Money Becomes

Programmable," foreword by Don Tapscott, Blockchain Research Institute, Sept. 28, 2017, rev. March 28, 2018, https://www.blockchainresearchinstitute .org/project/the-token-economy-when-money-becomes-programmable/.

43. Jay Walljasper, "Elinor Ostrom's Eight Principles for Managing a Commons," *On the Commons*, Oct. 2, 2011, https://www.onthecommons.org/magazine /elinor-ostroms-8-principles-managing-commmons.

44. "Digital Asset Outlook 2023," The Block, Dec. 20, 2022, https://www.tbstat .com/wp/uploads/2022/12/Digital-Asset-2023-Outlook.pdf.

45. Girri Palaniyapan, "NFT Marketplaces Are Centralized, and It's a Real Problem," NFT Now, April 21, 2022, https://nftnow.com/features/nft -marketplaces-are-centralized-and-its-a-real-problem/, accessed Nov. 25, 2022.

46. Ashley Pascual, "What Are Ancillary Rights and Why Are They Important?" *Beverly Boy Blog*, Aug. 10, 2021, https://beverlyboy.com/filmmaking/what-are -ancillary-rights-in-film-why-are-they-important/.

47. Jesse Nickson-Lopez and Torey Kohara, interview by Alex Tapscott via Zoom, Sept. 26, 2022.

48. Yat Siu, interview by Alex Tapscott via Zoom, Jan. 10, 2023.

49. The idea of "digital crumbs" and the "virtual you" were popularized by Ann Cavoukian and Don Tapscott in *Who Knows: Safeguarding Your Privacy in a Networked World* (New York: McGraw-Hill, 1996).

50. For more information on how public key infrastructure (PKI) establishes identity, see "Introduction to PKI," National Cyber Security Centre, Nov. 6, 2020, www.ncsc.gov.uk/collection/in-house-public-key-infrastructure /introduction-to-public-key-infrastructure, accessed Oct. 15, 2021. See also Phillip J. Windley, "Self-Sovereign Identity: The Architecture of Personal Autonomy and Generativity on the Internet," foreword by Don Tapscott, Blockchain Research Institute, March 10, 2022, https://www .blockchainresearchinstitute.org/project/self-sovereign-identity/.

51. OpenOrgs.info, https://openorgs.info/, accessed April 12, 2023.

52. Clayton M. Christensen, *The Innovator's Dilemma: When New Technologies Cause Great Firms to Fail* (Boston: Harvard Business School Press, 1997).

53. Christensen, 172.

54. Morgan Chittum, "Morgan Stanley Sees $8 Trillion Metaverse Market—In China Alone," Blockworks, Feb. 1, 2022, https://blockworks.co/morgan-stanley -sees-8-trillion-metaverse-market-eventually/.

55. Will Canny, "Metaverse-Related Economy Could Be as Much as $13T: Citi," *CoinDesk*, June 7, 2022, https://www.coindesk.com/business/2022/06/07 /metaverse-related-economy-could-be-as-much-as-13-trillion-citi/.

56. Aleksander Larsen, interview by Alex Tapscott via Zoom, Aug. 9, 2022.

57. https://aibc.world/people/dan-mapes/?from=europe.

58. Larsen interview by Alex Tapscott.

59. Ball, *The Metaverse*, 16.

60. Sami Kassab, "The DePIN Sector Map," Messari, Jan. 19, 2023, https://messari .io/report/the-depin-sector-map.

61. Aoyon Ashraf and Danny Nelson, "Canada Sanctions 34 Crypto Wallets Tied to Trucker 'Freedom Convoy,'" *CoinDesk*, Feb. 17, 2022, https://www.coindesk.com/policy/2022/02/16/canada-sanctions-34-crypto-wallets-tied-to-trucker-freedom-convoy/.

62. "Frequently Asked Questions," Silicon Valley Bridge Bank NA, Federal Deposit Insurance Corporation, March 30, 2023, https://www.fdic.gov/resources/resolutions/bank-failures/failed-bank-list/silicon-valley-faq.html.

63. Roneil Rumburg, email to Alex Tapscott, Nov. 18, 2022.

64. Rumburg email to Alex Tapscott.

65. Niall Ferguson, "FTX Kept Your Crypto in a Crypt Not a Vault," *Bloomberg Opinion*, Bloomberg LP, Nov. 20, 2022, https://www.bloomberg.com/opinion/articles/2022-11-20/niall-ferguson-ftx-kept-your-crypto-in-a-crypt-not-a-vault.

66. Chainalysis, "2022 Crypto Crime Report," Chainalysis Inc., Feb. 2022, https://go.chainalysis.com/2022-Crypto-Crime-Report.html. See also Chainalysis, "2023 Crypto Crime Report," Chainalysis Inc., Feb. 2023, https://go.chainalysis.com/2023-crypto-crime-report.html.

67. Owocki interview by Alex Tapscott.

68. Hester Peirce, "Remarks before the Digital Assets," Duke Conference, Washington DC, US Securities and Exchange Commission, Jan. 20, 2023, https://www.sec.gov/news/speech/peirce-remarks-duke-conference-012023#_ftnref15.

69. Niall Ferguson, "FTX Kept Your Crypto in a Crypt Not a Vault," *Bloomberg Opinion*, Bloomberg LP, Nov. 20, 2022, https://www.bloomberg.com/opinion/articles/2022-11-20/niall-ferguson-ftx-kept-your-crypto-in-a-crypt-not-a-vault.

70. Dixon interview by Alex Tapscott.

71. David Kushner, "A Brief History of Porn on the Internet, *Wired*, April 9, 2019, https://www.wired.com/story/brief-history-porn-Internet/.

72. Kidder, *The Soul of a New Machine*, 19.

73. Jack Schofield, "Ken Olsen Obituary," *Guardian*, Feb. 9, 2011, https://www.theguardian.com/technology/2011/feb/09/ken-olsen-obituary.

74. James Burnham, *The Managerial Revolution* (London: Lume Books, 1941), 84.

75. Maya Jaggi, "A Question of Faith," *Guardian*, Sept. 14, 2002, https://www.theguardian.com/books/2002/sep/14/biography.history.

Chapter 2: Blueprint for the Ownership Web

1. Walter Isaacson, *The Innovators: How a Group of Hackers, Geniuses, and Geeks Created the Digital Revolution* (New York: Simon & Schuster, 2014), x, https://www.amazon.com/Innovators-Hackers-Geniuses-Created-Revolution/dp/1476708703/, accessed Nov. 20, 2022.

2. Alan M. Turing, "Intelligent Machinery," Report 67/228, National Physical Laboratory, July 1948, https://www.npl.co.uk/getattachment/about-us/History/Famous-faces/Alan-Turing/80916595-Intelligent-Machinery.pdf, accessed Nov. 20, 2022.

3. Isaacson, *The Innovators*, 91, quoting Kurt Beyer, *Grace Hopper and the Invention of the Information Age* (Cambridge, MA: MIT Press, 2009).

4. Isaacson, 39.

5. Jesse Walden, interview by Alex Tapscott via Zoom, Oct. 25, 2022.

6. Isaacson, *The Innovators*, 35.

7. Isaacson, 181–83.

8. Charles Fishman, "How NASA Gave Birth to Modern Computing—and Gets No Credit for It," *Fast Company*, June 13, 2019, https://www.fastcompany.com /90362753/how-nasa-gave-birth-to-modern-computing-and-gets-no-credit -for-it.

9. *Gibbons v. Ogden* (1824), https://www.archives.gov/milestone-documents /gibbons-v-ogden.

10. Bhu Srinivasan, *Americana: A 400-Year History of American Capitalism* (New York: Penguin Press, 2017), 80–82 (railroads), 59–60 (steamships).

11. Ali Yahya, interview by Alex Tapscott via Zoom, Oct. 14, 2022.

12. Hallam Stevens, "Hans Peter Luhn and the Birth of the Hashing Algorithm," in *Spectrum*, IEEE, Jan. 30, 2018, https://spectrum.ieee.org/hans-peter-luhn-and -the-birth-of-the-hashing-algorithm; and W. Diffie and M. E. Hellman, "New Directions in Cryptography," *IEEE Transactions on Information Theory*, IT-22 (1976), 644–54, https://www.signix.com/blog/bid/108804/infographic-the -history-of-digital-signature-technology.

13. Annex 1, "Front-End Prototype Providers Technical Onboarding Package," ECB-PUBLIC, European Central Bank, Dec. 7, 2022, https://www.ecb .europa.eu/paym/digital_euro/investigation/profuse/shared/files/dedocs/ecb .dedocs221207_annex1_front_end_prototype_providers_technical_onboarding _package.en.pdf; and Metaco, "Quantum Resistance," March 23, 2021, https://www.metaco.com/digital-assets-glossary/quantum-resistance/.

14. M. Benda, "Turing's Legacy for the Internet," *IEEE Internet Computing* 1, no. 6 (Nov.–Dec. 1997): 75–77, https://ieeexplore.ieee.org/document/643940.

15. "IBM Virtual Machine Fiftieth Anniversary," IBM, last updated Aug. 3, 2022, https://www.vm.ibm.com/history/50th/index.html; and "Control Program," IBM, last updated Sept. 29, 2022, https://www.ibm.com/docs/en /zvm/7.2?topic=product-control-program-cp, accessed Dec. 9, 2022.

16. Kaveh Waddell, "The Long and Winding History of Encryption," *Atlantic*, Jan. 13, 2016, https://www.theatlantic.com/technology/archive/2016/01/the -long-and-winding-history-of-encryption/423726/.

17. Yahya interview by Alex Tapscott.

18. Albert Wenger, "Crypto Tokens and the Coming Age of Protocol Innovation," *Continuations Blog*, July 28, 2016, https://continuations.com/post/148098927445 /crypto-tokens-and-the-age-of-protocol-innovation; and Brad Burnham, "Protocol Labs," Union Square Ventures, May 18, 2017, https://www.usv.com /writing/2017/05/protocol-labs/, accessed Nov. 27, 2022.

19. Wenger, "Crypto Tokens and the Coming Age of Protocol Innovation."

20. "fungible things, n.," *Wex Online*, Legal Information Institute, Cornell Law School, updated July 2021, https://www.law.cornell.edu/wex/fungible_things#, accessed Nov. 27, 2022.

21. Campbell R. Harvey, Ashwin Ramachandran, and Joey Santoro, *DeFi and the Future of Finance* (Hoboken, NJ: Wiley, 2021), 23, 37, https://www.wiley.com /en-us/DeFi+and+the+Future+of+Finance-p-9781119836025.

22. "Double-Spending," Corporate Finance Institute, Oct. 9, 2022, https:// corporatefinanceinstitute.com/resources/cryptocurrency/double-spending/.

23. Leslie Lamport, Robert Shostak, and Marshall Pease, "The Byzantine Generals Problem," SRI International, June 11, 2000, https://lamport.azurewebsites.net /pubs/byz.pdf.

24. Red Sheehan, "Cardano: Slow and Steady Scales the Chain," Messari, Dec. 27, 2022, https://messari.io/report/cardano-slow-and-steady.

25. Nick Szabo, "Winning Strategies for Smart Contracts," foreword by Don Tapscott, Blockchain Research Institute, Dec. 4, 2017, https://www .blockchainresearchinstitute.org/project/smart-contracts.

26. Szabo.

27. Campbell R. Harvey, "DeFi Infrastructure," in *DeFi and the Future of Finance*, Duke University and NBER, 2022, https://people.duke.edu/~charvey/Teaching /697_2021/Public_Presentations_697/DeFi_2021_2_Infrastructure_697.pdf.

28. "About Gitcoin," n.d., https://gitcoin.co/about, accessed Feb. 2, 2023.

29. Scott Moore, interview by Alex Tapscott via Zoom, Sept. 8, 2022. See also Nathania Gilson, "What Is Conway's Law?" *Atlassian Teamwork Blog*, Dec. 28, 2021, https://www.atlassian.com/blog/teamwork/what-is-conways-law-acmi.

30. Moore interview by Alex Tapscott.

31. Moore interview by Alex Tapscott.

32. Licheng Wang, Xiaoying Shen, Jing Li, Jun Shao, and Yixian Yang, "Cryptographic Primitives in Blockchains," *Journal of Network and Computer Applications* 127 (2019): 43–58, https://www.sciencedirect.com/science/article /pii/S108480451830362X.

33. Yahya interview by Alex Tapscott.

34. Yahya interview by Alex Tapscott.

35. Yahya interview by Alex Tapscott.

36. Jake Hannah, interview by Alex Tapscott via Zoom for the *DeFi Decoded* podcast, Dec. 1, 2021.

37. Yahya interview by Alex Tapscott.

38. John Algeo and Adele Algeo, "Among the New Words," *American Speech* 63, no. 4 (1988): 345–52, https://www.jstor.org/stable/i219247, accessed Aug. 11, 2020. Authors referenced an article in *PC Week*, Jan. 5, 1988.

39. David Chaum, "Achieving Electronic Privacy," *Scientific American* 267, no. 2 (1992): 96–101, https://www.jstor.org/stable/24939181, accessed Aug. 11, 2020.

40. For BRI team's in-depth research on wallets, see Don Tapscott, "Toward a Universal Digital Wallet: A Means of Managing Payments, Data, and Identity," Blockchain Research Institute, Nov. 18, 2020, https://www .blockchainresearchinstitute.org/project/toward-a-universal-digital-wallet/.

41. Paul Andrews, "PC in Your Pocket: Bill Gates Previews Wallet That Knows You Well," *Seattle Times*, Feb. 2, 1993; Chris Tilley, "A Look Back to the Beginnings

of the Microsoft PDA Project," HPC Factor, Jan. 2005, https://www.hpcfactor
.com/reviews/editorial/walletpc; and Sean Gallagher, "Back to the Future:
Dusting off Bill Gates' *The Road Ahead*," *Ars Technica*, Feb. 4, 2014, https://www
.arstechnica.com/information-technology/2014/02/back-to-the-future-dusting
-off-bill-gates-the-road-ahead, accessed Aug. 25, 2020.

42. Bill Gates with Nathan Myhrvold and Peter Rinearson, *The Road Ahead* (New
York: Viking Penguin, 1995), 74–75.

43. Marc Andreessen, "From the Internet's Past to the Future of Crypto,"
interviewed by Katie Haun, *a16z Podcast*, Aug. 29, 2019, https://a16z
.com/2019/08/29/Internet-past-crypto-future-crypto-regulatory-summit/.

44. Kai Sedgwick, "Bitcoin History, Part 18: The First Bitcoin Wallet," Bitcoin.com,
Oct. 6, 2019, https://news.bitcoin.com/bitcoin-history-part-18-the-first-bitcoin
-wallet, accessed Aug. 25, 2020.

45. Gates, *The Road Ahead*, 76.

46. Don Tapscott and Alex Tapscott, *Blockchain Revolution: How the Technology
Behind Bitcoin and Other Cryptocurrencies Is Changing the World* (New York:
Penguin Portfolio, 2018), 14–16.

47. Olusegun Ogundeji, "[Andreas] Antonopoulos: Your Keys, Your Bitcoin.
Not Your Keys, Not Your Bitcoin," *Cointelegraph*, Aug. 10, 2016, https://
cointelegraph.com/news/antonopoulos-your-keys-your-bitcoin-not-your-keys
-not-your-bitcoin.

48. James Burnham, *The Managerial Revolution* (London: Lume Books, 1941), 84

49. Sidney Powell, email to Alex Tapscott, Nov. 25, 2022.

50. Powell email to Alex Tapscott.

51. Hester Peirce, "Remarks before the Digital Assets," Duke Conference,
Washington DC, US Securities and Exchange Commission, Jan. 20, 2023,
https://www.sec.gov/news/speech/peirce-remarks-duke-conference-012023#
_ftnref15.

52. Safe, "Unlock Digital Asset Ownership," Safe Ecosystem Foundation, as of
April 12, 2023, https://safe.global/.

53. Franck Barbier, "Composability for Software Components: An Approach
Based on the Whole-Part Theory," in *Proceedings of Eighth IEEE International
Conference on Engineering of Complex Computer Systems*, 2002, 101–6,
DOI:10.1109/ICECCS.2002.1181502.

54. Andrew Young, interview with Alex Tapscott via Zoom for the *DeFi Decoded*
podcast, Dec. 1, 2021.

55. Young interview with Alex Tapscott.

56. "Time Required to Start a Business (Days)," *Doing Business*, World Bank, 2019,
https://data.worldbank.org/indicator/IC.REG.DURS?end=2019&most_recent
_value_desc=true&start=2003.

57. "Time Required to Start a Business (Days)."

58. Oliver E. Williamson, "Public and Private Bureaucracies: A Transaction Cost
Economics Perspective," *Journal of Law, Economics & Organization* 15, no. 1
(1999): 306–42, https://www.jstor.org/stable/3554953.

59. Brian Ladd, *Autophobia: Love and Hate in the Automotive Age* (Chicago: University of Chicago Press, 2008), https://press.uchicago.edu/Misc/Chicago/467412.html.

60. *Pride of the West & Mars*, Jet Propulsion Laboratory, California Institute of Technology, Jan. 15, 2020, https://www.jpl.nasa.gov/images/pia24438-pride-of-the-west-mdash-and-mars.

61. Best Owie, "Solana's Network Blackout Puts It in Dire Straits Among Competitors," *Bitcoinist.com*, April 12, 2022, https://bitcoinist.com/solanas-network-blackout-puts-it-in-dire-straits-among-competitors/.

62. Walden interview by Alex Tapscott.

63. "The History of Car Technology," Jardine Motors Group, n.d., https://news.jardinemotors.co.uk/lifestyle/the-history-of-car-technology, accessed April 12, 2023.

64. Prashant Jha, "The Aftermath of Axie Infinity's $650M Ronin Bridge Hack," *Cointelegraph*, April 12, 2022, https://cointelegraph.com/news/the-aftermath-of-axie-infinity-s-650m-ronin-bridge-hack.

65. Ethan Buchman, interview by Alex Tapscott and Andrew Young via Zoom for the *DeFi Decoded* podcast, Nov. 17, 2021.

66. Buchman interview by Alex Tapscott and Andrew Young.

67. Sunny Aggarwal, interview by Alex Tapscott via Zoom, Aug. 8, 2022.

68. Aggarwal interview by Alex Tapscott.

69. Greg Osuri, interview by Alex Tapscott and Andrew Young, *DeFi Decoded* podcast, ep. 73, Dec. 15, 2021, https://podcasts-francais.fr/podcast/defi-decoded/defi-decoded-why-defi-needs-a-truly-decentralized-.

70. Jelena Djuric, interview by Alex Tapscott via Zoom, Jan. 12, 2022.

71. Djuric interview by Alex Tapscott.

72. Aggarwal interview by Alex Tapscott.

73. OpenAI, as of Dec. 6, 2022, https://openai.com/api/.

74. Stephanie Dunbar and Stephen Basile, "The Decentralized Science Ecosystem: Building a Better Research Economy," Messari, March 7, 2023, https://messari.io/report/the-decentralized-science-ecosystem-building-a-better-research-economy.

75. "Ocean Protocol: Tools for the Web3 Data Economy," technical white paper, Ocean Protocol Foundation Ltd. with BigchainDB GmbH, Sept. 1, 2022, https://oceanprotocol.com/technology/roadmap#papers.

76. Trent McConaghy, "How Does Ocean Compute-to-Data Related to Other Privacy-Preserving Approaches?" *Ocean Protocol Blog*, Ocean Protocol Foundation, May 28, 2020, https://blog.oceanprotocol.com/how-ocean-compute-to-data-relates-to-other-privacy-preserving-technology-b4e1c330483.

Chapter 3: Assets

1. "Great Domesday," Catalogue Reference: E 31/2, National Archives, United Kingdom, n.d., https://www.nationalarchives.gov.uk/domesday/discover-domesday/.

2. Robert Tombs, *The English and Their History* (New York: Vintage, 2015): 50.

3. Richard Mattessich, "The Oldest Writings, and Inventory Tags of Egypt," *The Accounting Historians Journal* 29, No. 1 (June 2002): 195–208, https://www.jstor .org/stable/40698264; Daniel C. Snell, *Ledgers and Prices: Early Mesopotamian Merchant Accounts* (New Haven: Yale University Press, 1982), https://babylonian -collection.yale.edu/sites/default/files/files/YNER%208%20Snell%2C%20 Ledgers%20and%20Prices%20-%20Early%20Mesopotamian%20Merchant%20 Accounts%2C%201982.PDF; Roger Atwood, "The Ugarit Archives," *Archaeology Magazine*, July/Aug. 2021, https://www.archaeology.org/issues/430-2107 /features/9752-ugarit-bronze-age-archive; and Sun Jiahui, "How Ancient Chinese Buried the Living Along with the Dead," *The World Of Chinese*, Nov. 12, 2021, https://www.theworldofchinese.com/2021/11/how-ancient -chinese-buried-the-living-along-with-the-dead/.

4. Jiahui, "How Ancient Chinese Buried the Living Along with the Dead"; and John Noble Wilford, "With Escorts to the Afterlife Pharaohs Proved Their Power," *New York Times*, March 16, 2004, https://www.nytimes.com/2004/03/16/science /with-escorts-to-the-afterlife-pharaohs-proved-their-power.html.

5. T. J. Stiles, *The First Tycoon* (New York: Vintage Books, 2010), 569.

6. Stiles, 569.

7. Jason Furman, "Financial Inclusion in the United States," *Obama White House Blog*, June 10, 2016, https://obamawhitehouse.archives.gov/blog/2016/06/10 /financial-inclusion-united-states; Lydia Saad and Jeffrey M. Jones, "What Percentage of Americans Own Stock?" *The Short Answer*, Gallup, May 12, 2022, https://news.gallup.com/poll/266807/percentage-americans-owns-stock.aspx.

8. "Traditional Sources of Economic Security," *Historical Background and Development of Social Security,* Social Security Administration, n.d., https:// www.ssa.gov/history/briefhistory3.html, accessed April 12, 2023.

9. Leander Heldring, James A. Robinson, and Sebastian Vollmer, "The Long-Run Impact of the Dissolution of the English Monasteries," Working Paper 21450, National Bureau of Economic Research, Aug. 2015, revised April 2021, https:// www.nber.org/system/files/working_papers/w21450/w21450.pdf.

10. "A Brief History of Mining," Earth Systems, 2006, https://www.earthsystems .com/history-mining/.

11. Stiles, 568.

12. Stiles, 568.

13. Mike Dudas, interview by Alex Tapscott via Zoom, Sept. 16, 2022.

14. Print and digital combined. "The New York Times Company Reports Second-Quarter 2022 Results," press release, *New York Times*, Aug. 3, 2022, https://nytco-assets.nytimes.com/2022/08/Press-Release-6.26.2022-Final -X69kQ5m3-2-1.pdf.

15. "Market Capitalization of Coinbase (COIN)," Companies Market Cap, as of April 12, 2023, https://companiesmarketcap.com/coinbase/marketcap/.

16. For current market capitalization of tokens, see CoinGecko, https://www .coingecko.com/. For example, Ethereum, the second largest cryptoasset platform

by value, has a market capitalization of $217 billion compared to Coinbase, the largest publicly traded Web3 company, which has a market capitalization of $15.5 billion. "Market Capitalization of Coinbase," Companies Market Cap, as of May 17, 2023, https://companiesmarketcap.com/coinbase/marketcap/.

17. Nathanial Popper, "Lost Passwords Lock Millionaires out of Their Bitcoin Fortunes," *New York Times*, Jan. 14, 2021, https://www.nytimes.com /2021/01/12/technology/bitcoin-passwords-wallets-fortunes.html.

18. Rick Delafont, "Chainalysis: Up to 3.79 Million Bitcoins May Be Lost Forever," *NewsBTC*, April 12, 2018, https://www.newsbtc.com/news/bitcoin/chainalysis -up-to/.

19. James Royal, "Are Your Lost Bitcoins Gone Forever? Here's How You Might Be Able to Recover Them," Bankrate, Feb. 11, 2022, https://www.bankrate.com /investing/how-to-recover-lost-bitcoins-and-other-crypto/; and Brian Nibley, "Tracking Down Lost Bitcoins and Other Cryptos," SoFi, Sept. 13, 2022, https://www.sofi.com/learn/content/how-to-find-lost-bitcoin/.

20. "Cryptocurrency Ownership Data," Triple A, April 5, 2023, https://triple-a.io /crypto-ownership-data/.

21. "Automobile Anecdotes," Stuttgart-Marketing GmbH, n.d., https://www.stuttgart -tourist.de/en/automobile/automotive-anecdotes-1, accessed April 12, 2023.

22. Lars Bosteen "Early Mis-Prediction of the Demand for Automobiles," History Stack Exchange, Aug. 18, 2021, https://history.stackexchange.com /questions/65780/early-mis-prediction-of-the-demand-for-automobiles.

23. L. Ceci, "Time Spent per Day on Smartphone," Statista, June 14, 2022, https:// www.statista.com/statistics/1224510/time-spent-per-day-on-smartphone-us/.

24. "Synthetixio," GitHub, accessed Dec. 18, 2022, https://github.com/Synthetixio.

25. Kain Warwick, interview by Alex Tapscott via Zoom, Aug. 15, 2022.

26. Kate Duguid and Nikou Asgari, "Central Banks Look to China's Renminbi to Diversify Foreign Currency Reserves," *Financial Times*, June 30, 2022, https:// www.ft.com/content/ce09687f-f7e5-499a-9521-d98cbd4c5ac1.

27. James Dale Davidson and Lord William Rees-Mogg, *The Sovereign Individual: Mastering the Transition to the Information Age* (New York: Simon & Schuster, 1997), 216.

28. Friedrich A. von Hayek, *Denationalization of Money* (London: Institute of Economic Affairs, 1976), 56.

29. Adrian Brink, interviewed by Alex Tapscott via Zoom for the *DeFi Decoded* podcast, March 31, 2022.

30. "Ukraine Government Turns to Crypto to Crowdfund Millions of Dollars," *Elliptic Blog*, March 11, 2022, https://www.elliptic.co/blog/live-updates -millions-in-crypto-crowdfunded-for-the-ukrainian-military, accessed March 31, 2022.

31. PartyBid App, PartyDAO, as of March 31, 2022, https://www.partybid.app /party/0x4508401BaDe71aE75fE70c97fe585D734f975502.

32. Andrew J. Hawkins, "The Anti-vaxx Canadian Truckers Want to Talk to You About Bitcoin," *The Verge*, Feb. 9, 2022 https://www.theverge

.com/2022/2/9/22925823/canadian-trucker-convoy-anti-vaxx-bitcoin-press -conference, accessed March 31, 2022.

33. Alex Wilson, interview by Alex Tapscott via Zoom, Aug. 9, 2022.

34. Amitoj Singh, "Ukraine Is Buying Bulletproof Vests and Night-Vision Goggles Using Crypto," *CoinDesk*, March 7, 2022, https://www.coindesk.com/policy /2022/03/07/ukraine-is-buying-bulletproof-vests-and-night-vision-goggles -using-crypto/, accessed March 31, 2022.

35. Sharon Braithwaite, "Zelensky Refuses US Offer to Evacuate, Saying 'I Need Ammunition, not a Ride,'" *CNN*, Cable News Network, Feb. 26, 2022, https:// www.cnn.com/2022/02/26/europe/ukraine-zelensky-evacuation-intl/index .html.

36. Chris Dixon, interview by Alex Tapscott via Zoom, Sept. 2, 2022.

37. "The Humble Hero: Containers Have Been More Important for Globalisation Than Freer Trade," *Economist*, May 18, 2013, https://www.economist.com /finance-and-economics/2013/05/18/the-humble-hero.

38. Dixon interview by Alex Tapscott.

39. Dixon interview by Alex Tapscott.

40. Dixon interview by Alex Tapscott.

41. Irene Vallejo, *Papyrus: The Invention of Books in the Ancient World*, trans. Charlotte Whittle (New York: Knopf, 2022), 22.

42. Design Services, Sigma Technology Group, n.d., https://sigmatechnology.com /service/design-services/, accessed Sept. 16, 2022.

43. Vallejo, *Papyrus*, 22.

44. Dixon interview by Alex Tapscott

45. Sunny Aggarwal, interview by Alex Tapscott via Zoom, Aug. 8, 2022.

46. Tim Beiko, interview by Alex Tapscott via Zoom, Aug. 9, 2022.

47. John Wu, interview by Alex Tapscott via Zoom, Aug. 2, 2022.

48. "The Uniswap Protocol Is a Public Good Owned and Governed by UNI Token Holders," Uniswap Governance, n.d., https://uniswap.org/governance.

49. "Stablecoins by Market Capitalization," CoinGecko, as of May 17, 2023, https:// www.coingecko.com/en/categories/stablecoins.

50. "State of the USDC Economy," *Circle*, Circle Internet Financial Ltd., March 10, 2023, https://www.circle.com/hubfs/PDFs/2301StateofUSDCEconomy_Web .pdf.

51. "Dai Price Chart (DAI)," CoinGecko, as of May 17, 2023, https://www .coingecko.com/en/coins/dai.

52. AngelList (@angellist), Twitter post, Sept. 28, 2021 (1:17 p.m.), https://twitter .com/AngelList/status/1442901252552101888, accessed Oct. 15, 2021.

53. Cryptorigami, "Introducing ERC 420—The Dank Standard," *PepeDapp Blog*, Medium, May 27, 2018, https://medium.com/pepedapp/erc-420%C2%B9 -the-dank-standard-83d7bb5fe18e; Eugene Mishura and Seb Mondet, "FA2—Multi-Asset Interface, 012," Software Freedom Conservancy, Jan. 24, 2020, https://gitlab.com/tezos/tzip/-/blob/master/proposals/tzip-12 /tzip-12.md; "Onflow/flow-nft," GitHub, n.d., https://github.com/onflow

/flow-nft; and Metaplex NFT, Metaplex Foundation, Sept. 19, 2022, https://z6uiuihwujnmmqy6obdswfnfoe4rcbavovcljbg4ki3vjfovftpa.arweave.net/z6iKIPaiWsZDHnBHKxWlcTkRBBV1RLSE3FI3VJXVLN4/index.html.

54. Campbell R. Harvey, Ashwin Ramachandran, and Joey Santoro, *DeFi and the Future of Finance* (Hoboken, NJ: Wiley, 2021), 27.

55. "The Digital Currencies That Matter: Get Ready for Fedcoin and the e-euro," *Economist*, May 8, 2021, https://www.economist.com/leaders/2021/05/08/the-digital-currencies-that-matter.

56. "The Digital Currencies That Matter."

57. Chris Giancarlo, interviewed by Alex Tapscott via Zoom, Dec. 13, 2022.

58. E. Glen Weyl, Puja Ohlhaver, and Vitalik Buterin, "Decentralized Society: Finding Web3's Soul," Social Science Research Network, May 10, 2022, https://dx.doi.org/10.2139/ssrn.4105763.

59. Dixon interview by Alex Tapscott.

60. "The Key to Industrial Capitalism: Limited Liability," *Economist*, Dec. 23, 1999, https://www.economist.com/finance-and-economics/1999/12/23/the-key-to-industrial-capitalism-limited-liability.

61. Frederick G. Kempin, Jr., "Limited Liability in Historical Perspective," *American Business Law Association Bulletin*, n.d., https://www.bus.umich.edu/KresgeLibrary/resources/abla/abld_4.1.11-33.pdf.

62. Julia Kagan, "C Corporation," *Investopedia*, July 22, 2022, https://www.investopedia.com/terms/c/c-corporation.asp, accessed Sept. 16, 2022.

63. Dixon interview by Alex Tapscott.

64. Dixon interview by Alex Tapscott.

65. "Matthew Effect," ScienceDirect, accessed Nov. 25, 2022, https://www.sciencedirect.com/topics/psychology/matthew-effect.

Chapter 4: People

1. Kelly Grovier, "The Most Terrifying Images in History?" BBC, Feb. 19, 2020, https://www.bbc.com/culture/article/20200214-the-art-of-terror-how-visions-of-fear-can-help-us-live.

2. Hua Hsu, "The End of White America?" *Atlantic*, Jan.–Feb. 2009, https://www.theatlantic.com/magazine/archive/2009/01/the-end-of-white-america/307208/.

3. Ben Sisario, "The Music Industry Is Wrestling with Race. Here's What It Has Promised," *New York Times*, July 1, 2020, https://www.nytimes.com/2020/07/01/arts/music/music-industry-black-lives-matter.html.

4. Elias Leight, "The Music Industry Was Built on Racism. Changing It Will Take More Than Donations," *Rolling Stone*, June 5, 2020, https://www.rollingstone.com/music/music-features/music-industry-racism-1010001/.

5. Tyler Winklevoss, interview by Alex Tapscott via Zoom, Sept. 12, 2022.

6. pplpleasr, interview by Alex Tapscott via Zoom, Nov. 1, 2022.

7. Ekin Genç, "An Ad for Uniswap Just Sold for $525,000 as an NFT," *DeCrypt*, March 27, 2021, https://decrypt.co/63080/an-ad-for-uniswap-just-sold-for-525000-as-an-nft-heres-why; pplpleasr interview by Alex Tapscott.

8. pplpleasr interview by Alex Tapscott.

9. pplpleasr interview by Alex Tapscott.

10. pplpleasr interview by Alex Tapscott.

11. Jessie Nickson-Lopez and Torey Kohara, interview by Alex Tapscott via Zoom, Sept. 26, 2022.

12. Dean Takahashi, "Bored Ape Company Yuga Labs Appoints Activision Blizzard's Daniel Alegre as CEO," *VentureBeat*, Dec. 19, 2022, https://venturebeat.com/games/bored-ape-company-yuga-labs-appoints-activision-blizzards-daniel-alegre-as-ceo/.

13. Sarah Emerson, "Seth Green Bored Ape NFT Returned," *BuzzFeed News*, June 9, 2022, https://www.buzzfeednews.com/article/sarahemerson/seth-green-bored-ape-nft-returned.

14. Nickson-Lopez and Kohara interview by Alex Tapscott.

15. Story, MV3: The Battle for Eluna, as of April 12, 2023, https://mv3hq.notion.site/Story-ecdaaa3a8a71447598726d8f8a2504fe.

16. Story, MV3: The Battle for Eluna.

17. Nickson-Lopez and Kohara interview by Alex Tapscott.

18. Nickson-Lopez and Kohara interview by Alex Tapscott.

19. Andres Guadamuz, "Non-fungible Tokens (NFTs) and Copyright," *WIPO*, Dec. 2021, https://www.wipo.int/wipo_magazine/en/2021/04/article_0007.html.

20. Creative Commons, "FAQ: CC and NFTs," Sept. 9, 2022, https://creativecommons.org/cc-and-nfts/.

21. Scott Kominers (@skominers), Twitter post, Aug. 3, 2022 (6:46 a.m.), https://twitter.com/skominers/status/1554780692067794945.

22. Lawrence Lessig, *Free Culture: How Big Media Uses Technology and the Law to Lock Down Culture and Control Creativity* (New York: Penguin Books, 2004), https://lessig.org/product/free-culture/.

23. Lessig, "About the Book," *Free Culture* website, n.d., https://lessig.org/product/free-culture/.

24. Flashrekt and Scott Duke Kominers, "Why NFT Creators Are Going cc0," *a16z Crypto Blog*, Aug. 3, 2022, https://a16zcrypto.com/cc0-nft-creative-commons-zero-license-rights/.

25. Ria Lu, interview by Alex Tapscott via Zoom, Oct. 12, 2022.

26. Pplpleasr, "Shibuya & White Rabbit Pilot," *Shibuya.xyz*, Feb. 28, 2022, https://medium.com/@shibuya.xyz/shibuya-white-rabbit-pilot-c901e8bb76a4.

27. pplpleasr interview by Alex Tapscott.

28. pplpleasr interview by Alex Tapscott.

29. pplpleasr interview by Alex Tapscott.

30. pplpleasr interview by Alex Tapscott.

31. Andrew Hayward, "Pplpleasr's Shibuya NFT Video Platform Raises $6.9M to Build the A24 of Web3," *Decrypt*, Dec. 8, 2022, https://decrypt.co/116749/pplpleasrs-shibuya-nft-video-platform-raises-6-9m-to-build-the-a24-of-web3.

32. Roneil Rumburg, interview by Alex Tapscott via Zoom, Aug. 11, 2022.

33. Rumburg interview by Alex Tapscott.

34. Roneil Rumburg, Sid Sethi, and Hareesh Nagaraj, "Audius: A Decentralized Protocol for Audio Content," white paper, Audius Inc., Oct. 8, 2020, https://whitepaper.audius.co/AudiusWhitepaper.pdf, accessed Nov. 27, 2022.

35. Rumburg interview by Alex Tapscott.

36. Aleksander Larsen, interview by Alex Tapscott via Zoom, Aug. 9, 2022.

37. "Digital Asset Outlook 2023," The Block, Dec. 20, 2022, https://www.tbstat.com/wp/uploads/2022/12/Digital-Asset-2023-Outlook.pdf.

38. Right Click Save, ClubNFT, n.d., https://www.rightclicksave.com/.

39. pplpleasr interview by Alex Tapscott.

40. Jesse Walden, interview by Alex Tapscott via Zoom, Oct. 25, 2022.

41. "Token-Gated Communities: $80,000+ Community, Soulbound NFTs and Web 2.5," Trends.vc, n.d., https://trends.vc/trends-0082-token-gated-communities/.

42. Walden interview by Alex Tapscott. For more on Twitch TV, see https://www.twitch.tv/p/en/about/.

43. Marshall McLuhan, *Understanding Media: The Extensions of Man*, introduction by Lewis H. Lapham (Cambridge, MA: MIT Press, 1994), mitpress.mit.edu/books/understanding-media.

44. Bill Gates, "Content Is King," Microsoft, Jan. 3, 1996, Wayback Machine, https://web.archive.org/web/20010126005200/http://www.microsoft.com/billgates/columns/1996essay/essay960103.asp, accessed Jan. 21, 2023. Syndicated by the New York Times Syndication Sales Corp. and archived in Nexis UNI as Bill Gates, "On the Internet, Content Is King. On the Internet, Cyberspace Content Is King," *Evening Post* (Wellington, New Zealand), Jan. 16, 1996.

45. Lex Sokolin, interview by Alex Tapscott via Zoom for the *DeFi Decoded* podcast, Feb. 1, 2022.

46. Yat Siu, interview by Alex Tapscott via Zoom, Jan. 10, 2023.

47. Some of this material first appeared in Alex Tapscott, "With NFTs, the Digital Medium Is the Message," *Fortune*, Oct. 4, 2021, https://fortune.com/2021/10/04/nfts-art-collectibles-medium-is-the-message/.

48. Siu interview by Alex Tapscott.

49. Enid Tsui, "Internet Whizz Yat Siu on Programming at 13 and Landing a Job at Atari as a Schoolboy," *South China Morning Post*, July 6, 2017, Wayback Machine, https://web.archive.org/web/20170706084545/https://www.scmp.com/magazines/post-magazine/long-reads/article/2101469/Internet-whizz-yat-siu-programming-13-and-landing.

50. Walter Isaacson, *The Innovators: How a Group of Hackers, Geniuses, and Geeks Created the Digital Revolution* (New York: Simon & Schuster, 2014), 214.

51. Siu interview by Alex Tapscott.

52. Siu interview by Alex Tapscott.

53. Siu interview by Alex Tapscott.

54. Siu interview by Alex Tapscott.

55. "Refunds are now available, you have two choices," ConstitutionDAO (2021), n.d., https://www.constitutiondao.com/.

56. Walden interview by Alex Tapscott.

57. Jesse Walden, "Tokens Are Products," Variant Fund, Aug. 24, 2022, https://variant.fund/articles/tokens-are-products/.

58. Ida Auken, "Welcome to 2030. I Own Nothing, Have No Privacy, and Life Has Never Been Better," World Economic Forum, Nov. 11, 2016, https://web.archive.org/web/20161125135500/https://www.weforum.org/agenda/2016/11/shopping-i-can-t-really-remember-what-that-is. The WEF originally indexed the piece under "Values" of Fourth Industrial Revolution on the Global Agenda but removed it from its website on May 6, 2021, https://web.archive.org/web/20210505052848/https://www.weforum.org/agenda/2016/11/how-life-could-change-2030/, accessed Nov. 27, 2022.

59. Walden interview by Alex Tapscott.

60. Auken, "Welcome to 2030."

61. Spencer High, "NAR Report Shows Share of Millennial Home Buyers Continues to Rise," National Association of Realtors, March 23, 2022, https://www.nar.realtor/newsroom/nar-report-shows-share-of-millennial-home-buyers-continues-to-rise.

62. John Locke, *Two Treatises of Government and A Letter Concerning Toleration*, 1690, 112.

63. Chris Dixon (@cdixon), Twitter post, Oct. 1, 2021 (6:50 p.m.), https://twitter.com/cdixon/status/1444072368859533316, accessed Oct. 15, 2021.

64. Chris Dixon (@cdixon), Twitter posts, Oct. 1, 2021 (6:50 p.m.), https://twitter.com/cdixon/status/1444072370788978691 and https://twitter.com/cdixon/status/1444072374798675970, accessed Oct. 15, 2021.

65. Jimmy Wales, interview by Alex Tapscott via Zoom, Feb. 24, 2023.

66. Wales interview by Alex Tapscott.

67. Muyao Shen, "Wikipedia Ends Crypto Donations as Environmental Concerns Swirl," *Bloomberg News*, Bloomberg LP, May 2, 2022, https://www.bloomberg.com/news/articles/2022-05-02/wikipedia-ends-crypto-donations-amid-environmental-concern, accessed April 12, 2023.

68. Wales interview by Alex Tapscott.

69. Wales interview by Alex Tapscott.

70. Larsen interview by Alex Tapscott.

71. James Burnham, *The Managerial Revolution* (London: Lume Books, 1941), 84.

72. Stepan Gershuni, interview by Alex Tapscott via Zoom, Jan. 26, 2023.

73. Ronald H. Coase, "The Nature of the Firm," *Economica* 4, no. 16 (Nov. 1937): 386–405, https://doi.org/10.2307/2626876.

74. Gershuni interview by Alex Tapscott.

75. Phillip J. Windley, "Framing and Self-Sovereignty in Web3," *Technometria Blog*, Feb. 15, 2022, https://www.windley.com/archives/2022/02/framing_and_self-sovereignty_in_web3.shtml, accessed March 31, 2022.

76. Ryan Selkis, interview by Alex Tapscott via Zoom, Aug. 24, 2022.

77. ENS Documentation, April 2022, https://docs.ens.domains/.

78. Gershuni interview by Alex Tapscott. See also https://kycdao.xyz/, https://www.violet.co/, and https://www.spectral.finance/, accessed April 12, 2023.

79. Gershuni interview by Alex Tapscott; and "ZK Badges," Sismo Docs, last updated May 12, 2023, https://docs.sismo.io/sismo-docs/readme/sismo-badges, accessed May 17, 2023.

80. Gitcoin Passport, n.d., https://passport.gitcoin.co/.

Chapter 5: Organizations

1. Jesse Walden, interview by Alex Tapscott via Zoom, Oct. 25, 2022.

2. Walden interview by Alex Tapscott.

3. Walden interview by Alex Tapscott.

4. Walden interview by Alex Tapscott.

5. Walden interview by Alex Tapscott.

6. GameKyuubi, "I AM HODLING," Bitcoin Forum, Simple Machines NPO, Dec. 18, 2013, https://bitcointalk.org/index.php?topic=375643 .msg4022997#msg4022997, accessed Nov. 29, 2022.

7. Walden interview by Alex Tapscott.

8. Walden interview by Alex Tapscott.

9. Jimmy Wales, interview by Alex Tapscott via Zoom, Feb. 24, 2023.

10. Walden interview by Alex Tapscott.

11. Yochai Benkler, *The Wealth of Networks: How Social Production Transforms Markets and Freedom* (New Haven, CT: Yale University Press, 2006), 9.

12. Matthew Campbell and Kit Chellel, *Dead in the Water: A True Story of Hijacking, Murder, and a Global Maritime Conspiracy* (New York: Penguin Portfolio, 2022), 38.

13. "Royal Charters," Privy Council Office, UK Government, n.d., https:// privycouncil.independent.gov.uk/royal-charters/; "The 1621 Charter of the Dutch West India Company," Historical Society of the New York Courts, n.d., https://history.nycourts.gov/about_period/charter-1621/, accessed April 13, 2023.

14. Charles Wright and C. Ernest Fayle, "A History of Lloyd's: From the Founding of Lloyd's Coffee-house to the Present Day," *Nature* 122 (Aug. 25, 1928): 267–268, https://doi.org/10.1038/122267a0.

15. Julia Kagan, "C Corporation," *Investopedia*, July 22, 2022, https://www .investopedia.com/terms/c/c-corporation.asp, accessed Sept. 16, 2022.

16. "The Key to Industrial Capitalism: Limited Liability," *Economist*, Dec. 23, 1999, https://www.economist.com/finance-and-economics/1999/12/23/the-key-to -industrial-capitalism-limited-liability.

17. Dixon interview by Alex Tapscott.

18. James Dale Davidson and Lord William Rees-Mogg, *The Sovereign Individual: Mastering the Transition to the Information Age* (New York: Simon & Schuster, 1997), 70.

19. Albert Wenger, *The World After Capital: Economic Freedom, Information Freedom, and Psychological Freedom*, Aug. 9, 2022, https://worldaftercapital.org/; Albert Wenger, interview by Alex Tapscott via Zoom, Dec. 16, 2022.

20. Wenger interview by Alex Tapscott.

21. Wenger interview by Alex Tapscott.

22. Hester Peirce, "Remarks before the Digital Assets," Duke Conference, Washington DC, US Securities and Exchange Commission, Jan. 20, 2023, https://www.sec.gov/news/speech/peirce-remarks-duke-conference-012023#_ftnref15.

23. Clayton M. Christensen, *The Innovator's Dilemma When New Technologies Cause Great Firms to Fail* (Boston: Harvard Business School Press, 1997), xv.

24. "Top 10 legal battles: Bell Telephone v Western Union (1879)," *Guardian*, Aug. 6 2007, https://www.theguardian.com/technology/2007/aug/06/bellvwestern; and Peter Baida, "Hindsight, Foresight, and No Sight," *American Heritage* 36, no. 4 (June–July 1985), https://web.archive.org/web/20200906141427/https://www.americanheritage.com/hindsight-foresight-and-no-sight.

25. Christensen, *The Innovator's Dilemma*, 147.

26. Christensen, *The Innovator's Dilemma*, 147.

27. Dixon interview by Alex Tapscott.

28. Dixon interview by Alex Tapscott.

29. Dixon interview by Alex Tapscott.

30. Donald Sull, "Why Good Companies Go Bad," *Harvard Business Review*, July–Aug. 1999, https://hbr.org/1999/07/why-good-companies-go-bad.

31. David Furlonger and Christophe Uzureau, *The Real Business of Blockchain: How Leaders Can Create Value in a New Digital Age* (Cambridge, MA: Harvard Business Review Press, 2019), 54–58.

32. Furlonger and Uzureau, 62–64.

33. Furlonger and Uzureau, 66.

34. Yat Siu, interview by Alex Tapscott via Zoom, Jan. 11, 2023.

35. Siu interview by Alex Tapscott.

36. Siu interview by Alex Tapscott.

37. Yorke E. Rhodes III, interview by Alex Tapscott via Zoom, Oct. 6, 2022.

38. Rhodes interview by Alex Tapscott.

39. Dixon interview by Alex Tapscott.

40. "How DigiCash Blew Everything," translated by Ian Grigg's colleagues, edited by Grigg, and emailed to Robert Hettinga mailing list, Feb. 10, 1999, https://cryptome.org/jya/digicrash.htm. See also "Hoe DigiCash Alles Verknalde," *Next!*, Jan. 1999, https://web.archive.org/web/19990427142412/http://www.nextmagazine.nl/ecash.htm.

41. Rhodes interview by Alex Tapscott.

42. "IBM Announces Blockchain Collaboration with GSF and Other Supply Chain Leaders to Address Food Safety," press release, Golden State Foods, Aug. 22, 2017, https://goldenstatefoods.com/news/ibm-announces-blockchain-collaboration-gsf-supply-chain-leaders-address-food-safety/; "IBM Food Trust Expands Blockchain Network to Foster a Safer, More Transparent and Efficient Global Food System," press release, IBM, Oct. 8, 2018, https://newsroom.ibm.com/2018-10-08-IBM-Food-Trust-Expands-Blockchain-Network-to-Foster-a-Safer-More-Transparent-and-Efficient-Global-Food-System-1; "US Food and Drug Administration Drug Supply Chain Security Act Blockchain

Interoperability Pilot Project Report," IBM, Feb. 2020, https://www.ibm
.com/downloads/cas/9V2LRYG5; and "About TradeLens," n.d., https://www
.tradelens.com/about, all accessed Nov. 11, 2022.

43. Gennaro "Jerry" Cuomo, interview by Alex Tapscott via Zoom, Aug. 29, 2022.

44. "International Business Machines Corporation," Computer History Museum,
n.d., https://www.computerhistory.org/brochures/g-i/international-business
-machines-corporation-ibm/; and "Chronological History of IBM," IBM,
accessed Nov. 11, 2022, https://www.ibm.com/ibm/history/history/history
_intro.html.

45. Cuomo interview by Alex Tapscott.

46. Patrick Lowry, "When Algorithms Fail: How an Algorithmic Stablecoin's
Collapse Fuelled a Crypto Bear Market," *Iconic Holding Blog*, Aug. 24, 2022,
https://iconicholding.com/when-algorithmic-stablecoins-fail/.

47. Rhodes interview by Alex Tapscott.

48. Alex Hughes, "ChatGPT: Everything You Need to Know About OpenAI's
GPT-4 tool," BBC Science Focus, April 3, 2023, https://www.sciencefocus.com
/future-technology/gpt-3/.

49. Greg Brockman "Microsoft Invests in and Partners with OpenAI to Support US
Building Beneficial AGI," OpenAI, July 22, 2019, https://openai.com/blog
/microsoft/.

50. David Becker, "Microsoft Got Game: Xbox Unveiled," CNET, Jan. 2, 2002,
https://www.cnet.com/culture/microsoft-got-game-xbox-unveiled/.

51. Matthew L. Ball, *The Metaverse: And How It Will Revolutionize Everything* (New
York: Liveright, 2022), 10–11.

52. "Minecraft Live Player Count and Statistic," ActivePlayer.io Game Statistics
Authority, as of April 13, 2023, https://activeplayer.io/minecraft/.

53. "United States of America Before the Federal Trade Commission in the Matter
of Microsoft Corp. and Activision Blizzard, Inc.," Docket No. 9412, Redacted
Public Version, Dec. 8, 2022, https://www.ftc.gov/system/files/ftc_gov/pdf
/D09412MicrosoftActivisionAdministrativeComplaintPublicVersionFinal.pdf.

54. "FTC Seeks to Block Microsoft Corp.'s Acquisition of Activision Blizzard Inc.,"
press release, Federal Trade Commission, Dec. 8, 2022, https://www.ftc.gov
/news-events/news/press-releases/2022/12/ftc-seeks-block-microsoft-corps
-acquisition-activision-blizzard-inc.

55. Duncan Riley, "Microsoft Bans Cryptocurrency Mining on Azure Without
Pre-approval," SiliconANGLE Media Inc., Dec. 15, 2022, https://siliconangle
.com/2022/12/15/microsoft-bans-cryptocurrency-mining-azure-without-pre
-approval/#.

56. Gurjot Dhanda, "How Nike won with NFTs," Covalent, Feb. 3, 2023, https://
www.covalenthq.com/blog/how-nike-won-with-nfts/#.

57. Christensen, *The Innovator's Dilemma*, xv.

58. Yorke E. Rhodes III, Faculty Directory, School of Professional Studies, New
York University, 2022, https://www.sps.nyu.edu/homepage/academics/faculty
-directory/14416-yorke-e-rhodes-iii.html#courses14416.

59. Klint Finley, "What Exactly Is GitHub Anyway?" *TechCrunch*, July 14, 2012, https://techcrunch.com/2012/07/14/what-exactly-is-github-anyway/; and Paul V. Weinstein, "Why Microsoft Is Willing to Pay So Much for GitHub," *Harvard Business Review*, June 6, 2018, https://hbr.org/2018/06/why-microsoft-is-willing-to-pay-so-much-for-github.

60. Benkler, *The Wealth of Networks*, 62.

61. Walden interview by Alex Tapscott.

62. Alvin Toffler, *Future Shock* (New York: Random House, 1970), 144.

63. Benkler, *The Wealth of Networks*, 50.

64. Vitalik Buterin "DAOs Are Not Corporations: Where Decentralization in Autonomous Organizations Matters," Vitalik Buterin's Website, Sept. 20, 2022, https://vitalik.ca/general/2022/09/20/daos.html.

65. Vitalik Buterin, "DAOs Are Not Corporations."

66. "About Aragon," Aragon Association, as of March 2023, https://aragon.org/about-aragon; Cryptopedia Staff, "Aragon (ANT): DAOs for Communities and Businesses," Gemini Trust Co. LLC, Oct. 21, 2021, https://www.gemini.com/cryptopedia/aragon-crypto-dao-ethereum-decentralized-government; and "Aragon," CoinMarketCap, n.d., https://coinmarketcap.com/currencies/aragon/, all accessed April 13, 2023.

67. "Security," *Tour TradeLens*, IBM Corp. and GTD Solution Inc., 2018, Wayback Machine, https://web.archive.org/web/20211028022622/https://tour.tradelens.com/security; and "TradeLens Data Sharing Specification," *TradeLens Documentation*, IBM Corp. and GTD Solution Inc., 2018, Wayback Machine, https://web.archive.org/web/20220608080928/https://docs.tradelens.com/reference/data_sharing_specification/, accessed April 13, 2023.

68. Cam Thompson, George Kaloudis, and Sam Reynolds, "The Final Word on Decentraland's Numbers," *CoinDesk*, Dec. 22, 2022, updated Jan. 3, 2023, https://www.coindesk.com/web3/2022/12/22/the-final-word-on-decentralands-numbers/.

69. Thompson, Kaloudis, and Reynolds.

70. "Decentraland," CoinMarketCap, n.d., https://coinmarketcap.com/currencies/decentraland/.

71. "Friends With Benefits," n.d., https://www.fwb.help/; "Friends With Benefits Pro," CoinMarketCap, n.d., https://coinmarketcap.com/currencies/friends-with-benefits-pro/; "Friends With Benefits," *Inside Venture Capital*, Inside.com Inc., Nov. 1, 2021, https://inside.com/campaigns/inside-venture-capital-30009/sections/fwb-raises-10m-from-a16z-257214; and "Friends With Benefits Treasury," Boardroom, n.d., https://boardroom.io/friendswithbenefits.eth/treasuryOverview, all accessed April 12, 2023.

72. "Join Friends With Benefits," FWB.com, n.d., https://www.fwb.help/join, accessed Dec. 19, 2022.

73. "Friends With Benefits," n.d., https://www.fwb.help/; "Friends With Benefits Pro," CoinMarketCap, n.d., https://coinmarketcap.com/currencies/friends-with-benefits-pro/; "Friends With Benefits," *Inside Venture Capital*, Inside.com

Inc., Nov. 1, 2021, https://inside.com/campaigns/inside-venture-capital-30009 /sections/fwb-raises-10m-from-a16z-257214; and "Friends With Benefits Treasury," Boardroom, n.d., https://boardroom.io/friendswithbenefits.eth /treasuryOverview, all accessed April 12, 2023.

74. Gregory Landua, interview by Alex Tapscott via Zoom, Aug. 24, 2022.

75. Landua interview by Alex Tapscott.

76. Balaji Srinivasan, "The Network State in One Essay," *The Network State: How to Start a New Country*, July 4, 2022, https://thenetworkstate.com/the-network -state-in-one-essay.

77. Alex Tapscott, "A Bitcoin Governance Network: The Multi-stakeholder Solution to the Challenges of Cryptocurrency," Global Solution Networks, 2014, https:// gsnetworks.org/wp-content/uploads/DigitalCurrencies.pdf.

78. "We're Building a Web3 City of the Future," CityDAO, n.d., https://www .citydao.io/.

79. Srinivasan, "The Network State in One Essay."

80. "Ocean Protocol," CoinMarketCap, n.d., https://coinmarketcap.com/currencies /ocean-protocol/, as of April 10, 2023.

81. Cryptopedia Staff, "Ocean Protocol (OCEAN): Decentralized Data as an Asset," Gemini Trust Co. LLC, Feb. 23, 2022, https://www.gemini .com/cryptopedia/ocean-protocol-web-3-0-ocean-market-ocean-token; and "Ocean Protocol Foundation Announces $140 Million USD in Grants for the Community-curated OceanDAO to Fund the Web3 Data Economy," Ocean Protocol Foundation Ltd., Oct. 7, 2021, https://oceanprotocol.com/press/2021 -10-07-ocean-protocol-foundation-announces-140M-USD.

82. "About SingularityNET," n.d., https://singularitynet.io/aboutus/, accessed April 12, 2023.

Chapter 6: Decentralizing Finance and Digitizing Money

1. David Emery, "Did Paul Krugman Say the Internet's Effect on the World Economy Would Be 'No Greater Than the Fax Machine's'?" *Snopes*, Snopes Media Group Inc., June 7, 2018, https://www.snopes.com/fact-check/paul -krugman-Internets-effect-economy/.

2. Yochai Benkler, *The Wealth of Networks: How Social Production Transforms Markets and Freedom* (New Haven, CT: Yale University Press, 2006), 215.

3. Benkler, 216.

4. Benkler, 216.

5. Benkler, 8.

6. James Burnham, *The Managerial Revolution* (London: Lume Books, 1941), 84.

7. Chris Dixon, interview by Alex Tapscott via Zoom, Sept. 2, 2022.

8. Dixon interview by Alex Tapscott.

9. Dixon interview by Alex Tapscott.

10. Marco Quiroz-Gutierrez, "Coinbase Says Apple Is Demanding 30% Cut of NFT Gas Fees Before Allowing Digital Wallet Update," *Fortune*, Dec. 1, 2022, https:// fortune.com/crypto/2022/12/01/coinbase-apple-30-percent-fee-digital-wallet/.

11. CoinbaseWallet, Twitter post, Dec. 1, 2022 (11:34 a.m.), https://twitter.com/CoinbaseWallet/status/1598354820905197576.

12. CoinbaseWallet, Twitter post, Dec. 1, 2022 (11:34 a.m.), https://twitter.com/CoinbaseWallet/status/1598354823501447168.

13. Jon Swartz, "Facebook Parent Meta Set to Take Nearly 50% Cut from Virtual Salesand Apple Is Calling It Out," *MarketWatch*, April 13, 2022, https://www.marketwatch.com/story/facebook-parent-meta-set-to-take-nearly-50-cut-from-virtual-sales-within-its-metaverse-11649885375.

14. Max Fisher, *The Chaos Machine: The Inside Story of How Social Media Rewired Our Minds and Our World* (New York: Little, Brown, 2022), 10.

15. "Innovative or Ancient? Is Cash Going the Way of the Dodo?" mod. Ellen Roseman, Royal Ontario Museum, Nov. 22, 2022, https://rom.akaraisin.com/ui/InnovativeOrAncient.

16. "Innovative or Ancient?"

17. "Remittances Grow 5% in 2022, Despite Global Headwinds," press release, World Bank, Nov. 30, 2022, https://www.worldbank.org/en/news/press-release/2022/11/30/remittances-grow-5-percent-2022.

18. "COVID-19 Boosted the Adoption of Digital Financial Services," World Bank, July 21, 2022, https://www.worldbank.org/en/news/feature/2022/07/21/covid-19-boosted-the-adoption-of-digital-financial-services.

19. "Know Your Money," US Secret Service, April 2016, rev. Dec. 2020, https://www.secretservice.gov/sites/default/files/reports/2020-12/KnowYourMoney.pdf; and "Learn How to Authenticate Your Money," US Currency Education Program, 2022, https://www.uscurrency.gov/.

20. John Locke, *Two Treatises of Government and A Letter Concerning Toleration*, 1690.

21. Louis Jordan, "Spanish Silver: General Introduction," *The Coins of Colonial and Early America*, Dept. of Special Collections, University of Notre Dame, last rev. Aug. 20, 2001, https://coins.nd.edu/colcoin/colcoinintros/sp-silver.intro.html.

22. Charles R. Bawden, "Kublai Khan," *Britannica*, updated Nov. 1, 2022, https://www.britannica.com/biography/Kublai-Khan; and "The First Paper Money," in "Top 10 Things You Didn't Know About Money," *Time*, April 2010, https://content.time.com/time/specials/packages/article/0,28804,1914560_1914558_1914593,00.html.

23. "Bitcoin," CoinMarketCap, as of Dec. 11, 2022, https://coinmarketcap.com/currencies/bitcoin/; and MasterCard, Companies Market Cap, as of Dec. 11, 2022, https://companiesmarketcap.com/.

24. Scott Alexander Siskind, "Why I'm Less Than Infinitely Hostile to Cryptocurrency," *Astral Codex Ten Blog*, Dec. 8, 2022, https://astralcodexten.substack.com/p/why-im-less-than-infinitely-hostile.

25. Alex Gladstein, interview by Alex Tapscott via Zoom, Jan. 12, 2023.

26. Gabriel Abed, interview by Alex Tapscott via Zoom, March 15, 2023.

27. Gladstein interview by Alex Tapscott.

28. Ari Paul (@Ari DavidPaul), Twitter post, Feb. 13, 2019 (9:18 a.m.), https://twitter.com/AriDavidPaul/status/1095688683280351233.

29. "Tether," CoinMarketCap, as of Dec. 11, 2022, https://coinmarketcap.com /currencies/usd-coin/ and https://coinmarketcap.com/currencies/tether/.

30. Zachary Warmbrodt, "Jerome Powell: Facebook's Libra Poses Potential Risk to Financial System," *Politico*, July 10, 2019, https://www.politico .com/story/2019/07/10/jerome-powell-facebook-libra-1578306; and Alan Rappeport and Nathaniel Popper, "Cryptocurrencies Pose National Security Threat, Mnuchin Says," *New York Times*, July 15, 2019, https://www.nytimes .com/2019/07/15/us/politics/mnuchin-facebook-libra-risk.html, accessed Dec. 11, 2022.

31. Gladstein interview by Alex Tapscott.

32. James Dale Davidson and Lord William Rees-Mogg, *The Sovereign Individual: Mastering the Transition to the Information Age* (New York: Simon & Schuster, 1997), 216.

33. Davidson and Rees-Mogg, 216.

34. Adrian Brink, interviewed by Alex Tapscott, *DeFi Decoded* podcast, March 31, 2022, https://www.youtube.com/watch?v=528EV-y2VKQ.

35. Jeremy Allaire, interview by Alex Tapscott via Zoom, Feb. 6, 2023.

36. Allaire interview by Alex Tapscott.

37. Don Tapscott and Alex Tapscott, *Blockchain Revolution: How the Technology Behind Bitcoin and Other Cryptocurrencies Is Changing the World* (New York: Penguin Portfolio, 2018), 71–72.

38. "State of the USDC Economy," *Circle*, Circle Internet Financial Limited, Mar. 10, 2023, https://www.circle.com/hubfs/PDFs/2301StateofUSDCEconomy _Web.pdf, accessed April 12, 2023, 8.

39. "State of the USDC Economy," 8.

40. "State of the USDC Economy," 8.

41. "State of the USDC Economy," 12.

42. "State of the USDC Economy," 14.

43. Allaire interview by Alex Tapscott.

44. Allaire interview by Alex Tapscott.

45. Allaire interview by Alex Tapscott.

46. Allaire interview by Alex Tapscott.

47. Christopher J. Waller, "Reflections on Stablecoins and Payments Innovations," at *Planning for Surprises, Learning from Crises*, 2021 Financial Stability Conference, cohosted by the Federal Reserve Bank of Cleveland and the Office of Financial Research, Cleveland, Ohio, Nov. 17, 2021, https://www.federalreserve.gov /newsevents/speech/waller20211117a.htm.

48. For a full survey of the Golden Nine and the impact of DeFi on every facet of financial services, I recommend checking out my book *Digital Asset Revolution*.

49. Rune Christensen, interviewed by Alex Tapscott, July 24, 2019.

50. Matt Huang (@matthuang), Twitter post, Feb. 27, 2021 (6:44 p.m.), https:// twitter.com/matthuang/status/1365809948417007617.

51. Hayden Adams, "A Crypto-exchange Founder Makes His Case for Decentralised Finance," *Economist*, Dec. 6, 2022, https://www.economist.com

/by-invitation/2022/12/06/a-crypto-exchange-founder-makes-his-case-for
-decentralised-finance.

52. Adams, "A Crypto-exchange Founder Makes His Case for Decentralised
Finance."

53. Campbell R. Harvey, Ashwin Ramachandran, and Joey Santoro, *DeFi and the
Future of Finance* (Hoboken, NJ: Wiley, 2021), 51.

54. The "bancor" was economist John Maynard Keynes's name for a multinational
currency issued by a global bank and used to measure a country's trade deficit or
trade surplus. Sandra Kollen Ghizoni, "Creation of the Bretton Woods System,
July 1944," *Federal Reserve History*, Federal Reserve Bank of Atlanta, Nov. 22,
2013, https://www.federalreservehistory.org/essays/bretton-woods-created; and
E. F. Schumacher, "Multilateral Clearing," *Economica* 10, no. 38 (1943): 150–65,
https://doi.org/10.2307/2549461.

55. Galia Benartzi, interview by Alex Tapscott and Andrew Young via Zoom for the
DeFi Decoded podcast, Nov. 2, 2021.

56. Benartzi interview by Alex Tapscott and Andrew Young.

57. Harvey, Ramachandran, and Santoro, *DeFi and the Future of Finance*, 57.

58. Harvey, Ramachandran, and Santoro, 57.

59. Harvey, Ramachandran, and Santoro, 60.

60. Anonymous, *The Book Buyer: A Monthly Review of American and Foreign
Literature*, vol. 6, p. 57, https://www.google.com/books/edition/The_Book
_Buyer/rV5bxQEACAAJ?hl=en.

61. Sidney Powell, interview by Alex Tapscott via Zoom, Aug. 19, 2022.

62. Powell interview by Alex Tapscott.

63. Powell interview by Alex Tapscott.

64. Samuel Haig, "Vitalik Urges DeFi to Embrace Real World Assets," *The Defiant*,
Dec. 7, 2022, https://thedefiant.io/vitalik-urges-defi-to-embrace-real-world
-assets.

65. Linda Hardesty, "T-Mobile Allows the Helium Mobile 'Crypto Carrier' to Ride
on Its 5G Network Fierce Wireless," Sept. 20, 2022, https://www.fiercewireless
.com/5g/t-mobile-allows-helium-mobile-crypto-carrier-ride-its-5g-network.

66. Sishir Varghese, interview by Alex Tapscott via Zoom, Aug. 31, 2022.

67. Varghese interview by Alex Tapscott.

68. Alex Johnson, "Steal from the Rich and Live Off the Interest," *Fintech Newsletter*,
Aug. 28, 2022, https://workweek.com/2022/08/28/steal-from-the-rich-and-live
-off-the-interest/.

69. Stepan Gershuni, interview by Alex Tapscott via Zoom, Jan. 26, 2023.

70. Gershuni interview by Alex Tapscott.

71. Harvey, Ramachandran, and Santoro, *DeFi and the Future of Finance*, 24.

72. Habtamu Fuje, Saad Quayyum, and Tebo Molosiwa, "Africa's Growing Crypto
Market Needs Better Regulations," *IMF Blog*, International Monetary Fund,
Nov. 22, 2022, https://www.imf.org/en/Blogs/Articles/2022/11/22/africas
-growing-crypto-market-needs-better-regulations; and Aditya Narain and
Marina Moretti, "Regulating Crypto," *Finance and Development*, International

Monetary Fund, Sept. 2022, https://www.imf.org/en/Publications/fandd /issues/2022/09/Regulating-crypto-Narain-Moretti.

73. Ethan Buchman, interview by Alex Tapscott for the *DeFi Decoded* podcast, Nov. 17, 2021.

74. Irene Vallejo, *Papyrus: The Invention of Books in the Ancient World*, trans. Charlotte Whittle (New York: Knopf, 2022), 23.

75. Lex Sokolin, interview by Alex Tapscott, *DeFi Decoded* podcast, Feb. 1, 2022.

76. Ronald H. Coase, "The Nature of the Firm," *Economica* 4, no. 16 (Nov. 1937): 386–405, https://doi.org/10.1111/j.1468-0335.1937.tb00002.x.

77. Sirio Aramonte, Wenqian Huang, and Andreas Schrimpf, "DeFi Risks and the Decentralisation Illusion," *BIS Quarterly Review*, Dec. 6, 2021, https://www.bis .org/publ/qtrpdf/r_qt2112b.htm.

78. Matt Levine, "Making Crypto Hacking Less Lucrative," *Bloomberg News*, Bloomberg LP, Oct. 20, 2022, https://www.bloomberg.com/opinion/articles /2022-10-20/making-crypto-hacking-less-lucrative.

79. Levine, "Making Crypto Hacking Less Lucrative."

80. CertiK, "Facebook's 'Move' Programming Language: How Does It Compare to Solidity and DeepSEA?" *Certik Blog*, June 21, 2019, https://medium.com/certik /facebooks-move-programming-language-how-does-it-compare-to-solidity-and -deepsea-42cff1ba4c10.

81. Ali Yahya, interview by Alex Tapscott via Zoom, Oct. 14, 2022.

82. Yahya interview by Alex Tapscott.

83. John Robison, Aryan Sheikhalian, and Alex Tapscott, "Decentralized Finance Analysis: How to Identify Value Within the Crypto Ecosystem," Blockchain Research Institute, Feb. 9, 2023, https://www.blockchainresearchinstitute.org /project/decentralized-finance-analysis/.

84. James Beck and Mattison Asher, "What Is EIP-1559? How Will It Change Ethereum?" Consensus Systems, June 22, 2021, https://consensys.net/blog /quorum/what-is-eip-1559-how-will-it-change-ethereum/; and Vitalik Buterin et al., "EIP-1559: Fee Market Change for ETH 1.0 Chain," Ethereum Improvement Proposals, April 13, 2019, https://eips.ethereum.org/EIPS/eip -1559.

85. timbeiko.eth (@TimBeiko), Twitter post, Jan. 16, 2023 (3:40 p.m.), https:// twitter.com/TimBeiko/status/1615086494317973504.

86. "Tether," CoinMarketCap, as of April 14, 2022, https://coinmarketcap.com /currencies/tether/; and Raynor de Best, "Quarterly TPV (Total Payment Volume) of Venmo in USD 2017–2022," Statista, Feb. 10, 2023, https://www .statista.com/statistics/763617/venmo-total-payment-volume/.

87. "State of the USDC Economy."

Chapter 7: Gaming

1. David Curry, "Roblox Revenue and Usage Statistics (2023)," *Business of Apps*, Soko Media Ltd., last updated Feb. 28, 2023, https://www.businessofapps.com /data/roblox-statistics/, accessed May 17, 2023.

2. Yat Siu, interview by Alex Tapscott via Zoom, Jan. 11, 2023.
3. Siu interview by Alex Tapscott.
4. J. Clement, "Mobile Gaming Market in the United States: Statistics and Facts," Statista, Oct. 18, 2022, https://www.statista.com/topics/1906/mobile-gaming/#topicOverview.
5. Siu interview by Alex Tapscott.
6. Siu interview by Alex Tapscott.
7. Siu interview by Alex Tapscott.
8. Siu interview by Alex Tapscott.
9. Ria Lu, interview by Alex Tapscott via Zoom, Oct. 12, 2022.
10. Lu interview by Alex Tapscott.
11. Aleksander Larsen, interview by Alex Tapacott and Andrew Young for the *DeFi Decoded* podcast, April 18, 2023.
12. "A Digital Pet Collecting and Farming Game, Built on Blockchain," Crypto Unicorns, as of April 12, 2023, https://www.cryptounicorns.fun/.
13. Lu interview by Alex Tapscott.
14. Lu interview by Alex Tapscott.
15. Siu interview by Alex Tapscott.
16. Lu interview by Alex Tapscott.
17. Lu interview by Alex Tapscott.
18. Aleksander Larsen, interview by Alex Tapscott via Zoom, Aug. 9, 2022.
19. Katrina Wolfe, interview by Alex Tapscott via Zoom, Oct. 14, 2022.
20. Sascha Darius Mojtahedi, interview by Alex Tapscott via Zoom, Aug. 9, 2022.
21. Mojtahedi interview by Alex Tapscott.
22. Ben Lee, interview by Alex Tapscott and Andrew Young for the *DeFi Decoded* podcast, March 8, 2022.
23. Lee interview by Alex Tapscott and Andrew Young.
24. Lee interview by Alex Tapscott and Andrew Young.
25. Lee interview by Alex Tapscott and Andrew Young.
26. Larsen interview by Alex Tapscott.
27. "Axie Infinity Live Player Count and Statistics," ActivePlayer.io Game Statistics Authority, https://activeplayer.io/axie-infinity/, accessed April 14, 2022.
28. Larsen interview by Alex Tapscott.
29. Vittoria Elliott, "Workers in the Global South Are Making a Living Playing the Blockchain Game Axie Infinity," *Rest of World*, Aug. 19, 2021, https://restofworld.org/2021/axie-players-are-facing-taxes/, accessed Oct. 15, 2021.
30. Vittoria Elliott, "Some Axie Infinity Players Amassed Fortunes—Now the Philippine Government Wants Its Cut," *Rest of World*, Sept. 30, 2021, https://restofworld.org/2021/axie-players-are-facing-taxes/, accessed Oct. 15, 2021.
31. Erin Plante, "$30 Million Seized: How the Cryptocurrency Community Is Making It Difficult for North Korean Hackers to Profit," *Chainalysis Blog*, Sept. 8, 2022, https://blog.chainalysis.com/reports/axie-infinity-ronin-bridge-dprk-hack-seizure/.
32. Andrew Thurman, "Axie Infinity's Ronin Network Suffers $625M Exploit,"

CoinDesk, March 29, 2022, https://www.coindesk.com/tech/2022/03/29
/axie-infinitys-ronin-network-suffers-625m-exploit/; and Plante, "$30 Million
Seized."

33. Axie Infinity, "Axie Passed Google Play Store Review!" *The Lunacian*, Dec. 22,
2022, https://axie.substack.com/p/googleplaystore.

34. Beryl Li, interview by Alex Tapscott via Zoom, Oct. 4, 2022.

35. "Digital Asset Outlook 2023," The Block, Dec. 20, 2022, https://www.tbstat
.com/wp/uploads/2022/12/Digital-Asset-2023-Outlook.pdf.

36. Dean Takahashi, "Game Boss Interview: Epic's Tim Sweeney on Blockchain,
Digital Humans, and Fortnite," *VentureBeat*, Aug. 30, 2017, https://venturebeat
.com/games/game-boss-interview-epics-tim-sweeney-on-blockchain-digital
-humans-and-fortnite/, accessed Nov. 18, 2022.

37. Sean Murray, "Epic CEO Tim Sweeney Says 'Developers Should Be Free to
Decide' If They Want NFTs in Their Games," *The Gamer*, July 22, 2022, https://
www.thegamer.com/epic-ceo-tim-sweeney-free-to-decide-nft-games/.

38. Pete Evans, "Fortnite Maker Epic Games to Pay $520M in Fines and Rebates for
Duping Users into Downloading Paid Content," *CBC News*, CBC/Radio-Canada,
Dec. 19, 2022, https://www.cbc.ca/news/business/fornite-ftc-fines-1.6690777.

39. Evans, "Fortnite Maker Epic Games."

40. "Epic FTC Settlement and Moving Beyond Long-Standing Industry Practices,"
press release, Epic Games, Dec. 19, 2022, https://www.epicgames.com/site
/en-US/news/epic-ftc-settlement-and-moving-beyond-long-standing-industry
-practices.

41. Matthew L. Ball, *The Metaverse: And How It Will Revolutionize Everything* (New
York: Liveright, 2022), 234.

42. Ball, 201.

43. Ball, 218.

44. Mojtahedi interview by Alex Tapscott.

45. Li interview by Alex Tapscott.

46. Li interview by Alex Tapscott.

47. Lu interview by Alex Tapscott.

48. Lu interview by Alex Tapscott.

49. Dean Takahashi, "Bored Ape Company Yuga Labs Appoints Activision
Blizzard's Daniel Alegre as CEO," *VentureBeat*, Dec. 19, 2022, https://
venturebeat.com/games/bored-ape-company-yuga-labs-appoints-activision
-blizzards-daniel-alegre-as-ceo/.

50. Jordan Novet and Lauren Feiner, "FTC Sues to Block Microsoft's Acquisition of
Activision Blizzard," CNBC Universal, Dec. 8, 2022, https://www.cnbc
.com/2022/12/08/ftc-sues-to-block-microsofts-acquisition-of-game-giant
-activision-blizzard.html.

51. Elizabeth Howcroft, "Bored Ape NFT Company Raises around $285 Million of
Crypto in Virtual Land Sale," Reuters, May 1, 2022, https://www.reuters.com
/technology/bored-ape-nft-company-raises-around-285-million-crypto-virtual
-land-sale-2022-05-01/.

52. Ryan Selkis, interview by Alex Tapscott via Zoom, Aug. 24, 2022.
53. Marshall McLuhan, "Oracle of the Electric Age," interviewed by Robert Fulford, CBC/Radio-Canada, 1966, https://www.cbc.ca/player/play /1809367561.
54. "Earn Tokens by Using Crypto Applications," RabbitHole Studios Inc., n.d., https://rabbithole.gg/, accessed April 12, 2023.
55. "Digital Asset Outlook 2023," The Block.
56. Oleg Fomenko, interview by Alex Tapscott, Jan. 20, 2023.
57. Fomenko interview by Alex Tapscott.
58. Fomenko interview by Alex Tapscott.
59. Fomenko interview by Alex Tapscott.

Chapter 8: The Metaverse

1. William Gibson, *Neuromancer* (New York: Ace Books, 1984), https://www .goodreads.com/quotes/14638-cyberspace-a-consensual-hallucination -experienced-daily-by-billions-of-legitimate.
2. Aldous Huxley, *Brave New World* (London: Chatto and Windus, 1932), chapter 3.
3. A. Brad Schwartz, "The Infamous *War of the Worlds* Radio Broadcast Was a Magnificent Fluke," *Smithsonian Magazine*, May 6, 2015, https://www .smithsonianmag.com/history/infamous-war-worlds-radio-broadcast-was -magnificent-fluke-180955180/.
4. Marshall McLuhan, "The World Is a Global Village," *The Future of Health Technology*, HealthcareFuture, March 24, 2009, https://www.youtube.com /watch?v=HeDnPP6ntic.
5. Matthew L. Ball, *The Metaverse: And How It Will Revolutionize Everything* (New York: Liveright, 2022), 57.
6. Ball, 16.
7. Dean Takahashi, "Epic Graphics Guru Tim Sweeney Foretells How We Can Create the Open Metaverse," *Venture Beat*, Dec. 9, 2016, https://venturebeat .com/games/the-deanbeat-epic-boss-tim-sweeney-makes-the-case-for-the-open -metaverse/.
8. Yat Siu, interview by Alex Tapscott via Zoom, Jan. 11, 2023.
9. Siu interview by Alex Tapscott.
10. Siu interview by Alex Tapscott.
11. Ball, *The Metaverse*, 188.
12. Ball, 10.
13. Kate Birch, "JP Morgan Is First Leading Bank to Launch in the Metaverse," *FinTech Magazine*, BizClik, Feb. 17, 2022, https://fintechmagazine.com /banking/jp-morgan-becomes-the-first-bank-to-launch-in-the-metaverse.
14. "Digital Asset Outlook 2023," The Block, Dec. 20, 2022, https://www.tbstat .com/wp/uploads/2022/12/Digital-Asset-2023-Outlook.pdf.
15. Ball, *The Metaverse*, 200.
16. Ball, 201.
17. Brett Winton, interview by Alex Tapscott via Zoom, Aug. 25, 2022.

18. Winton interview by Alex Tapscott.

19. Winton interview by Alex Tapscott.

20. Ball, *The Metaverse*, 208.

21. "Digital Asset Outlook 2023," The Block.

22. "Digital Twin," *Gartner Glossary*, Gartner Inc., n.d., https://www.gartner.com /en/information-technology/glossary/digital-twin, accessed April 12, 2023.

23. Sascha Darius Mojtahedi, interview by Alex Tapscott via Zoom, Aug. 9, 2022.

24. Anatoly Yakovenko, interview by Alex Tapscott and Andrew Young via Zoom for the *DeFi Decoded* podcast, July 27, 2022.

25. Yakovenko interview by Alex Tapscott and Andrew Young.

26. Yakovenko interview by Alex Tapscott and Andrew Young.

27. Yakovenko interview by Alex Tapscott and Andrew Young.

28. Jules Urbach, interview by Alex Tapscott via Zoom, Jan. 24, 2022.

29. Urbach interview by Alex Tapscott.

30. RNDR Team, "Q1-Q3 Data Update: [Behind the Network (BTN)]," Render Network, Dec. 2, 2022, https://medium.com/render-token/q1-q3-data-update -december-2nd-2022-behind-the-network-btn-b627c0d8841e.

31. Phillip Gara, email exchange, Jan. 24, 2023.

32. Render Network (@RenderToken), Twitter post, May 12, 2022 (11:48 a.m.), https://twitter.com/RenderToken/status/1524778641573527553.

33. Metaverse Standards Forum, Khronos Group Inc., n.d., https://metaverse -standards.org/, accessed April 12, 2023.

34. Urbach interview by Alex Tapscott.

35. Urbach interview by Alex Tapscott.

36. Urbach interview by Alex Tapscott.

37. Sami Kassab, "Using Crypto to Build Real-World Infrastructure," Messari, Aug. 4, 2022, https://messari.io/report/using-crypto-to-build-real-world -infrastructure.

38. Kassab email interview by Alex Tapscott.

39. Kassab email interview by Alex Tapscott.

40. "State of Storage Market," Storage.Market, as of Feb. 6, 2023, https://file.app/.

41. "Filecoin Project," GitHub, https://github.com/filecoin-project; and https:// storage.filecoin.io/, as of Feb. 6, 2023.

42. Kassab, "Using Crypto to Build Real-World Infrastructure."

43. Greg Osuri, interview by Alex Tapscott and Andrew Young for the *DeFi Decoded* podcast, Dec. 15, 2021.

44. Osuri interview by Alex Tapscott and Andrew Young.

45. Osuri interview by Alex Tapscott and Andrew Young.

46. Linda Hardesty, "T-Mobile Allows the Helium Mobile 'Crypto Carrier' to Ride on Its 5G Network Fierce Wireless," Sept. 20, 2022, https://www.fiercewireless .com/5g/t-mobile-allows-helium-mobile-crypto-carrier-ride-its-5g-network.

47. Filecoin had 557,244,178,562,884,100 BYTES (494.9323 PIB) of total data stored, as of Jan. 8, 2023, https://storage.filecoin.io/. See also https://file.app/.

48. Ariel Seidman, interview by Alex Tapscott via Zoom, Jan. 20, 2023.

49. NYPL Staff, "The Great War and Modern Mapping: WWI in the Map Division," New York Public Library, May 15, 2015, https://www.nypl.org /blog/2015/05/15/wwi-map-division.

50. Paul Berger, "'It Takes Over Your Life': Waze Volunteers Work for the Love of Maps; Thousands of Them Spend Hours Updating Maps for Company; Rising through the Ranks," *Wall Street Journal*, March 20, 2019; or Paul Berger, "Waze to Win: Employ Army of Map Nerds—Unpaid Thousands Help Edit the Google Service," *Wall Street Journal*, Eastern Edition, March 21, 2019, https://www.wsj .com/articles/the-Internets-most-devoted-volunteers-waze-map -editors-11553096956.

51. Seidman interview by Alex Tapscott.

52. Paolo Bonato, "Wearable Sensors and a Web-Based Application to Monitor Patients with Parkinson's Disease in the Home Environment," Funded Study, Michael J. Fox Foundation for Parkinson's Research, 2008, https://www .michaeljfox.org/grant/wearable-sensors-and-web-based-application-monitor -patients-parkinsons-disease-home-0.

53. Hirsh Chitkara, "Worldcoin Emerges from Stealth to Pursue Its UBI Infrastructure Ambitions," *Protocol*, PROTOCOL LLC, Oct. 12, 2021, https:// www.protocol.com/bulletins/worldcoin-ubi-infrastructure.

54. Joe Light, "ChatGPT's Sam Altman Is Getting $100 Million for Worldcoin Crypto Project," *Barron's*, Dow Jones & Co. Inc., May 15, 2023, https://www .barrons.com/articles/worldcoin-sam-altman-crypto-ff4632ba.

Chapter 9: Civilization

1. "Africa Life Expectancy 1950–2023," Macrotrends LLC, as of April 12, 2023, https://www.macrotrends.net/countries/AFR/africa/life-expectancy.

2. "Africa Infant Mortality Rate 1950–2023," Macrotrends LLC, as of April 12, 2023, https://www.macrotrends.net/countries/AFR/africa/infant-mortality-rate.

3. "COVID-19 Boosted the Adoption of Digital Financial Services," World Bank, July 21, 2022, https://www.worldbank.org/en/news/feature/2022/07/21/covid -19-boosted-the-adoption-of-digital-financial-services; and "State of the USDC Economy," *Circle*, Circle Internet Financial Limited, March 10, 2023, https:// www.circle.com/hubfs/PDFs/2301StateofUSDCEconomy_Web.pdf.

4. James Dale Davidson and Lord William Rees-Mogg, *The Sovereign Individual: Mastering the Transition to the Information Age* (New York: Simon & Schuster, 1997), 196.

5. Ani Petrosyan, "Worldwide Digital Population 2023," Statista, April 3, 2023, https://www.statista.com/statistics/617136/digital-population-worldwide/.

6. Chainalysis Team, "2021 Global Crypto Adoption Index," *Chainalysis Blog*, Oct. 14, 2021, https://blog.chainalysis.com/reports/2021-global-crypto -adoption-index/.

7. NFT.NYC, PeopleBrowsr Inc., April 2022, https://www.nft.nyc/.

8. April and Sevi Agregado, interview by Alex Tapscott via Zoom, Oct. 14, 2022.

9. Alex Hawgood, "Six-Figure Artworks, by a Fifth Grader," *New York Times*,

Sept. 26, 2022, https://www.nytimes.com/2022/09/26/style/andres-valencia-art-paintings.html.

10. Pedro Herrera, "2021 Dapp Industry Report," *DappRadar Blog*, Dec. 17, 2021, https://dappradar.com/blog/2021-dapp-industry-report.

11. April and Sevi Agregado interview by Alex Tapscott.

12. April and Sevi Agregado interview by Alex Tapscott.

13. April and Sevi Agregado interview by Alex Tapscott.

14. Katrina Wolfe, interview by Alex Tapscott via Zoom, Oct. 14, 2022.

15. Wolfe interview by Alex Tapscott.

16. Ria Lu, interview by Alex Tapscott via Zoom, Oct. 12, 2022.

17. Lu interview by Alex Tapscott.

18. Lu interview by Alex Tapscott.

19. Lu interview by Alex Tapscott.

20. Lu interview by Alex Tapscott.

21. Dickson Nsofor, interview by Alex Tapscott via Zoom for the *DeFi Decoded* podcast, July 12, 2022.

22. Alex Gladstein, interview by Alex Tapscott via Zoom, Jan. 12, 2023.

23. "Cryptocurrency Information about Nigeria," Triple A, 2021, https://triple-a.io/crypto-ownership-nigeria-2022/.

24. Victor Oluwole, "Top Five African Countries with the Most Cryptocurrency Holders," *Business Insider,* June 21, 2022, https://africa.businessinsider.com/local/markets/top-5-african-countries-with-the-most-cryptocurrency-holders/2tvh7r5.

25. Arianna Simpson, interview by Alex Tapscott via Zoom, Sept. 13, 2022.

26. Simpson interview by Alex Tapscott.

27. Simpson interview by Alex Tapscott.

28. Hija Kamran, "State Bank of Pakistan Decides to Ban Cryptocurrencies; Submits Report in Court," Digital Rights Monitor, Jan. 12, 2022, https://digitalrightsmonitor.pk/state-bank-of-pakistan-decides-to-ban-cryptocurrencies-submits-report-in-court/.

29. Nsofor interview by Alex Tapscott.

30. Mariam Saleh, "Population of Africa in 2021, by Age Group," *Statista*, Nov. 21, 2022, https://www.statista.com/statistics/1226211/population-of-africa-by-age-group/.

31. "Nigeria's Informal Economy Size," *World Economics*, as of April 13, 2023, https://www.worldeconomics.com/National-Statistics/Informal-Economy/Nigeria.aspx.

32. Ogwah Oreva, "Nigeria Payments System Vision 2025," Central Bank of Nigeria, Nov. 18, 2022, https://www.cbn.gov.ng/Out/2022/CCD/PSMD%20vision%202025%20EDITED%20FINAL.pdf.

33. "UNHCR Launches Pilot Cash-Based Intervention Using Blockchain Technology for Humanitarian Payments to People Displaced and Impacted by the War in Ukraine," press release, Dec. 15, 2022, https://www.unhcr.org/ua/en/52555-unhcr-launches-pilot-cash-based-intervention-using-blockchain

-technology-for-humanitarian-payments-to-people-displaced-and-impacted-by
-the-war-in-ukraine-unhcr-has-launched-a-first-of-its-kind-integ.html.

34. Leo Schwartz, "Coinbase CEO Says USDC Will Become 'De Facto Central
Bank Digital Currency,' Company Posts Weak Q3 Earnings," *Fortune*, Fortune
Media IP Limited, Nov. 3, 2022, https://fortune.com/crypto/2022/11/03
/coinbase-ceo-says-usdc-will-become-de-facto-cbdc/.

Chapter 10: Web3's Implementation Challenges

1. AngelList (@angellist), Twitter post, Sept. 28, 2021 (1:17 p.m.), https://twitter
.com/AngelList/status/1442901252552101888, accessed Oct. 15, 2021.

2. Raj Dhamodharan, "Why Mastercard Is Bringing Crypto onto Its Network,"
Mastercard International, Feb. 10, 2021, https://www.mastercard.com/news
/perspectives/2021/why-mastercard-is-bringing-crypto-onto-our-network,
accessed Oct. 15, 2021.

3. "Digital Currency Comes," *VISA Everywhere Blog*, Visa, March 26, 2021,
https://usa.visa.com/visa-everywhere/blog/bdp/2021/03/26/digital-currency
-comes-1616782388876.html, accessed Oct. 15, 2021.

4. Ryan Weeks, "PayPal Has Held Exploratory Talks About Launching a
Stablecoin: Sources," Block Crypto, May 3, 2021, https://www.theblockcrypto
.com/post/103617/paypal-has-held-exploratory-talks-about-launching-a
-stablecoin-sources, accessed Oct. 15, 2021.

5. Jeff John Roberts, "Visa Unveils 'Layer 2' Network for Stablecoins, Central Bank
Currencies," *Decrypt*, Sept. 30, 2021, https://decrypt.co/82233/visa-universal
-payment-channel-stablecoin-cbdc, accessed Oct. 15, 2021.

6. "The Digital Currencies That Matter: Get Ready for Fedcoin and the e-euro,"
Economist, May 8, 2021, https://www.economist.com/leaders/2021/05/08/the
-digital-currencies-that-matter.

7. Hester Peirce, "Remarks before the Digital Assets," Duke Conference,
Washington DC, US Securities and Exchange Commission, Jan. 20, 2023,
https://www.sec.gov/news/speech/peirce-remarks-duke-conference-012023#
_ftnref15.

8. Peirce, "Remarks before the Digital Assets."

9. Tobixen, "A Brief History of the Bitcoin Block Size War," *Steemit*, Nov. 7, 2017.
steemit.com/bitcoin/@tobixen/a-brief-history-of-the-bitcoin-block-size-war,
accessed Oct. 15, 2021.

10. Kain Warwick, interview by Alex Tapscott via Zoom, Aug. 15, 2022.

11. Albert Wenger, interviewed by Alex Tapscott via Zoom, Dec. 16, 2022.

12. Moxie Marlinspike, "My First Impressions of Web3," *Moxie Blog*, Jan. 7, 2022,
https://moxie.org/2022/01/07/web3-first-impressions.html.

13. Moxie Marlinspike, "My First Impressions of Web3."

14. Charles Hoskinson, interview by Alex Tapscott via Zoom, Jan. 5, 2023.

15. Sal Bayat, Tim Bray, Grady Booch, et al., "Letter in Support of Responsible
Fintech Policy," to US Congressional Leadership, Committee Chairs, and
Ranking Members, June 1, 2022, https://concerned.tech/.

16. Roneil Rumburg, email to Alex Tapscott, Nov. 18, 2022.

17. Warwick interview by Alex Tapscott.

18. Tyler Winklevoss, interview by Alex Tapscott via Zoom, Sept. 12, 2022.

19. "Understanding the Problem Crusoe Solves," *Crusoe Blog*, Crusoe Energy, Sept. 23, 2021, https://www.crusoeenergy.com/blog/3MyNTKiT6wqs EWKhP0BeY/understanding-the-problem-crusoe-solves.

20. Chainalysis Team, "Crypto Crime Summarized: Scams and Darknet Markets Dominated 2020 by Revenue, But Ransomware Is the Bigger Story," *Chainalysis Blog*, Jan. 19, 2021, https://blog.chainalysis.com/reports/2021-crypto-crime -report-intro-ransomware-scams-darknet-markets; and Michael J. Morell, "Report: An Analysis of Bitcoin's Use in Illicit Finance," *Cipher Brief*, April 13, 2021, https://www.thecipherbrief.com/report-an-analysis-of-bitcoins-use-in -illicit-finance, accessed Oct. 15, 2021.

21. Niall Ferguson, "FTX Kept Your Crypto in a Crypt Not a Vault," *Bloomberg Opinion*, Bloomberg LP, Nov. 20, 2022, https://www.bloomberg.com/opinion /articles/2022-11-20/niall-ferguson-ftx-kept-your-crypto-in-a-crypt-not-a-vault.

22. Ria Lu, email to Alex Tapscott, Nov. 21, 2022.

23. Lu email to Alex Tapscott.

24. Jennifer Sor, "Sam Bankman-Fried Is a World-class Manipulator and the Implosion of FTX Is an 'Old-school Fraud,' Congressman Says," *Business Insider*, Yahoo Finance, Dec. 13, 2022, https://finance.yahoo.com/news/sam-bankman -fried-world-class-180256987.html.

25. Rep. Patrick McHenry (R-NC), "FTX CEO Testifies on Cryptocurrency Company's Collapse," C-SPAN, National Cable Satellite Corp., Dec. 13, 2022 (00:07:12), https://www.c-span.org/video/?524743-1/ftx-ceo-testifies -cryptocurrency-companys-collapse.

26. "Crypto Crash: Why the FTX Bubble Burst and the Harm to Consumers," Full Committee Hearing, US Senate Committee on Banking, Housing, and Urban Affairs, Dirksen Senate Office Building G50, Dec. 14, 2022 (10:00 a.m.), https://www.banking.senate.gov/hearings/crypto-crash-why-the-ftx-bubble -burst-and-the-harm-to-consumers.

27. Senator Elizabeth Warren, "ICYMI: At Hearing, Warren Warns about Crypto's Use for Money Laundering by Rogue States, Terrorists, and Criminals," press release, Dec. 15, 2022, https://www.warren.senate.gov/newsroom/press-releases /icymi-at-hearing-warren-warns-about-cryptos-use-for-money-laundering-by -rogue-states-terrorists-and-criminals.

28. Peter Van Valkenburgh, "The Digital Asset Anti-Money Laundering Act," Coin Center, Dec. 14, 2022, https://www.coincenter.org/the-digital-asset -anti-money-laundering-act-is-an-opportunistic-unconstitutional-assault -on-cryptocurrency-self-custody-developers-and-node-operators/.

29. Valkenburgh, "The Digital Asset Anti-Money Laundering Act."

30. Peter Van Valkenburgh, "How Does Tornado Cash Actually Work?" Coin Center, Aug. 25, 2022, https://www.coincenter.org/how-does-tornado-cash -actually-work/; and Jerry Brito and Peter Van Valkenburgh, "Coin Center Is

Suing OFAC over Its Tornado Cash Sanction," Coin Center, Oct. 12, 2022, https://www.coincenter.org/coin-center-is-suing-ofac-over-its-tornado-cash-sanction/.

31. Jerry Brito and Peter Van Valkenburgh, "US Treasury Sanction of Privacy Tools Places Sweeping Restrictions on All Americans," Coin Center, Aug. 8, 2022, https://www.coincenter.org/u-s-treasury-sanction-of-privacy-tools-places-sweeping-restrictions-on-all-americans/.

32. Daniel Kuhn, "What Happens When You Try to Sanction a Protocol Like Tornado Cash," Coin Center, Aug. 10, 2022, https://www.coindesk.com/layer2/2022/08/10/what-happens-when-you-try-to-sanction-a-protocol-like-tornado-cash/.

33. Chainalysis Team, "How 2022's Biggest Cryptocurrency Sanctions Designations Affected Crypto Crime," *Chainalysis Blog*, Jan. 9, 2023, https://blog.chainalysis.com/reports/how-2022-crypto-sanction-designations-affected-crypto-crime/.

34. "Digital Asset Outlook 2023," The Block, Dec. 20, 2022, https://www.tbstat.com/wp/uploads/2022/12/Digital-Asset-2023-Outlook.pdf.

35. Sheila Warren, interview by Alex Tapscott via Zoom, Oct. 6, 2022.

36. Tom Emmer (@RepTomEmmer), Twitter post, Oct. 5, 2021 (2:51 p.m.), https://twitter.com/RepTomEmmer/status/1445461701567160320, accessed Oct. 15, 2021.

37. Chris Dixon (@cdixon), Twitter post, Oct. 1, 2021 (6:50 p.m.), https://twitter.com/cdixon/status/1444072368859533316, accessed Oct. 15, 2021.

38. Chris Dixon (@cdixon), Twitter post, Oct. 1, 2021 (6:50 p.m.), https://twitter.com/cdixon/status/1444072370788978691 and https://twitter.com/cdixon/status/1444072374798675970, accessed Oct. 15, 2021.

39. Arianna Simpson, interview by Alex Tapscott via Zoom, Sept. 13, 2022.

40. "DAO Jobs: Find Great Crypto Jobs at a DAO," Cryptocurrency Jobs, accessed Nov. 5, 2021, https://cryptocurrencyjobs.co/dao.

41. Beryl Li, interview by Alex Tapscott via Zoom, Oct. 4, 2022.

42. Katrina Wolfe, interview by Alex Tapscott via Zoom, Oct. 14, 2022.

43. "Digital Asset Outlook 2023," The Block.

44. Kyung Taeck Minn, "Towards Enhanced Oversight of 'Self-Governing' Decentralized Autonomous Organizations: Case Study of the DAO and Its Shortcomings," *NYU Journal of Intellectual Property and Entertainment Law* 9, no. 1 (Jan. 24, 2020), https://jipel.law.nyu.edu/vol-9-no-1-5-minn, accessed Oct. 15, 2021.

45. Roy Learner, "Blockchain Voter Apathy," *Wave Financial Blog*, March 29, 2019, https://medium.com/wave-financial/blockchain-voter-apathy-69a1570e2af3. See also Nic Carter, "A Cross-Sectional Overview of Cryptoasset Governance and Implications for Investors" (diss., University of Edinburgh Business School, 2016–17), https://niccarter.info/papers, accessed Oct. 15, 2021.

46. Taras Kulyk and Ben Gagnon, "Global Bitcoin Mining Data Review: Q4 2022," Presentation, Bitcoin Mining Council, Jan. 18, 2023, https://

bitcoinminingcouncil.com/wp-content/uploads/2023/01/BMC-Q4-2022
-Presentation.pdf.

47. Warren interview by Alex Tapscott.

Conclusion

1. Many have alleged that Lenin made this observation, but we found no authoritative source.
2. Clayton M. Christensen, *The Innovator's Dilemma: When New Technologies Cause Great Firms to Fail* (Boston: Harvard Business School Press, 1997), 39.
3. Charles Hoskinson, interview by Alex Tapscott via Zoom, Jan. 5, 2023.
4. Robert Wilde, "Steam in the Industrial Revolution," July 25, 2019, https://www
.thoughtco.com/steam-in-the-industrial-revolution-1221643.
5. Tony Judt, *Postwar: A History of Europe since 1945* (New York: Penguin, 2005), 257.
6. Judt, 257.
7. "The Internet's First Message Sent from UCLA: 1969," *UCLA 100*, Univ. of California at Los Angeles, n.d., https://100.ucla.edu/timeline/the-Internets
-first-message-sent-from-ucla; and "Digital Around the World," *DataReportal*, Kepios Pte. Ltd., April 2023, https://datareportal.com/global-digital-overview.
8. Albert Wenger, interview by Alex Tapscott via Zoom, Dec. 16, 2022.
9. Wenger interview by Alex Tapscott.
10. Charles Hoskinson, interview by Alex Tapscott via Zoom, Jan. 5, 2023.
11. Wenger interview by Alex Tapscott.
12. Mark McSherry-Forbes, "Let's Hope Churchill Was Wrong About Americans," National Churchill Museum, Oct. 3, 2013, https://www
.nationalchurchillmuseum.org/10-07-13-lets-hope-churchill-was-wrong-about
-americans.html, accessed April 14, 2022.
13. Kristin Smith, interview by Alex Tapscott via Zoom, Aug. 23, 2022.
14. Alex Tapscott, "What Is Decentralized Finance?" Ninepoint Partners, YouTube, Jan. 10, 2022, https://www.youtube.com/watch?v=j6_Wm-gjh4s&t=7s, accessed March 31, 2022.
15. Janell Ross, "Inside the World of Black Bitcoin, Where Crypto Is About Making More Than Just Money," *Time*, TIME USA LLC, Oct. 15, 2021, https://time
.com/6106706/bitcoin-black-investors/, accessed March 31, 2022.
16. Morning Star, Aug. 17, 2021, https://morningconsult.com/2021/08/17/trust
-awareness-paynents-unbanked-underbanked/.
17. Avik Roy, "In El Salvador, More People Have Bitcoin Wallets Than Traditional Bank Accounts," *Forbes*, Oct. 7, 2021, https://www.forbes.com/sites
/theapothecary/2021/10/07/in-el-salvador-more-people-have-bitcoin-wallets
-than-traditional-bank-accounts/.
18. Christian Nunley, "People in the Philippines Are Earning Cryptocurrency During the Pandemic by Playing a Video Game," *CNBC*, NBCUniversal, May 14, 2021, https://www.cnbc.com/2021/05/14/people-in-philippines-earn-cryptocurrency
-playing-nft-video-game-axie-infinity.html, accessed March 31, 2022.

19. Caitlin Ostroff and Jared Malsin, "Turks Pile Into Bitcoin and Tether to Escape Plunging Lira," *Wall Street Journal*, Jan. 12, 2022, https://www.wsj.com/articles/turks-pile-into-bitcoin-and-tether-to-escape-plunging-lira-11641982077, accessed March 31, 2022.

20. "Top Stablecoin Tokens by Market Capitalization," CoinMarketCap, as of Dec. 22, 2022, https://coinmarketcap.com/view/stablecoin/.

21. Smith interview by Alex Tapscott.

22. Smith interview by Alex Tapscott.

23. Smith interview by Alex Tapscott.

24. "A Brief History of NSF and the Internet," Fact Sheet, National Science Foundation, Aug. 13, 2003, https://www.nsf.gov/news/news_summ.jsp?cntn_id=103050.

25. "Cyberporn," *Congressional Record* 141, no. 105 (Senate: June 26, 1995): S9017–S9023, https://www.congress.gov/congressional-record/volume-141/issue-105/senate-section/article/S9017-2.

26. Wireline Competition Bureau, "Telecommunications Act of 1996," Federal Communications Commission, last updated June 20, 2013, https://www.fcc.gov/general/telecommunications-act-1996, accessed April 14, 2022.

27. Bob Kerrey was among the proponents. "E-Rate and Education: A History," Federal Communications Commission, last updated Jan. 8, 2004, https://www.fcc.gov/general/e-rate-and-education-history.

28. Sec. 706, "Advanced Telecommunications Incentives," Telecommunications Act of 1996, 104th Congress (Jan. 3, 1996): 119–20, https://transition.fcc.gov/Reports/tcom1996.pdf.

29. Smith interview by Alex Tapscott.

30. Smith interview by Alex Tapscott.

31. Smith interview by Alex Tapscott.

32. Smith interview by Alex Tapscott.

33. Smith interview by Alex Tapscott.

34. Smith interview by Alex Tapscott.

35. Smith interview by Alex Tapscott.

36. Smith interview by Alex Tapscott.

37. Hester Peirce, "Remarks before the Digital Assets," Duke Conference, Washington DC, US Securities and Exchange Commission, Jan. 20, 2023, https://www.sec.gov/news/speech/peirce-remarks-duke-conference-012023#_ftnref15.

38. vitalik.eth (@VitalikButerin), Twitter post, Aug. 9, 2022 (4:49 a.m.), https://twitter.com/VitalikButerin/status/1556925602233569280.

39. Chainalysis Team, "How 2022's Biggest Cryptocurrency Sanctions Designations Affected Crypto Crime," *Chainalysis Blog*, Jan. 9, 2023, https://blog.chainalysis.com/reports/how-2022-crypto-sanction-designations-affected-crypto-crime/.

40. Jerry Brito and Peter Van Valkenburgh, "US Treasury Sanction of Privacy Tools Places Sweeping Restrictions on all Americans," Coin Center, Aug. 8, 2022,

https://www.coincenter.org/u-s-treasury-sanction-of-privacy-tools-places
-sweeping-restrictions-on-all-americans/.

41. Chris Giancarlo, interview by Alex Tapscott via Zoom, Dec. 13, 2022.

42. Giancarlo interview by Alex Tapscott.

43. Giancarlo interview by Alex Tapscott.

44. Giancarlo interview by Alex Tapscott.

45. Peirce, "Remarks before the Digital Assets."

46. Sheila Warren, interview by Alex Tapscott via Zoom, Oct. 6, 2022.

47. Kain Warwick, interview by Alex Tapscott via Zoom, Aug. 15, 2022.

48. Peirce, "Remarks before the Digital Assets."

49. Jerry Brito and Peter Van Valkenburgh, "Coin Center Is Suing OFAC over Its
    Tornado Cash Sanction," Coin Center, Oct. 12, 2022, https://www.coincenter
    .org/coin-center-is-suing-ofac-over-its-tornado-cash-sanction/.

50. Wenger interview by Alex Tapscott.

51. Jai Massari, "Why Cryptoassets Are Not Securities," Harvard Law School
    Forum on Corporate Governance, Dec. 6, 2022, https://corpgov.law.harvard
    .edu/2022/12/06/why-cryptoassets-are-not-securities/.

52. Peirce, "Remarks before the Digital Assets."

53. Wenger interview by Alex Tapscott.

54. Mark Gurman, "Apple to Allow Outside App Stores," *Bloomberg News*, Dec. 13,
    2022, https://www.bloomberg.com/news/articles/2022-12-13/will-apple-allow
    -users-to-install-third-party-app-stores-sideload-in-europe.

55. "Digital Markets Act," press release, European Commission, Oct. 31, 2022,
    https://ec.europa.eu/commission/presscorner/detail/en/IP_22_6423.

56. "Digital Markets Act."

57. "Digital Markets Act."

58. James Dale Davidson and Lord William Rees-Mogg, *The Sovereign Individual:
    Mastering the Transition to the Information Age* (New York: Simon & Schuster,
    1997), 19.

59. Davidson and Rees-Mogg, 203.

60. Yochai Benkler, *The Wealth of Networks: How Social Production Transforms
    Markets and Freedom* (New Haven, CT: Yale University Press, 2006), 9.

61. Pindar Wong, interview by Don Tapscott and Alex Tapscott, April 7, 2017,
    quoted in Don Tapscott and Alex Tapscott, "Realizing the Potential of
    Blockchain: A Multistakeholder Approach to the Stewardship of Blockchain
    and Cryptocurrencies," white paper, World Economic Forum, June 2017, https://
    www3.weforum.org/docs/WEF_Realizing_Potential_Blockchain.pdf, accessed
    30 Sept. 2021.

62. Warren interview by Alex Tapscott.

63. Yat Siu, interview by Alex Tapscott via Zoom, Jan. 11, 2023.

64. Siu interview by Alex Tapscott.

65. Siu interview by Alex Tapscott. See, for example, "Japan's NFT Strategy for the
    Web 3.0 Era," white paper, Headquarters for the Promotion of a Digital Society,

Liberal Democratic Party, April 2022, https://www.taira-m.jp/Japan%27s%20
NFT%20Whitepaper_E_050122.pdf, accessed April 12, 2023.

66. Richard A. D'Aveni, "The Trade War with China Could Accelerate 3-D
Printing in the United States," *Harvard Business Review*, Oct. 18, 2018, https://
hbr.org/2018/10/the-trade-war-with-china-could-accelerate-3-d-printing-in
-the-u-s.

67. Timothy Leary, "The Effects of Psychotropic Drugs," Department of
Psychology, Harvard College, n.d., https://psychology.fas.harvard.edu/people
/timothy-leary, accessed Oct. 15, 2021.

INDEX

About the Author

Alex Tapscott is a globally recognized writer, speaker, and investor focused on the impact of blockchain and Web3 on business, society, and government. He is the coauthor of the critically acclaimed nonfiction bestseller *Blockchain Revolution: How the Technology Behind Bitcoin and Other Cryptocurrencies Is Changing the World*, which has been translated into more than twenty languages. Alex is also the managing director of the Digital Asset Group at Ninepoint Partners, a leading independent investment firm. He is regularly sought after by global business audiences for his insights on Web3 and other emerging technologies. In 2017, Alex cofounded the Blockchain Research Institute, a multimillion-dollar think tank that is investigating blockchain strategies, use cases, and opportunities. Alex is a Chartered Financial Analyst (CFA) charterholder. He lives in Toronto.